英国文学学习辅导教程
（新升级版）

A Coursebook for the Study and Review of English Literature
(Newly Upgraded)

主　编：李正栓
Chief Compiler: Li Zhengshuan

副主编：梁　辰
Deputy Chief Compiler: Liang Chen

编　者：许桓鸣　仇　安　颜亚蕾
Co-compilers: Xu Huanming　Qiu An　Yan Yalei

图书在版编目（CIP）数据

英国文学学习辅导教程：新升级版：英文 / 李正栓主编 . —北京：商务印书馆，2023
ISBN 978-7-100-20220-6

Ⅰ.①英… Ⅱ.①李… Ⅲ.①英语—阅读教学—高等学校—教材 ②英国文学—文学欣赏 Ⅳ.① H319.4：Ⅰ

中国国家版本馆 CIP 数据核字（2023）第 128912 号

权利保留，侵权必究。

英国文学学习辅导教程（新升级版）
李正栓 主编

商 务 印 书 馆 出 版
（北京王府井大街36号 邮政编码100710）
商 务 印 书 馆 发 行
北京新华印刷有限公司印刷
ISBN 978-7-100-20220-6

2024 年 1 月第 1 版　　开本 710×1000　1/16
2024 年 1 月北京第 1 次印刷　印张 27¼

定价：69.80 元

内容提要

《英国文学学习辅导教程（新升级版）》共分为两编。上编为文学史基础知识部分，下编为经典文学作品选读部分。按照英国文学史发展阶段，上编针对每个发展阶段的时代特征、重要作家及其代表作品设计了多种题型的练习，主要有填空、单项选择、作家作品匹配、文学术语解释、简答论述等形式。下编涵盖了英国文学经典作品选段，选材详尽、全面，具有代表性，填空、选择、翻译、简评等题目的设计涵盖国内出版的众多英国文学教材的内容。此外，针对部分文学作品选段，设计了中西文学作品对比赏析练习，在提高学生英国文学欣赏能力的同时，弘扬中国文学的博大精深，将"课程思政"有机融入英国文学的学习中。本书有两个附录。附录一是英国文学主要作家作品简录，按历史年代顺序，总结各个时期的作家及其作品，供学生快速背诵。附录二是常用文学术语。这两个附录的设计是为了帮助学生对英国文学及作品有较全面的掌握。

本书作为一本实用参考书，适用于英语专业本科生、商务英语专业本科生、翻译专业本科生、自学考试英语专业本科生、报考英语语言文学专业研究生的广大考生以及广大英国文学爱好者。同时，本书也为广大英国文学教师进行教学和测试提供了必要参考。

前　言

我国高校英语专业高年级、高等教育自学考试英语专业本科段、英语专业函授本科均开设英美文学史及选读课，文学史与文学选读分别开设或合在一起，英国文学与美国文学分别开设或合在一起，视具体师资和学时而定。

2013年，教育部开始编制本科各专业教学质量国家标准，对课程进行严格要求。2018年，《普通高等学校本科专业类教学质量国家标准（外国语言文学类）》（以下简称《国标》）问世。2020年，《普通高等学校本科外国语言文学类专业教学指南》（以下简称《指南》）问世。这两个文件成为英语专业建设的重要依据。教育部认为，在树人过程中必须加强立德，培养具有中国情怀和国际视野的合格人才。2020年，教育部印发了《高等学校课程思政建设指导纲要》（以下简称《纲要》）。

《国标》将英语文学课程设置为英语专业核心课程，旨在提高学生对外国文学作品的主要内容和主题思想的理解和评论能力。《指南》指出，英语文学这个概念和范围扩大了传统的英美文学概念，但由于学时和师资有限，各学校仍以英国文学和美国文学构成英语专业重要的课程，更符合专业建设实际情况。多学固然好，学透更重要。在培养方案中，英国文学史和美国文学史作为必修课出现。《纲要》要求把"立德树人"根本任务落实到教学的方方面面，全面推进高校课程思政建设。讲授英国文学和美国文学的同时，还得加强课程思政建设，即把英美文学教学和中国文化教学与思考融通起来。

国家自2000年以来对英语专业教学大纲不断修订，表明了对英语专业教育的重视以及对英语专业人才要求的不断提高。教育部指示，要重视课程体系化，要重视课程质量，更要重视课程的德育培养作用。高校英语专业教学不仅要传授语言和文学等专业知识，更要承担起传承和传播中华文明和中华文化的神圣使命，将中西方意识形态和价值观念比较融入教学中，使专业教育和德育教育同向同行，从而建立外语人才的文化自信和文化认同感，培养学生的国际视野、家国情怀和跨文化交际能力。

应当说，英美文学相关课程是我国高校英语院系的传统课程，是培养英语语言文学专业本科生及研究生基本功的必经途径，更是帮助外语人才树立正确的世界观、价值观和人生观，提升道德修养的重要阵地。近年来，全国各级各类出版社出版了大量优秀的有关教材，为学生学习和教师教学提供了诸多选择。但在日常教学中，经常有学生说英美文学课高深莫测，想要学懂实属不易，加之市面上可供练习的书相对较少，难以检验学习效果，更不能满足考前复习的需要。此外，我们在教学实践中发现，如果能在英国文学的学习过程中，加入同时代、同题材、同风格的中国文学相关内容，会增加学生文学学习的兴趣，更有助于培养学生对不同意识形态和价值观念的批判思维能力，在学好英国文学的同时，能更好地引导学生深刻领悟中国文化的博大精深。

我曾先后主编出版过数本英美文学练习书籍，受到学生和教师的厚爱，成为学生津津乐道的应试宝典，也成为教师考试命题的重要参考，被有的学校选入本科阶段必读书目和研究生入学考试参考书目。更令我欣慰的是，不少教师见到我后告诉我，他们是通过我编的练习考上了硕士，并为读博士打下了坚实的基础。近年来，英美文学教材又有新发展，在"新文科"建设背景下，在"课程思政"指导思想下，有必要编写一套最新的学习辅导教程，以适应新时代和新读者。

本书以外语教学与研究出版社出版的《英国文学史及选读》（第二版）和其他几本主要的英国文学教材为蓝本。为了使本书适应性强，能让使用不同教材的学生都能使用本书进行复习和巩固，我参考并吸收了多家出版社出版的英国文学教材的知识点，争取做到集各家之长，满足日常学习之需，全方位应对各类考试。有不少考上研究生的同学过分夸大了我主编的此类文学练习教材，说认真做书中的练习就能考上研究生。但我认为，还要学好本校教师为你选定的教材。学习教材之余大量地做我主编的书中的练习，复习效果和考试成绩肯定非常好。

本书共分为两编。上编为文学史基础知识练习，下编为经典文学作品选读练习。按照英国文学史时间发展脉络，上编由以下十部分组成："The Anglo-Saxon Period and the Anglo-Norman Period" "The Age of Geoffrey Chaucer" "The 15th Century: The Age of Popular Ballads" "The 16th Century: The Age of Drama and Poetry" "The 17th Century: Revolution, Restoration and New Poetic Expression" "The 18th Century: The Enlightenment, Neo-classicism and Pre-romanticism" "The 19th Century (First Half): The Romantic Period" "The 19th Century (Second Half): The Victorian Age and Critical Realism" "The 20th Century: Transition from the 19th to the 20th Century Before 1945" "The 20th Century: Contemporary Literature Since 1945"，针对每个发展阶段的时代特征、重要作家及其代表作品设计了多种题型的练习，主要有填空、单项选择、作家作品匹配、文学术语解释、简答论述等形式。下编涵盖了英国文学从古英语时期到现当代的经典作品选段，填空、选择、翻译、简评等题目的设计涵盖国内出版的众多英国文学教材的内容。本书题量丰富，实现了基本点、重点、难点、创新点的全覆盖。

本书后共有两个附录。附录一是英国文学主要作家作品简录，按历史年代顺序，总结各个时期的作家及其代表作品；作家作品是中英文对照，附有出版或发表年代，非常方便学生快速学习和背诵记忆。附录二是常用文学术语，包括英汉对照的术语及其定义、解释、例子等。这两个附录的设计是为了帮助学生对英国文学及作品有较全面的掌握。值得一提的是，本书对重点作家及作品做了整理和简录，紧跟时代要求，帮助学生精准定位重点与非重点。文学基础知识对增加和巩固考生的文学知识大有裨益。文学术语或文学批评知识仅供进一步的选读，略有难度，是为适应某些学校研究生命题而做的特殊安排。经验证明，这两个附录非常有必要。两个附录均参考了一些专家的成果（自1986年到2022年出版的主要教材），已在参考文献部分注明。我们在此代表广大读者向各位专家表示衷心的感谢。

本着实用、好用的原则，本书不单独介绍研究生阶段才学习的复杂、深奥的文学批评知识，而是将文学基础知识和文学术语合并，高度浓缩，呈现精华；因此本书条目更精简，内容更实际，并伴有实例，便于学生理解和记忆，对文学练习部分是有益的补充。

《英国文学学习辅导教程（新升级版）》注重满足各种不同教学形式、教学层次以及自主学习的需要。希望广大的英语专业本科生、自学考试本科生、函授本科生及报考英语语言文学专业研究生的同学学习本书后有很大收获。

由于编者水平有限，错误或不当之处仍在所难免，望不吝指正。

李正栓
2024 年 1 月

目 录
CONTENTS

内容提要 ·· i
前言 ·· iii

上编　英国文学史练习
Part One　Exercises on the History of English Literature

Part I　The Anglo-Saxon Period and the Anglo-Norman Period ············ 3
Part II　The Age of Geoffrey Chaucer ·· 8
Part III　The 15th Century: The Age of Popular Ballads ····················· 12
Part IV　The 16th Century: The Age of Drama and Poetry ·················· 16
Part V　The 17th Century: Revolution, Restoration and New Poetic Expression
　　　　 ·· 28
Part VI　The 18th Century: The Enlightenment, Neo-classicism and
　　　　 Pre-romanticism ··· 38
Part VII　The 19th Century (First Half): The Romantic Period ············· 56
Part VIII　The 19th Century (Second Half): The Victorian Age and Critical
　　　　 Realism ·· 69
Part IX　The 20th Century: Transition from the 19th to the 20th Century
　　　　 Before 1945 ·· 93
Part X　The 20th Century: Contemporary Literature Since 1945 ··········· 108

下编　英国文学选段练习
Part Two　Exercises on Selected Readings of English Literature

Exercise 1 ·· 115
Exercise 2 ·· 115

· vii ·

Exercise 3	116
Exercise 4	117
Exercise 5	118
Exercise 6	119
Exercise 7	120
Exercise 8	121
Exercise 9	122
Exercise 10	123
Exercise 11	123
Exercise 12	124
Exercise 13	124
Exercise 14	126
Exercise 15	127
Exercise 16	128
Exercise 17	129
Exercise 18	130
Exercise 19	131
Exercise 20	131
Exercise 21	132
Exercise 22	133
Exercise 23	134
Exercise 24	134
Exercise 25	135
Exercise 26	136
Exercise 27	137
Exercise 28	137
Exercise 29	138
Exercise 30	139
Exercise 31	140
Exercise 32	140
Exercise 33	141
Exercise 34	141

Exercise 35	142
Exercise 36	143
Exercise 37	145
Exercise 38	145
Exercise 39	146
Exercise 40	147
Exercise 41	148
Exercise 42	149
Exercise 43	150
Exercise 44	151
Exercise 45	152
Exercise 46	153
Exercise 47	156
Exercise 48	157
Exercise 49	161
Exercise 50	162
Exercise 51	163
Exercise 52	165
Exercise 53	168
Exercise 54	169
Exercise 55	170
Exercise 56	171
Exercise 57	172
Exercise 58	173
Exercise 59	174
Exercise 60	174
Exercise 61	176
Exercise 62	177
Exercise 63	178
Exercise 64	178
Exercise 65	180
Exercise 66	180

Exercise 67 ·· 181
Exercise 68 ·· 182
Exercise 69 ·· 183
Exercise 70 ·· 184
Exercise 71 ·· 185
Exercise 72 ·· 186
Exercise 73 ·· 187
Exercise 74 ·· 188
Exercise 75 ·· 189
Exercise 76 ·· 191
Exercise 77 ·· 192
Exercise 78 ·· 193
Exercise 79 ·· 194
Exercise 80 ·· 195
Exercise 81 ·· 196
Exercise 82 ·· 198
Exercise 83 ·· 199
Exercise 84 ·· 200
Exercise 85 ·· 201
Exercise 86 ·· 201
Exercise 87 ·· 202
Exercise 88 ·· 203
Exercise 89 ·· 204
Exercise 90 ·· 205
Exercise 91 ·· 206
Exercise 92 ·· 206
Exercise 93 ·· 207
Exercise 94 ·· 208
Exercise 95 ·· 209

上编参考答案
Key to Exercises of Part One

Part I　　The Anglo-Saxon Period and the Anglo-Norman Period ················213

Part II	The Age of Geoffrey Chaucer	220
Part III	The 15th Century: The Age of Popular Ballads	224
Part IV	The 16th Century: The Age of Drama and Poetry	227
Part V	The 17th Century: Revolution, Restoration and New Poetic Expression	251
Part VI	The 18th Century: The Enlightenment, Neo-classicism and Pre-romanticism	260
Part VII	The 19th Century (First Half): The Romantic Period	273
Part VIII	The 19th Century (Second Half): The Victorian Age and Critical Realism	278
Part IX	The 20th Century: Transition from the 19th to the 20th Century Before 1945	296
Part X	The 20th Century: Contemporary Literature Since 1945	314

下编参考答案
Key to Exercises of Part Two

Exercise 1	321
Exercise 2	321
Exercise 3	322
Exercise 4	323
Exercise 5	323
Exercise 6	325
Exercise 7	325
Exercise 8	325
Exercise 9	326
Exercise 10	326
Exercise 11	327
Exercise 12	327
Exercise 13	327
Exercise 14	328
Exercise 15	328
Exercise 16	329

Exercise 17 ·················· 330
Exercise 18 ·················· 330
Exercise 19 ·················· 330
Exercise 20 ·················· 331
Exercise 21 ·················· 332
Exercise 22 ·················· 332
Exercise 23 ·················· 332
Exercise 24 ·················· 333
Exercise 25 ·················· 333
Exercise 26 ·················· 333
Exercise 27 ·················· 334
Exercise 28 ·················· 334
Exercise 29 ·················· 334
Exercise 30 ·················· 335
Exercise 31 ·················· 335
Exercise 32 ·················· 335
Exercise 33 ·················· 336
Exercise 34 ·················· 337
Exercise 35 ·················· 337
Exercise 36 ·················· 337
Exercise 37 ·················· 338
Exercise 38 ·················· 338
Exercise 39 ·················· 338
Exercise 40 ·················· 339
Exercise 41 ·················· 339
Exercise 42 ·················· 340
Exercise 43 ·················· 340
Exercise 44 ·················· 340
Exercise 45 ·················· 341
Exercise 46 ·················· 341
Exercise 47 ·················· 342
Exercise 48 ·················· 342

Exercise 49	342
Exercise 50	343
Exercise 51	343
Exercise 52	344
Exercise 53	345
Exercise 54	345
Exercise 55	345
Exercise 56	346
Exercise 57	346
Exercise 58	347
Exercise 59	347
Exercise 60	347
Exercise 61	348
Exercise 62	348
Exercise 63	348
Exercise 64	349
Exercise 65	349
Exercise 66	349
Exercise 67	350
Exercise 68	350
Exercise 69	351
Exercise 70	351
Exercise 71	352
Exercise 72	352
Exercise 73	353
Exercise 74	353
Exercise 75	354
Exercise 76	354
Exercise 77	355
Exercise 78	355
Exercise 79	355
Exercise 80	356

Exercise 81 ·· 356
Exercise 82 ·· 356
Exercise 83 ·· 357
Exercise 84 ·· 357
Exercise 85 ·· 358
Exercise 86 ·· 358
Exercise 87 ·· 359
Exercise 88 ·· 360
Exercise 89 ·· 360
Exercise 90 ·· 361
Exercise 91 ·· 361
Exercise 92 ·· 362
Exercise 93 ·· 362
Exercise 94 ·· 362
Exercise 95 ·· 363

附录一　英国文学主要作家作品简录·· 364
附录二　常用文学术语·· 382

参考文献·· 416

上编
英国文学史练习

Part One
Exercises on the History of English Literature

Part I

The Anglo-Saxon Period and the Anglo-Norman Period

I. Fill in the Blanks.

1. For nearly four hundred years, Britain was ruled by _____.
2. After the Roman troops withdrew from it in 410 A.D., Britain was successively conquered by _____ (449), and later by _____.
3. The literature of the Anglo-Saxon period falls into two divisions— _____ and _____.
4. Among the early Anglo-Saxon poets, two are worth mentioning. One is _____ who wrote a poetic paraphrase of the Bible, the other is _____ who wrote poems on religious subjects.
5. _____ is the first national epic written in national language rather than in Latin in the history of Europe.
6. _____ is represented by the poetry, or sagas, of the Anglo-Saxons originally in oral form.
7. In Anglo-Saxon period, *The Song of Beowulf* represented the _____ poetry.
8. The _____ period witnessed a transition from tribal society to feudalism.
9. In the year of _____, at the battle of _____, the Anglo-Saxons were defeated by the _____.
10. After the _____ Conquest, feudal system was established in English society.
11. English literature of the Anglo-Norman period was also a combina-

tion of _____ and _____ elements.
12. The Norman Conquest brought a linguistic shock to the Anglo-Saxons. Both language and culture were influenced by _____.
13. The didactic poem *The Christ* was produced by _____.
14. The early inhabitants in the island now we call England were _____, a tribe of _____.
15. The story of _____ is the culmination of the Arthurian romances.
16. The theme of _____ to king and lord was repeatedly emphasized in romance.
17. In terms of matter, romance can be divided into three classes, they are _____, _____, and _____.
18. The most famous cycle of English ballads centers on the stories about a legendary outlaw called _____.
19. The prevailing form of literature in the feudal England is _____, which represents a courtly and chivalric age.
20. After the Norman Conquest, three languages existed in England at that time, the Normans spoke _____; the lower class spoke _____; and the scholar and clergymen spoke _____.

II. Choose the Best Answer for Each Question.

1. The original settlers of British Isles is _____.
   A. the Angles and Saxons   B. the Jutes
   C. the Celtics   D. the Romans
2. The only existing manuscript of *The Song of Beowulf* was discovered in the _____.
   A. 10th century   B. 6th century.
   C. 17th century   D. 18th century
3. *The Song of Beowulf* describes the deeds of the hero _____.
   A. Beowulf   B. Hrothgar
   C. Grendel   D. Danes

4. _____ is the half-human monster injured and killed thirty warriors in *The Song of Beowulf*.
   A. Beowulf   B. Hrothgar
   C. Grendel   D. Danes

5. _____ is represented by the writings developed under teaching of the monks who copied the works, in the course of which they made some changes to cater to their religious taste.
   A. The Christian literature   B. The pagan literature
   C. The Bible   D. *Iliad*

6. Which of the following is NOT the feature of *The Song of Beowulf*?
   A. Alliteration
   B. The epic of Rome
   C. Written in the vernacular language of a nation
   D. Oral form

7. In the 8th century, Anglo-Saxon prose appeared. The famous prose writers of the period were Venerable Bede and _____.
   A. Cynewulf   B. Caedmon
   C. Julius Caesar   D. Alfred the Great

8. When we speak of the old English prose, the first name that comes into our minds is _____, who is the first scholar in English literature and has been regarded as father of English learning.
   A. William, Duke of Normandy   B. Beowulf
   C. Julius Caesar   D. Venerable Bede

9. The most important work of Alfred the Great is _____, which is regarded as the best monument of the old English prose.
   A. *The Song of Beowulf*
   B. *The Anglo-Saxon Chronicles*
   C. *Sir Gawain and the Green Knight*
   D. *Piers Plowman*

10. _____ is the first important religious poet in English literature.
    A. Caedmon   B. Geoffrey Chaucer
    C. Cynewulf   D. Beowulf

11. *Beowulf* describes the exploits of a _____ hero, Beowulf, in fighting against the monster Grendel, his revengeful mother, and a fire-breathing dragon.
    A. Denmark   B. Scandinavian
    C. England   D. Norway
12. *Sir Gawain and the Green Knight* is a verse romance of _____.
    A. 3,182 lines   B. 2,530 lines
    C. 1,326 lines   D. 4,100 lines
13. _____ describes a series of wonderful dreams the author dreamed.
    A. *The Song of Beowulf*
    B. *The Canterbury Tales*
    C. *Sir Gawain and the Green Knight*
    D. *Piers Plowman*
14. *Piers Plowman* describes a picture of the life in the _____ England.
    A. primitive   B. feudal
    C. bourgeois   D. tribal
15. _____ was the greatest of English religious reformers and the translator of the first complete English Bible.
    A. William Langland   B. John Gower
    C. John Wycliffe   D. Geoffrey Chaucer
16. The prevailing form of literature in the feudal England was _____.
    A. the romance   B. the epic
    C. the prose   D. the poetry

III. Match-Making

	Column A		Column B
1.	Venerable Bede	a.	*The Anglo-Saxon Chronicles*
2.	Alfred the Great	b.	*Beowulf*

3. An unknown scribe
4. Cynewulf
5. William Langland

c. *The Christ*
d. *Piers Plowman*
e. *The Ecclesiastical History of the English People*

IV. Define the Literary Terms.

1. Alliteration
2. Epic
3. Romance

V. Answer the Following Questions Briefly.

1. Give an account of the history of Britain from the Celtic settlement to the Norman Conquest.
2. What are the main characteristics of Anglo-Saxon literature?
3. What is the difference between pagan literature and Christian literature?
4. Please briefly describe the plots of *The Song of Beowulf*.
5. What are the features of *The Song of Beowulf*?
6. What social significance does *The Song of Beowulf* express?
7. Please briefly describe the plots of *Sir Gawain and the Green Knight*.
8. What are the main features of English literature in the period of Norman Conquest?
9. Make a brief comment on *Sir Gawain and the Green Knight*.
10. The great majority of the romances fall into three groups, what are they?

Part II

The Age of Geoffrey Chaucer

I. Fill in the Blanks.

1. Geoffrey Chaucer was called the "_____" and one of the greatest narrative poets of England.
2. Geoffrey Chaucer had a wide range of knowledge, all the best poems and histories in Latin, _____ and _____ were well known to him.
3. Geoffrey Chaucer's works reflect vividly the changes that had taken root in English culture of the second half of the _____ century.
4. *The Canterbury Tales* is a collection of _____ told by people of different background of that time.
5. In *The Canterbury Tales*, the ideas of _____ are shown in Chaucer's praising of man's energy, intellect, wit and love of life.
6. There should be 120 stories in *The Canterbury Tales*, but actually only _____ were written.
7. The foundations of the feudal system had already begun to crumble in the 14th century. The people's uprising of 1388 raised the question as to the abolition of _____.
8. In *The Canterbury Tales*, people's right to pursue _____ is affirmed by Geoffrey Chaucer.
9. By serving as a page to Elizabeth, Countess of Ulster, Geoffrey Chaucer came into contact with the _____.
10. *The Canterbury Tales* is Geoffrey Chaucer's masterpiece, and the

greater part of it is written in _____ couplet.
11. Geoffrey Chaucer died on the 25th of October 1400, and was buried in the "_____" at Westminster Abbey.
12. With his vivid portrait of people of all walks of life, Geoffrey Chaucer began the realistic tradition, thus was properly and rightly praised by Gorky as "_____".
13. The Prologue to *The Canterbury Tales* is a _____ of the English society of Chaucer's time.
14. _____ provides a framework of *The Canterbury Tales*, and it includes vivid sketches of typical medieval figures.
15. Geoffrey Chaucer's use of _____ promoted the position of language used by common people and refined it into an acceptable literary one.
16. *The Canterbury Tales* contains _____ and 24 tales, of which two are left unfinished.
17. With Geoffrey Chaucer's vivid portrait of people of all walks of life, he began the _____ tradition.
18. Geoffrey Chaucer greatly enriched the rhyme schemes by introducing from France the rhymed stanzas of various types. The rhymed couplet of _____ is the form he was most at home with.
19. In *The Canterbury Tale*, the character of _____ is a vivid sketch of a woman of the middle class, whose life represents the domestic life of that class in Chaucer's time.

II. Choose the Best Answer for Each Question.

1. *The Canterbury Tales* consists of about _____ lines.
   A. 15,000   B. 17,000   C. 20,000   D. 23,000
2. *The Canterbury Tales* represents the spirit of the rising _____.
   A. bourgeoisie B. proletariat C. feudalist   D. peasantry
3. In *The Canterbury Tales*, Geoffrey Chaucer showed his _____

for the poor to some extent.

A. indifference B. satire C. sympathy D. prejudice

4. *The Canterbury Tales* displays Geoffrey Chaucer's acceptance and influence he received from _____, which describes the stories told by some ladies and young men who were fleeing the Black Death.

A. Dante Alighieri's *Divine Comedy*

B. Boccaccio's *Decameron*

C. Francesco Petrarch's sonnets

D. Homer's *Iliad*

5. Geoffrey Chaucer's poetry traces out a path to the literature of _____.

A. English realism   B. Italian Renaissance

C. English romanticism   D. English Renaissance

6. _____ was the first to be buried in the "Poet's Corner" at Westminster Abbey.

A. William Shakespeare   B. Thomas Percy

C. Geoffrey Chaucer   D. Walter Scott

7. Geoffrey Chaucer was influenced by three literatures except _____.

A. French literature   B. English literature

C. Italian literature   D. German literature

8. The representative work of the first period of Geoffrey Chaucer's literary career is _____.

A. *The Romance of the Rose*

B. *Troilus and Criseyde*

C. *The Canterbury Tales*

D. *Reliques of Ancient English Poetry*

9. In the _____ period of Geoffrey Chaucer's literary career, he borrowed foreign themes but showed his own creativeness.

A. first   B. second   C. third   D. fourth

10. _____, the "father of English poetry" and one of the greatest narrative poets of England, was born in London about 1340.

A. Geoffrey Chaucer   B. Sir Gawain

C. Francis Bacon　　　　　　D. John Dryden

11. Geoffrey Chaucer's works reflect vividly the changes that had taken root in English culture of the _____ century.
    A. first half of the 13th　　B. second half of the 13th
    C. first half of the 14th　　D. second half of the 14th
12. Geoffrey Chaucer composed a long narrative poem named _____ based on Boccaccio's poem *Filostrato*.
    A. *Troilus and Criseyde*　　B. *The Canterbury Tales*
    C. *The Romance of the Rose*　　D. *The Faerie Queene*
13. Geoffrey Chaucer greatly enriched the rhyme schemes by introducing from France the rhymed stanzas of various types. The rhymed couplet of _____ is the form he was most at home with.
    A. iambic tetrameter　　B. iambic pentameter
    C. iambic trimester　　D. iambic hexameter
14. The spoken English of Geoffrey Chaucer's time consisted of several dialects, and Geoffrey Chaucer did much in making the dialect of _____ the standard for the modern English speech.
    A. London　　B. Cambridge　　C. Oxford　　D. Scotland
15. Geoffrey Chaucer adopted an attitude of opposition against _____ and attacked the corruption of the contemporary church government in his work.
    A. Christianity　　B. Catholicism　　C. Islamism　　D. Buddhism

III. Answer the Following Questions Briefly.

1. Summarize Geoffrey Chaucer's contribution to the English literature.
2. Give a brief introduction of *The Canterbury Tales*.
3. What is the social significance of *The Canterbury Tales*?
4. What is the function of the Prologue to *The Canterbury Tales*?

Part III

The 15th Century: The Age of Popular Ballads

I. Fill in the Blanks.

1. Popular ballads belong to the domain of _____.
2. Ballads were found all over Europe in Middle Ages. But a particularly fertile soil was the border area between _____ and _____.
3. A ballad is a story told through singing, usually in _____ consisting of four lines, with the second line rhyming with the fourth line.
4. Around the _____ century, ballads were widely spread among the common people.
5. _____ is among the first to take a literary interest in ballads.
6. In English history, Robin Hood is a partly _____ and partly _____ figure.
7. The greatest collection of ballads is _____ first published in 1882.
8. The most famous cycle of the English ballads deal with the stories of a legendary outlaw named _____, a Saxon by birth.
9. The _____ spirit of Robin Hood and his companions often inspired the English people in the struggle against their oppressors.
10. _____ gained great popularity in the second half of the 14th century, at the time of the struggle of the peasants and artisans against their masters and exploiters.
11. *Get up and Bar the Door* is a good example of a _____ ballad.
12. The most commonly-seen ballad stanza is the abcb-schemed stan-

za, consisting usually of alternating iambic _____ and _____ lines.

13. Many of the "_____" were devoted to historical events which reflect the age-long struggle between the Scots and the English.
14. The first mention of Robin Hood in literature is in William Langland's _____.
15. The ballads are usually in various _____ and _____ dialects.
16. Some ballads are highly lyrical, some fantastical, and some very humorous, giving the reader a feeling of _____ and _____.
17. Ballads were widespread among the common people of England and Scotland. They were created and preserved by the people and that is why they are termed "_____".
18. Robin Hood's hatred for the cruel _____ is the result of his love for the poor and downtrodden.
19. The most commonly-seen ballad stanzas are the _____ schemed stanza and _____ schemed stanza, consisting usually of alternating iambic tetrameter and trimester lines.
20. Around the 15th century, ballads were widespread among the common people. But as a matter of fact, ballads already existed in the _____ and _____ centuries.

II. Choose the Best Answer for Each Question.

1. There are ballads in almost every country. And most ballads are popular and easily accepted by _____ who may not be very learned and cultured.
   A. ruling class　　　　　　B. common people
   C. the King　　　　　　　 D. outlaws
2. Which of the following is Thomas Percy's work?
   A. *Piers Plowman*
   B. *The English and Scottish Popular Ballads*

C. *Minstrelsy of the Scottish Border*

D. *Reliques of Ancient English Poetry*

3. The most famous cycle of English ballads centers on the stories about a legendary outlaw called _____.

   A. Little John   B. Piers
   C. Robin Hood   D. Kubla Khan

4. William Langland's _____ is written in the form of a dream vision.

   A. *Piers Plowman*
   B. *The English and Scottish Popular Ballads*
   C. *Minstrelsy of the Scottish Border*
   D. *Reliques of Ancient English Poetry*

5. Many of the _____ were devoted to historical events which reflect the age-long struggle between the Scots and the English.

   A. humorous ballads   B. border ballads
   C. popular ballads   D. legendary ballads

6. The author of *The English and Scottish Popular Ballads* (1882) is _____.

   A. F. J. Child   B. Thomas Percy
   C. Walter Scott   D. William Langland

7. _____ is a good example of a humorous ballad.

   A. *Piers Plowman*
   B. *The Rime of the Ancient Mariner*
   C. *Get up and Bar the Door*
   D. *Minstrelsy of the Scottish Border*

8. The spring tide of English ballad arrived in the _____ century.

   A.12th   B.13th   C.15th   D.18th

9. The ballads of Robin Hood gained great popularity in the second half of the _____ century, at the time of the struggle of the peasants and artisans against their masters and exploiters.

   A. 14th   B. 12th   C.15th   D.18th

10. Some historical books say that Robin Hood and his friend Little

John lived during the reign of _____.
A. William I   B. Edward I
C. George III   D. Richard I the Lion-Hearted

III. Define the Literary Term.

1. Ballad

IV. Answer the Following Questions Briefly.

1. Summarize the various themes of the ballads.
2. Make comments on the character Robin Hood.

Part IV

The 16th Century: The Age of Drama and Poetry

I. Fill in the Blanks.

1. In England, the 16th century was a period breaking up _____ and establishing the foundations of _____.
2. The "_____ movement" drove many peasants to towns where they gradually settled down.
3. At the beginning of the 16th century, King Henry VIII broke off with the Pope, and became the head of the _____.
4. When the old aristocracy had been greatly weakened in the _____, a new nobility, totally dependent on the King's power, came onto the stage.
5. Henry VIII obtained the support of the merchants and handicraftsmen who were developing into a new class— _____.
6. The rapid progress of _____ made England powerful and enabled her to defeat the Spanish Armada in 1588.
7. The 16th century saw the contradiction between the wealth of the _____ and the poverty of the people.
8. Together with the development of bourgeois relationships and formation of the English national state, the 16th century is marked by a flourishing of national culture known as the _____.
9. The term Renaissance means a revival of classical (Greek and Roman) learning, including _____, _____ and _____ after the Middle Ages.

10. In England, Renaissance found its best expression in _____ and _____.
11. _____ held their chief interest not in ecclesiastical knowledge, but in man, his environment and doings.
12. At the beginning of the 16th century the outstanding humanist Thomas More wrote his *Utopia* in which he gave a profound and truthful picture of _____ and put forward his ideal of _____.
13. "Liberty, Fraternity and Equality" were first uttered in the book _____.
14. At the end of the 16th century, the great English scientist and philosopher _____ wrote his famous philosophical and literary works.
15. In the first half of the 16th century there appeared lyrical poems by _____ and _____ who translated Italian poetry into English to prove that English is as beautiful and flexible as Italian.
16. Thomas Wyatt and Henry Howard, Earl of Surrey translated many of _____ and wrote their own sonnets, in most of which there flourished the theme of _____.
17. The poems that the man speaker always complains about the love frustrated by the coldness and even cruelty of the beautiful lady are called _____.
18. In the second half of the 16th century _____ became widespread in England.
19. _____ gave rise to the term "euphuism", designating an affected style of court speech.
20. _____ tendencies developed in Thomas Deloney's and Thomas Nashe's novels, devoted to the everyday life of craftsmen, merchants and other representatives of the lower classes.
21. The greatest of the pioneers of English drama was _____ who reformed that genre in England and perfected the language and verse of dramatic works.
22. _____, together with Henry Howard, Earl of Surrey, was gen-

erally regarded as the founder of the golden age in English poetry under the reign of Elizabeth I.

23. Sir Thomas Wyatt's greatest contribution to English literature is that he introduced into England the _____, a 14-line poem with a complicated rhyme scheme, rhyming abba abba cdecde or abba abba cdcdee.

24. Thomas Wyatt's poetry modeled on classical and Italian poets, but he also admired _____ and borrowed his vocabulary.

25. _____ became Earl of Surrey in 1524 when his grandfather died and his father became Duke of Norfolk.

26. Henry Howard was the first English poet to publish _____ in his translation of the second and fourth books of Virgil's *Aeneid*.

27. The Italian sonnets are usually composed of two parts. The first part is called the _____ (two quatrains) in which a problem is presented. The second part is called the _____ (two tercets), in which a resolution is provided.

28. _____, the greatest non-dramatic poet of the English Renaissance, was called "the poet's poet".

29. _____ was Edmund Spenser's first major work, a series of pastoral poems arranged according to the months of the year.

30. *The Faerie Queene* made Edmund Spenser "_____".

31. Edmund Spenser was buried in _____, near Chaucer, his great medieval forerunner.

32. In 1594, Edmund Spenser married Elizabeth Boyle, the lady in his sonnet sequence _____.

33. The dominating thoughts of *The Faerie Queene* are _____ (seen from the celebration of Queen Elizabeth), _____ (seen from the strong opposition to Roman Catholicism), and _____ (shown in its moral teachings).

34. Edmund Spenser created a 9-line stanza form, called _____, rhymed abab bcbc c.

35. _____ was the founder of Virginia and the introducer of tobacco

into Europe.
36. _____ was regarded by Edmund Spenser as "the noble and virtuous gentleman most worthy of all titles both of learning and chivalry".
37. *Astrophel and Stella* is the masterpiece of _____.
38. As a child, _____ was called by Elizabeth her "Little Lord Keeper".
39. Of Francis Bacon's literary works, the most important are the _____.
40. _____ is regarded as the greatest of the pioneers in English drama, first making blank verse the principal instrument of English drama.
41. *The Passionate Shepherd to His Love* is one of _____'s lyrics.
42. Some people say Christopher Marlowe's works paved the way for plays of the greatest English dramatist _____.
43. _____, _____, _____, and _____ are generally regarded as William Shakespeare's four great tragedies.
44. Francis Bacon's works may be divided into three classes, the _____, the _____, and the _____ works.
45. *Of Revenge* and *Of Friendship* are the essays on questions of _____.
46. "Come live with me and be my love, And we will all the pleasures prove" are the lines from one of _____'s lyrics.
47. During the twenty-two years of William Shakespeare's literary work, he produced 37 plays, _____ narrative poems and 154 sonnets.
48. _____, _____, _____, and _____ are generally regarded as William Shakespeare's four great comedies.
49. The film *The Lion King*, *Night Feast* and some other such films bear similarities with the plot of William Shakespeare's play _____.
50. _____ first praised Shakespeare as a man belonging to all ages.
51. Ben Jonson advocated classicism, modeling on the old Greek and

Roman masters, taking a firm stand for the _____ in play-writing.
52. William Shakespeare was born and died in _____.
53. "What a piece of work is a man! How noble in reason! How infinite in faculty" are famous lines in _____.
54. Alexander Pope described _____ as "the wisest, brightest, meanest of mankind".
55. Three Unities consists of the Unity of _____, the Unity of _____ and the Unity of _____.
56. _____ was made poet-laureate in 1616.

II. Choose the Best Answer for Each Question.

1. _____ was a time when, as Thomas More put it, "sheep devoured men."
   A. The 14th century   B. The 15th century
   C. The 16th century   D. The 17th century
2. _____ broke off with the Pope, and became the head of the Church of England.
   A. King Henry VIII   B. Queen Elizabeth
   C. King Edward III   D. The Pope
3. Absolute monarchy reached its summit during the reign of _____ between 1558 and 1603.
   A. King Henry VIII   B. Queen Elizabeth
   C. King Edward III   D. the Pope
4. The victory over _____ consolidated England's might and power on the seas and in world trade.
   A. Spain   B. Italy   C. Germany   D. France
5. Renaissance reached _____ the latest because people were involved in the War of Roses.
   A. Spain   B. Italy   C. England   D. France
6. At the beginning of the 16th century, _____ created *Utopia*.

A. Francis Bacon   B. Thomas More
   C. Ben Jonson   D. Edmund Spenser
7. _____ fought bravely for the emancipation of man from the tyranny of the church and religious dogmas.
   A. The humanists   B. The King
   C. The ruling classes   D. The bourgeoisie
8. _____ was the first to introduce the sonnet into English literature.
   A. William Shakespeare   B. Edmund Spenser
   C. Thomas Wyatt   D. Christopher Marlowe
9. _____ invented the blank verse which would make its greatest contribution to English literature.
   A. William Shakespeare   B. Henry Howard
   C. Thomas Wyatt   D. Christopher Marlowe
10. John Lyly's *Euphues* is a(n) _____.
    A. novel   B. poetry   C. drama   D. essay
11. It was _____ who made blank verse the principal vehicle of expression in drama.
    A. William Shakespeare   B. Henry Howard
    C. Thomas Wyatt   D. Christopher Marlowe
12. Thomas Wyatt's sonnets first appeared in _____.
    A. *Tottle's Miscellany*
    B. *The Long Love That in My Thought Doth Harbor*
    C. *George Green, the Pinner of Wakefield*
    D. *Yet Was I Never of Your Love Aggrieved*
13. _____ was the first English poet to publish blank verse.
    A. William Shakespeare   B. Henry Howard
    C. Thomas Wyatt   D. Edmund Spenser
14. A sonnet is a _____ complete poem usually using iambic pentameter.
    A. 12-line   B. 14-line   C. 16-line   D. 18-line
15. _____ was called "the poet's poet".
    A. William Shakespeare   B. Henry Howard

C. Thomas Wyatt   D. Edmund Spenser

16. _____ made Edmund Spenser "the prince of poets in his time".
    A. *The Faerie Queene*   B. *The Shepherd's Calendar*
    C. *Amoretti*   D. *Prothalamion*

17. _____ consists of twelve pastoral eclogues, one for each month.
    A. *The Faerie Queene*   B. *The Shepherd's Calendar*
    C. *Amoretti*   D. *Prothalamion*

18. Edmund Spenser's masterpiece *The Faerie Queene* consists of _____ books.
    A. three   B. six   C. eight   D. twelve

19. The publication of _____ marked the budding of the Renaissance flower in England.
    A. *Childe Harold's Pilgrimage*   B. *The Shepherd's Calendar*
    C. *Amoretti*   D. *Revolt of Islam*

20. _____ was the first master to make English (Modern English) the natural music of his poetic writing.
    A. Edmund Spenser   B. Thomas Wyatt
    C. Philip Sidney   D. William Shakespeare

21. _____, together with Shakespeare's sonnets and *Astrophel and Stella* were, and still are, regarded as the most famous sonnet sequences of the Elizabethan Age.
    A. *The Faerie Queene*   B. *Amoretti*
    C. *Tottle's Miscellany*   D. *Euphues*

22. _____ was imprisoned in the Tower of London by King James and was executed.
    A. Walter Raleigh   B. Christopher Marlowe
    C. John Donne   D. Philip Sidney

23. _____ is the first of the great Elizabethan sonnet sequences modeling on Petrarch and other Italian and French poets of the Renaissance.
    A. *Amoretti*
    B. *Tottle's Miscellany*

    C. *The Passionate Shepherd to His Love*
    D. *Astrophel and Stella*
24. _____ died in battle at the age of thirty-two, the whole country mourned his death.
    A. Philip Sidney   B. Walter Raleigh
    C. Henry Howard   D. Edmund Spenser
25. The largest and most important of Francis Bacon's professional works are the treatises entitled _____.
    A. *Advancement of Learning*
    B. *Novum Organum*
    C. *Maxims of the Law and Reading on the Statute of Uses*
    D. *De Augmentis Scientiarum*
26. Which of the following is not Christopher Marlowe's play?
    A. *The Jew of Malta*   B. *Tamburlaine the Great*
    C. *Doctor Faustus*   D. *Troilus and Cressida*
27. At the inn of the widow Bull, _____ was killed in an argument over the bill.
    A. Walter Raleigh   B. Christopher Marlowe
    C. Edmund Spenser   D. Philip Sidney
28. Who is not regarded as the "University Wits"?
    A. John Lyly   B. William Shakespeare
    C. Christopher Marlowe   D. Thomas Kyd
29. Which of the following is not Francis Bacon's work?
    A. *Advancement of Learning*   B. *Essays*
    C. *The New Instrument*   D. *Measure for Measure*
30. In the Elizabethan Period, _____ was the greatest playwright of England.
    A. William Shakespeare   B. Christopher Marlowe
    C. Ben Jonson   D. Walter Raleigh
31. Which of the following essays is on problems of statesmanship?
    A. *Of Truth*
    B. *Of Revenge*

C. *Of the True Greatness of Kingdoms and Estates*
D. *Of Friendship*

32. *Venus and Adonis* is William Shakespeare's _____.
    A. comedy   B. tragedy
    C. sonnet   D. narrative poem

33. Which of the following is not one of the four tragedies of William Shakespeare?
    A. *Hamlet*   B. *Othello*
    C. *Romeo and Juliet* D. *King Lear*

34. _____ is the summit of William Shakespeare's art.
    A. *Hamlet*   B. *Romeo and Juliet*
    C. *The Merchant of Venice* D. *The Taming of the Shrew*

35. Which of the following dramatic works is Ben Jonson's comedy of humors?
    A. *Sejanus*   B. *Every Man in His Humor*
    C. *Volpone*   D. *The Alchemist*

36. *The Rape of Lucrece* is William Shakespeare's _____.
    A. tragedy   B. comedy
    C. sonnet   D. narrative poem

37. Ben Jonson is famous for his analysis of _____ in his comedies.
    A. humor   B. satire   C. greed   D. humanism

38. The first complete English Bible was translated by _____.
    A. William Tyndal   B. James I
    C. John Wycliffe   D. Bishop Lancelot Andrewes

III. Match-Making

Group One

	Column A		Column B
1.	Christopher Marlowe	a.	*Utopia*
2.	William Shakespeare	b.	*The Jew of Malta*

3. Edmund Spenser				c. *The Faerie Queene*
4. Thomas More				d. *The Merchant of Venice*
5. John Lyly				e. *Euphues*

Group Two
Column A				Column B
1. Francis Bacon				a. *The New Instrument*
2. Ben Jonson				b. *Volpone*
3. Thomas Kyd				c. *Discovery of Guiana*
4. Walter Raleigh				d. *The Spanish Tragedy*
5. Sir Philip Sidney				e. *Astrophel and Stella*

Group Three
Column A				Column B
1. *Hamlet*				a. Juliet
2. *Romeo and Juliet*				b. Cordelia
3. *The Merchant of Venice*				c. Ophelia
4. *Othello*				d. Desdemona
5. *King Lear*				e. Portia

Group Four
Column A				Column B
1. *As You Like it*				a. Mephistophilis
2. *Doctor Faustus*				b. Viola
3. *Twelfth Night*				c. Malcolm
4. *Macbeth*				d. Hermia
5. *A Midsummer Night's Dream*				e. Rosalind

IV. Define the Literary Terms.

1. Renaissance

2. Humanism
3. Sonnet
4. Stanza
5. Spenserian stanza
6. Blank verse
7. Essay
8. Comedy
9. Tragedy
10. Morality plays
11. History plays
12. Three Unities
13. Euphuistic style
14. University Wits
15. Epigram
16. Farce
17. Allegory
18. Soliloquy

V. Answer the Following Questions Briefly.

1. What are the main features of European Renaissance?
2. What are the features of Renaissance in England?
3. Summarize the English literature in the Renaissance period.
4. What contribution did Thomas Wyatt make to the English literature?
5. What are the characteristics of Edmund Spenser's poetry?
6. Summarize the main story of *The Faerie Queene*.
7. What are the writing features of Edmund Spenser's masterpiece *The Faerie Queene*?
8. Comment on Thomas More's *Utopia*.
9. Francis Bacon's work can be divided into three classes, what are they?

10. What is the writing style of Francis Bacon's essays?
11. Summarize the social significance of Christopher Marlowe's plays.
12. Summarize the periods of William Shakespeare's literary creation.
13. In which period did William Shakespeare write his main comedies? What did he tell us in his comedies?
14. In which period did William Shakespeare write his main tragedies? What did he write about in his tragedies?
15. What did William Shakespeare express in his historical plays?
16. What are the features of William Shakespeare's plays?
17. Comment on William Shakespeare's sonnets.
18. Make a brief comment on the character of Hamlet.
19. What is the theme of *The Merchant of Venice*?
20. Make a brief comment on Ben Jonson's works.
21. Make a brief comment on Christopher Marlowe's *The Tragical History of Doctor Faustus*.
22. What are the limitations in *Utopia*?

Part V

The 17th Century: Revolution, Restoration and New Poetic Expression

I. Fill in the Blanks.

1. In the early decades of the 17th century, a group of poets called "_____ poets" appeared.
2. Against the royal arrogance after 1625, the Puritans offered another theory of divine right, the divine right of _____.
3. Under the leadership of _____, England became a commonwealth after the execution of Charles I.
4. After the Restoration, _____ influence was most marked in drama.
5. In John Donne's middle years, he experienced a period of searching, uncertainty and unhappiness, because of the huge _____.
6. John Donne's poems always impress his readers with his _____, _____ and _____.
7. Robert Herrick got his B. A. and M. A. degree in _____.
8. In Robert Herrick's publication of poems in 1648, for the secular poems he entitled them as _____, and for the sacred ones _____.
9. *To the Virgins, to Make Much of Time* is the best example of the carpe diem tradition in _____'s poems.
10. Pamphlets are important works of John Milton, whose purpose is dedicated to _____.
11. John Suckling attended _____, Cambridge.
12. Andrew Marvell's poetry is playful, casual, and witty in tone, and

always light on metrical feet and exact in diction, which is best revealed in his work _____.
13. Until after _____, with Herbert J. C. Grierson's _____ and _____'s *Andrew Marvell* that the modern high estimation of his poetry began to prevail.
14. _____ is a war that Puritan struggle for liberty.
15. Two books namely _____ and _____ contribute a lot to John Bunyan's poems.
16. _____ was probably written in the jail by John Bunyan and was published in _____.
17. George Herbert wrote his poems by _____ from Bible and _____.
18. _____ traveled abroad in the continent from 1642 to 1647 to avoid Civil War.
19. *Paradise Regained* further explores the theme of _____ and _____.
20. The Revolution Period is also called the _____ Age, because the English Revolution was carried out under a religious cloak.
21. After the death of Oliver Cromwell, the Parliament recalled Charles II to England in 1660; then followed the _____ period.
22. English literature of the 17th century witnessed a _____ on the whole.
23. In the field of prose writing of the Puritan Age, _____ occupied the most important place.
24. _____ gives a vivid and satirical description of Vanity Fair which is the symbol of London at the time of Restoration.
25. During this period of revolution and counter-revolution, _____ turned with the tide and always placed himself on the winning side. Thus, he has been called a time-server by some critics.
26. A _____ is a far-fetched metaphor in which a very unlikely connection between two things is established. John Donne employs them extensively in his poetry.
27. John Dryden wrote about 27 plays. The famous one is _____,

a tragedy dealing with the same story as William Shakespeare's *Antony and Cleopatra*.

28. After the victory of the English Revolution, the movement of the _____ broke out. The leader of this revolt is Gerard Winstanley.
29. John Donne is a poet of peculiar _____, having his own way of reasoning and comparison.
30. Puritans fighting against the Cavaliers who helped the king was commonly called the English _____.
31. In 1653 Oliver Cromwell imposed _____ on the country.
32. After Oliver Cromwell died, monarchy was again restored (1660), which was called the period of the _____.
33. John Milton's _____ is a poetic drama modeled on the Greek tragedies.
34. During _____, the Puritans dispossessed Robert Herrick.
35. _____ had a life of devotion to both God and people.
36. _____, which the Puritans did not quite notice at first, was a recurrent theme in Robert Herrick's verses.
37. At the top of his poetic production, in _____, Robert Herrick wrote a major lyric on the central theme of his life, the happy reconciliation of nature and nature's god.
38. _____ is a poem describing happiness, which was written by John Milton.
39. John Milton thought of himself as "_____", who felt that his verse originated in and was guided by the _____.
40. After losing his sight, John Milton dictated _____ and _____, a play telling the story of Samson, the champion of Israel, who, like John Milton himself, passed his last days in blindness.
41. John Suckling left England for a time to fight with the French army against the _____.
42. _____ was supposed to have been written in prison by Richard Lovelace.
43. _____ was once the assistant of John Milton who was blind by

1651.

II. Choose the Best Answer for Each Question.

1. Which of the following poets is not metaphysical poet?
   A. John Donne   B. Andrew Marvell
   C. Alexander Pope   D. John Cleveland
2. Oliver Cromwell's military dictatorship was against the expectation of many people, which can be seen in _____.
   A. John Milton's *Paradise Lost*
   B. John Donne's *A Valediction: Forbidding Mourning*
   C. Robert Herrick's *To the Virgins, to Make Much of Time*
   D. George Herbert's *Virtue*
3. Which of the poet's former belief is Catholicism?
   A. John Milton   B. John Donne
   C. Thomas Carew   D. Richard Crashaw
4. The following classical forms were used by John Donne, except _____.
   A. satire   B. elegy   C. epistle   D. epic
5. Which of the following is George Hebert's volume?
   A. *Temple*   B. *Hesperides*
   C. *An Essay of Dramatic Poesy* D. *All for Love*
6. Which of the following is not John Milton's short poem?
   A. *L'Allegro*   B. *Lycidas*
   C. *Il Penseroso*   D. *Holy Sonnets*
7. In order to attack on the censorship of the press, John Milton wrote _____.
   A. *Areopagitica or Speech for the Liberty of Unlicensed Printing*
   B. *Eikonoklastes*
   C. *Defense for the English People*
   D. *The Anatomy of Melancholy*

8. Who is a firm supporter of the King during the Civil War?
   A. John Milton   B. Richard Lovelace
   C. George Herbert   D. John Donne
9. When were all of Andrew Marvell's lyric poems written?
   A. 1640s   B. 1650s   C. 1660s   D. 1670s
10. Who was once an open-air preacher?
    A. John Milton   B. John Donne
    C. John Bunyan   D. Richard Lovelace
11. John Bunyan died in _____.
    A. 1686   B. 1687   C. 1688   D. 1689
12. *The Pilgrim's Progress* was _____.
    A. written in the old-fashioned, medieval form of allegory and dream
    B. not popular after its publication
    C. published right after he finished it
    D. written in 1684
13. *Song and Sonnets* _____.
    A. was written by John Milton
    B. contains cynical comments on inconstancy of women in love
    C. is the dialogue with his mistress or wife
    D. reveals the author's meditation on death and religion
14. Which of the poet often associates the short life of flowers with the transitory nature of human life and human affairs?
    A. John Milton   B. John Bunyan
    C. George Herbert   D. Robert Herrick
15. Until about 1590, the bourgeoisie had many interests in common with those of the monarchy in the struggles against the following except _____.
    A. Spain
    B. the Roman Catholic Church
    C. noble houses ruining the country with their civil wars
    D. the common people
16. In 1642, a civil war broke out. The opposition leaders in _____

were supported by contributions of merchants, the mass demonstrations of artisans and apprentices in the city, and by the peasants' riots against enclosures in the countryside. While around the king clustered the conservative gentry, the big landlords and the monopolists.

    A. Parliament   B. Royalist party

    C. Elizabeth I   D. Charles I

17. *Paradise Lost* is John Milton's masterpiece. It is a great epic in 12 books written in _____ about the heroic revolt of Satan against God's authority.

    A. blank verse   B. Spenserian stanza

    C. sonnet   D. heroic couplet

18. In the famous pamphlet _____, John Milton thus wrote: "Our king made not us, but we him. Nature has given fathers to us all, but we ourselves appointed our own king; so that the people are not for the king, but the king for them."

    A. *Second Defence of the English People*

    B. *The Ready and Easy Way to Establish a Free Commonwealth*

    C. *Of Reformation in England*

    D. *Defence of the People of England*

19. The finest thing in *Paradise Lost* is the description of hell, and _____ is regarded as the real hero of this part of the poem.

    A. God   B. Satan   C. Adam   D. Raphael

20. The main literary form in the 17th century is _____.

    A. drama   B. poetry   C. prose   D. novel

21. John Milton is famous for his _____, which is the result of his lifelong classical and biblical study.

    A. grand style   B. euphemism

    C. mighty lines   D. lucid style

22. _____ wrote the lives of John Donne, George Herbert and other personages to his liking, which marked a new departure in the development of English biography, based on observation and research

and containing records of personal traits.

A. Robert Burton   B. Sir Thomas Browne

C. Jeremy Taylor   D. Izaak Walton

23. "After the Restoration, he was flung into Bedford prison in 1660, for refusing to obey the law prohibiting religious meetings. He was told that, if he gave up preaching, he would be instantly set free. His answer was, 'If you let me out today, I will preach again tomorrow.' This enraged the reactionaries so much that they kept him in prison for 12 years." Whom does "he" refer to in the above lines?

A. John Milton   B. John Bunyan

C. John Dryden   D. Alexander Pope

24. _____ has been one of the most popular pieces of Christian writing produced during the Puritan Age.

A. *Paradise Lost*   B. *The Pilgrim's Progress*

C. *All for Love*   D. *Song and Sonnets*

25. The revolution of 1688 meant the following things except _____.

A. the supremacy of Parliament

B. the beginning of modern England

C. the triumph of the principle of political liberty

D. the Restoration of monarchy

26. William Shakespeare and Ben Jonson wrote their best works in the _____ century.

A. 16th   B. 17th   C. 18th   D. 19th

27. All the achievements in literature in the 17th century is based on _____.

A. the government's support

B. social awareness about literature

C. writers' concern about the society

D. King's support

28. When Elizabeth I died in 1603, _____ was chosen from Scotland and succeeded Elizabeth.

A. William I   B. Charles I   C. James I   D. James II

29. The _____ Period is also called Age of Milton because it produced a great poet whose name is John Milton.
    A. Revolution   B. Caroline   C. Elizabethan   D. Restoration
30. _____ does not belong to the Cavalier group.
    A. John Suckling   B. Richard Lovelace
    C. George Herbert   D. Robert Herrick
31. The poem _____, as we are told at the outset, was "to justify the ways of God to man", i.e. to advocate submission to the Almighty.
    A. *Paradise Regained*   B. *Samson Agonistes*
    C. *Paradise Lost*   D. *L'Allegro*
32. *The Flea* is one of _____'s famous poems.
    A. John Donne   B. George Herbert
    C. Andrew Marvell   D. Richard Crashaw
33. _____ entered the Anglican Church in 1615.
    A. Ben Jonson   B. George Herbert
    C. John Donne   D. Richard Crashaw
34. Which of the following didn't Robert Herrick invent?
    A. Imaginary mistress
    B. Hectic
    C. Imaginary novels
    D. Bewitching creature with exotic names
35. Which is the best example of the carpe diem tradition?
    A. *The Flea*
    B. *To the Virgins, to Make Much of Time*
    C. *Virtue*
    D. *Easter Wings*
36. _____ was the forerunner of the English classical school of literature in the 18th century.
    A. John Milton   B. John Bunyan
    C. John Dryden   D. Alexander Pope
37. The works of _____ are characterized, generally speaking, by

mysticism in content and fantasticality in form.
A. the metaphysical poets   B. the Cavalier poets
C. John Milton   D. John Dryden

III. Match-Making

Group One
Column A   Column B
1. Richard Lovelace   a. *On His Blindness*
2. John Milton   b. *The Constant Lover*
3. John Suckling   c. *To Lucasta, Going to the Wars*
4. George Herbert   d. *To His Coy Mistress*
5. Andrew Marvell   e. *Easter Wings*

Group Two
Column A   Column B
1. John Donne   a. *Virtue*
2. Robert Herrick   b. *A Valediction: Forbidding Mourning*
3. John Milton   c. *Why So Pale and Wan*
4. George Herbert   d. *To the Virgins, to Make Much of Time*
5. John Sucking   e. *On His Deceased Wife*

IV. Define the Literary Terms.

1. Puritan Age
2. Metaphysical poetry
3. Cavalier poet
4. *Paradise Lost*

5. Conceit
6. Restoration literature

V. Answer the Following Questions Briefly.

1. Describe the features of metaphysical poetry in the 17th century.
2. What does Glorious Revolution symbolize?
3. Make a brief comment on *Paradise Lost*.
4. What do you think contributed to John Bunyan's ideas?
5. Make a brief comment on John Bunyan's *The Pilgrim's Progress*.
6. What are the different aspects between the literature of the Elizabethan Period and the literature of the Revolution Period?
7. What are the differences between John Milton and John Donne in terms of religious sensibility?
8. What are the features of John Milton's poetry?
9. What's the feature of the literature after Restoration?
10. Make a comparison between *The Pilgrim's Progress* and *Journey to the West*, one of China's classical novels.

Part VI

The 18th Century: The Enlightenment, Neo-classicism and Pre-romanticism

I. Fill in the Blanks.

1. The 18th century has witnessed great development in _____.
2. After people controlled the government, they divided them into two parties: _____ and _____.
3. _____ played an important role when the two parties traded places.
4. A huge change in the 18th century in social life is that a large number of _____ appeared in London.
5. The Enlightenment, on the whole, was an expression of struggle of _____ against _____.
6. The realization of _____ led to the crisis of the Enlightenment at the end of the 18th century.
7. Joseph Addison (1672-1719) and Richard Steele (1672-1729) are the publishers of a moralistic journal _____.
8. The essays and stories of Joseph Addison and Richard Steele were devoted to _____, _____ and _____.
9. The development of _____ brought to the fore men of a new stamp, who had to be typified in the new literature.
10. The image of an enterprising Englishman of the 18th century was created by _____ in his famous novel _____.
11. _____ and _____ were the real founders of the genre of the bourgeois realistic novel in England and Europe.

12. In _____'s novel _____, he ruthlessly exposed the dirty mercenary essence of bourgeois relationships.
13. Pre-romanticism found its most manifest expression in the _____, because the greater part of such romances were devoted to the _____ times.
14. As a so-called time-server, _____ wrote Heroic Stanzas praising _____ within two years.
15. John Dryden's finest works are his long poems in rhymed couplets on _____, _____, and _____ themes.
16. _____ discovered modern novel.
17. Daniel Defoe made good use of _____, thus crowds flocked to cheer him in the pillory.
18. Robinson Crusoe saved a man from cannibals and called him _____.
19. Johnathan Swift's first notable work _____ is a keen satire upon the classics and modern literature in the controversy.
20. Johnathan Swift was courted and flattered by every side due to his book, _____, after that, _____ went out of power, thus he returned to Ireland and wrote his best-known literary work, _____.
21. In the country of Houyhnhnm, it is governed by _____, and their servants are _____ that possess every conceivable evil.
22. Joseph Addison and Richard Steele made great contribution in the field of _____.
23. After Richard Steele stopped _____, he started a new paper he called _____ published every morning instead of three times a week.
24. Alexander Pope's literature work, _____, brought him much fame, and the publication of his _____ in 1712 made him well-known and much honored in England.
25. Alexander Pope translated _____ and _____, which are characterized by elegant and artificial language of his day.
26. *The Rape of the Lock* is a _____ poem, which exhibits Alexander Pope's startling faculty as a satirist.

27. Alexander Pope can be regarded as a typical representative of _____.
28. From 1729 to 1737, Henry Fielding produced 26 plays, among which, _____ and _____ are his best works.
29. After the tour in Europe, Thomas Gray lived for a short time at Stoke Poges, where he wrote his _____, and probably sketched his _____.
30. Although in his day, Thomas Gray was considered England's foremost poet, he refused the title of _____.
31. In Oliver Goldsmith's poetry, he was much influenced by _____, however, in his sympathy for nature and human life, he belongs to the school of _____.
32. _____ presents a brilliant portrayal of England's high society and a biting satire on the morals and manners of that age, which also tells the story of a group of backbiters who busied themselves with malicious gossip.
33. _____ made breakthrough into the Romantic Movement, thus he is called a _____ poet.
34. In William Blake's first collection of poems *Poetical Sketches*, he tried Spenserian _____, Shakespearean and Miltonic _____, the ballad form and lyric meters.
35. _____ can be regarded as a peasant poet or farmer poet as well as the national hero of Scotland.
36. There appeared two groups of English enlighteners. One was the moderate group; the other was the _____.
37. The main literary stream of the 18th century was _____. What the writers described were mainly social realities.
38. One of the special features of *Tristram Shandy* is its art of _____. It seems that Laurence Sterne tried to catch the actual flow of human mind and sentiment in ordinary life, in the manner of a modern "_____ of consciousness" novelist.
39. _____ is Oliver Goldsmith's best poem. It contains some charm-

ing descriptions of village life, but the poet laments a state of society where "wealth accumulates and men decay."

40. The name of sentimentalism came from _____'s novel *A Sentimental Journey*.
41. Before newspapers appeared, the _____ had become a mighty power in England, and any writer with a talent for _____ or _____ was almost certain to be hired by party leaders.
42. Along with the depiction of _____ and social mode of life the writers of the Enlightenment began to display an interest in the _____ of an individual.
43. _____ and actual vices of aristocratic society are derided in the plays of Richard B. Sheridan, particularly in his comedy _____.
44. The most outstanding figure of English sentimentalism was _____. His representative works are *Tristram Shandy* and *Sentimental Journey*, the style and structure of which are the very antithesis of rationally composed novels, revealing a purely emotional approach to life on the part of the narrator.
45. The task of upholding revolutionary struggle of the people for their rights in the 18th century was undertaken by _____ and later taken up in the 19th century by the writers of _____.
46. John Dryden's long poetic career spanned the four decades from _____ in 1660 to the end of the 17th century.
47. _____ is a witty attack on Thomas Shadwell, a minor poet and playwright.
48. In poetry, John Dryden set an enduring style with his neat "_____" — paired lines of rhymed iambic pentameter.
49. In 1702 Daniel Defoe published a remarkable pamphlet called _____, supporting the claims of the free churches against the "High Fliers", i.e. Tories and Anglicans.
50. The whole name of Danial Defoe's *Robinson Crusoe* is _____.
51. Joseph Addison was born into the family of a _____ in a little village in Wilstshire.

52. Joseph Addison once became a member of _____ and later was sent to Ireland as _____.
53. Richard Steele started his first newspaper called _____.
54. With his great zeal and art, Joseph Addison helped Richard Steele establish a new genre of literature, which is _____.
55. Alexander Pope was born into a _____ family in London in the year of the _____.
56. The _____ was a progressive intellectual movement throughout Western Europe in the 18th century.
57. _____, written in heroic couplet by Alexander Pope, was a manifesto of English neo-classicism as Alexander Pope put forward his aesthetic theories in it.
58. Jonathan Swift is a representative of _____ in the 18th century.
59. _____ was so well received by the English readers that wherever there was a Bible, there was a copy of this book.
60. _____ is a satirical novel, in which the author Henry Fielding exposes the English bourgeois aristocratic society and mocks at its political system.
61. Richard Brinsley Sheridan's *The School for Scandal* has been called a great comedy of _____. It gives a brilliant portrayal and a biting satire of English high society.
62. _____, repudiating the high society for its vanity, greed and hypocrisy, has been regarded as the best English comedy since Shakespeare.

II. Choose the Best Answer for Each Question.

1. When did the Glorious Revolution happen?
   A. 1686　　　B. 1687　　　C. 1688　　　D. 1689
2. Which of the following best describes liberal Whigs?
   A. They were determined to safeguard popular liberty.

B. They wanted to leave as much authority as possible in the royal hands.

C. Their third party is called Jacobites.

D. They aimed to bring the Stuarts back to the throne.

3. Which of the following didn't work for the two parties?

   A. Daniel Defoe   B. Richard Steele

   C. Jonathan Swift   D. John Dryden

4. The difference between English and French Enlighteners is that _____.

   A. English philosophers and writers cleared the minds of men for the coming revolution

   B. English Enlighteners set no revolutionary aims before them

   C. France has gone through its bourgeois revolution in the 17th century

   D. French philosophers and writers emphasized more on liberty and freedom

5. Which is not included in the three main divisions of the 18th century writings?

   A. The reign of so-called classicism

   B. The New Poetic Generation

   C. The revival of Romantic poetry

   D. The beginning of the modern novel

6. What is the main contribution the first representatives of the English Enlightenment made?

   A. They criticized different aspects of the past England.

   B. They set themselves the task of struggling against the existing order of life.

   C. They use radical language to intensify social conflicts and arouse people's awareness.

   D. They attempted to smooth over social contradictions by moralizing and proclaiming.

7. Who was regarded as the highest authority on literary art by his

contemporaries?

A. Alexander Pope B. Richard Steele

C. Joseph Addison D. Jonathan Swift

8. What contribution is not made by Alexander Pope?

   A. He made great contribution to the theory and practice of prosody.

   B. He elaborated certain regulations for the style of poetical works.

   C. He published *The Spectator* together with other poets.

   D. He made popular the so-called heroic couplets.

9. Which category does the novel *Robinson Crusoe* belong to?

   A. Classic   B. Adventure   C. Fantasy   D. Realistic

10. What is the common feature of Henry Fielding and T. G. Smollet's novels?

    A. They both described the panorama of life in all sections of English society.

    B. They both exposed the depraved aristocracy and the avaricious bourgeoisie.

    C. They both contrasted the life of the ruling classes to the lack of rights and misery of the people.

    D. They both exposed all kinds of political charlatans and mocked at the state system.

11. Which of the following is T. G. Smollet's first novel?

    A. *Pamela*

    B. *The Adventures of Roderick Random*

    C. *The Adventures of Peregrine Pickle*

    D. *The Expedition of Humphrey Clinker*

12. Which of the following novels did not reveal psychological analysis?

    A. *The History of a Young Lady*   B. *Virtue Rewarded*

    C. *Gulliver's Travels*   D. *The Vicar of Wakefield*

13. Which is not the work of sentimentalism?

    A. *The Vicar of Wakefield*   B. *Tristram Shandy*

    C. *Gulliver's Travels*   D. *The Deserted Village*

14. Which kind of novel can also be called "a novel of horrors"?
    A. Novel of sentimentalism   B. Gothic novel
    C. Realistic novel   D. Classic novel
15. Who thought "a man should be learned in several sciences to be a complete and excellent poet"?
    A. Oliver Cromwell   B. Daniel Defoe
    C. Jonathan Swift   D. John Dryden
16. Which one is John Dryden's greatest work of literary criticism?
    A. *An Essay of Dramatic Poesy* B. *Heroic Stanzas*
    C. *A Song for St. Cecilia's Day* D. *Astrea Redux*
17. Which of the following is not the feature of Daniel Defoe?
    A. He was a jack-of-all-trades, as well as a writer.
    B. He was a radical Nonconformist in religion.
    C. He was a journalist and pamphleteer.
    D. He mainly focused on the life of royal family.
18. In which country did Robinson Crusoe become a sugar-planter?
    A. Guinea   B. Turkey   C. Britain   D. Brazil
19. Which word can best describe the character of Robinson Crusoe?
    A. Caring   B. Adventurous C. Realistic   D. Strong
20. *The Tale of a Tub* and *The Battle of the Books* were both published in _____.
    A. 1702   B. 1703   C. 1704   D. 1705
21. Which of the following can be regarded the greatest satires in the English language?
    A. *Robinson Crusoe*   B. *Gulliver's Travels*
    C. *Journal to Stella*   D. *The Tatler*
22. Which is the right sequence of Gulliver's travel?
    A. Lilliput—Brobdingnag—Flying island of Laputa—Houyhnhnm
    B. Brobdingnag—Lilliput—Flying island of Laputa—Houyhnhnm
    C. Houyhnhnm—Flying island of Laputa—Brobdingnag—Lilliput
    D. Flying island of Laputa—Lilliput—Brobdingnag—Houyhnhnm
23. Who went to travel in Europe and learned the politics of other Euro-

pean countries?

    A. Richard Steele   B. Joseph Addison

    C. Alexander Pope   D. Henry Fielding

24. Which is not true about *The Spectator*?

    A. It was limited to the doings of the women.

    B. It contained much comment on books.

    C. It was published every morning.

    D. It brought literature down to everyday life.

25. Which is true about *An Essay on Criticism*?

    A. It is written by John Dryden.

    B. It contains 744 lines and is divided into two parts.

    C. It is written in heroic couplets.

    D. It is a comparative study of the criticism on prose.

26. Which of the following authors worked in the field of literature, politics and finance?

    A. Joseph Addison   B. Henry Fielding

    C. Thomas Gray   D. Oliver Goldsmith

27. Which novel describes a faithful and virtuous wife in contrast with her unworthy husband?

    A. *The Life of Mr. Jonathan Wild the Great*

    B. *The History of Tom Jones, a Foundling*

    C. *Joseph Andrews*

    D. *Amelia*

28. When did Oliver Goldsmith publish his first original book *An Enquiry into the Present State of Polite Learning in Europe*?

    A. 1749   B. 1759   C. 1769   D. 1779

29. Which is not true about *The Deserted Village*?

    A. It is written in heroic couplets and can be regarded as Oliver Goldsmith's best poem.

    B. It begins with the poet's happy reminiscences of his home village.

    C. It blames the enclosure movement.

D. It is based on his own wandering experiences.
30. Which play of the 18th century isn't kept alive upon the modern stage?
   A. *Rivals*   B. *She Stoops to Conquer*
   C. *The Good-Natured Man*   D. *The School for Scandal*
31. Which of the following plays was first performed in 1779?
   A. *The Rivals*   B. *The Duenna*
   C. *The School for Scandal*   D. *The Critic*
32. Which poem depicts the happy condition of a child before it knows anything about the pains of existence?
   A. *Songs of Innocence*   B. *Songs of Experience*
   C. *Poetical Sketches*   D. *The French Revolution*
33. Which poem voices the new Romantic estimate of humanity?
   A. *Poems Chiefly in the Scottish Dialect*
   B. *A Man's a Man for That*
   C. *The Epistle to a Young Friend*
   D. *The Vision*
34. _____ was a progressive intellectual movement throughout Western Europe in the 18th century.
   A. The Renaissance   B. The Enlightenment
   C. The Religious Reformation D. The Chartist Movement
35. Most of the English writers in the 18th century were Enlighteners. They fell into two groups: _____.
   A. the moderate group and the radical group
   B. the passive Romantic poets and the active Romantic poets
   C. the metaphysical poets and the Cavalier poets
   D. the lakers and the sentimentalists
36. *Lives of Poets* is one of _____'s main works, which consists of some of the best-known pictures of the early English poets.
   A. Samuel Johnson   B. James Boswell
   C. Henry Fielding   D. Ben Jonson
37. The 18th century was an age of _____.

A. prose　　　B. novel　　　C. poetry　　　D. drama

38. In the 18th century, satire was much used in writing. English literature of this age produced some excellent satirists. Among them, _____ is the greatest.
    A. Alexander Pope　　　　B. Jonathan Swift
    C. Henry Fielding　　　　D. Daniel Defoe

39. _____ is Alexander Pope's poem which indicates the poet's political and philosophical viewpoint. It deals with man's relation to the universe, to society, to himself and to happiness.
    A. *The Rape of the Lock*　　B. *Essay on Man*
    C. *The Dunciad*　　　　D. *Essay on Criticism*

40. _____ was a member of Johnson's literary club. He has been known for his biography of Johnson entitled *Life of Johnson*.
    A. Samuel Johnson　　　　B. James Boswell
    C. Henry Fielding　　　　D. Ben Jonson

41. "To err is human, to forgive, divine" is a famous line from Alexander Pope's poem _____.
    A. *The Rape of the Lock*　　B. *Essay on Man*
    C. *The Dunciad*　　　　D. *Essay on Criticism*

42. _____ is the most important representative of the English classical poetry. He was at his best in satire and epigram.
    A. Jonathan Swift　　　　B. Samuel Richardson
    C. Alexander Pope　　　　D. Joseph Addison

43. "Proper words in proper places, makes the true definition of a style." This sentence is said by _____, one of the greatest masters of English prose.
    A. Alexander Pope　　　　B. Henry Fielding
    C. Daniel Defoe　　　　D. Jonathan Swift

44. _____'s best-known pamphlet was *The Trueborn Englishman—A Satire*, which contained a caustic exposure of the aristocracy and the tyranny of the church.
    A. Alexander Pope　　　　B. Henry Fielding

C. Daniel Defoe   D. Jonathan Swift

45. In May 1737, a Licensing Act was passed in Parliament. It prohibited the production of any play unless it had received the sanction of the English Government. As a result, _____'s career as a playwright was brought abruptly to an end.
    A. Richard Brinsley Sheridan   B. Henry Fielding
    C. David Garrick   D. John Gay

46. _____ and *The Idler* were periodicals edited by Samuel Johnson.
    A. *The Review*   B. *The Rambler*
    C. *The Tatler*   D. *The Spectator*

47. Oliver Goldsmith's _____ is a comedy of character, written as a counterblast of the "weeping comedy," i.e. the comedy full of sentimental moralizing.
    A. *She Stoops to Conquer*   B. *The Deserted Village*
    C. *The Vicar of Wakefield*   D. *The Good-Natured Man*

48. William Blake and Robert Burns are the representative poets of _____.
    A. pre-romanticism   B. romanticism
    C. sentimentalism   D. naturalism

49. In the 18th century English literature, the representative writers of realism include the following except _____.
    A. Daniel Defoe   B. Henry Fielding
    C. Tobias Smollett   D. Oliver Goldsmith

50. The 18th century England witnessed unprecedented technical innovations which equipped industry with steam, the new moving force, and new tools, and rapid growth of industry and commerce, which influenced the way of social life as a whole. This is called the "_____".
    A. Glorious Revolution   B. Industrial Revolution
    C. Bourgeois Restoration   D. Renaissance

51. _____ was Alexander Pope's poem which satirized the idle and artificial life of the aristocracy.

A. *The Rape of the Lock*　　B. *The Rape of Lucrece*
C. *The School for Scandal*　　D. *Every Man in His Humor*

52. The Enlighteners intended to reform social life according to a more reasonable principle, though this principle could never go beyond the limit of _____ interests.
    A. feudal　　B. capitalist
    C. bourgeois　　D. proletariat

53. Sentimentalism turned to the countryside for its material, and so was in striking contrast to _____, which had confined itself to the clubs and drawing-rooms, and to the social and political life of London.
    A. realism　　B. sentimentalism
    C. classicism　　D. romanticism

54. _____'s comedies are examples of the brief revival of the English comedy in the 1770s.
    A. Henry Fielding　　B. Samuel Johnson
    C. Oliver Goldsmith　　D. Richard Brinsley Sheridan

55. As a satirist, _____'s greatest power of satire is shown in his brilliant play *The Historical Register for the Year 1736*, which is daring in the extreme as a political satire.
    A. Henry Fielding　　B. Samuel Johnson
    C. Oliver Goldsmith　　D. Richard Brinsley Sheridan

56. Tobias Smollett wrote the following picaresque novels except _____.
    A. *The Adventure of Roderick Random*
    B. *The Adventure of Peregrine Pickle*
    C. *The Expedition of Humphrey Clinker*
    D. *Gulliver's Travels*

57. Henry Fielding's first work, _____ (1741), is a parody of *Pamela*, featuring a heroine who artfully manipulates her honor in order to secure a husband.
    A. *Shamela*　　B. *Joseph Andrews*
    C. *Clarissa*　　D. *The Conscious Lovers*

58. Which of the following is not the feature of the 18th century?
    A. Social had a rapid development.
    B. It is a time of prose.
    C. Young authors tended to write prose like Joseph Addison, or verse like Alexander Pope.
    D. Country life has had great refinement.
59. The middle of the 18th century in England saw the beginning of a new literary current, which is _____.
    A. sentimentalism   B. realism
    C. romanticism   D. the Enlightenment
60. Why did sentimentalism come into being?
    A. Because there was a bitter discontent on the part of certain Enlighteners in social reality.
    B. Because the common people were unsatisfied about the King.
    C. Because authors were enthusiastic about certain type of genre.
    D. Because some writers advocated that type of writing genre.
61. What was John Dryden's best poetry often inspired by?
    A. Family member   B. His beloved one
    C. Particular occasion   D. Social background
62. Which of the following is wrong about *A Song for St. Cecilia's Day*?
    A. It was an inventive testimony to the power of music.
    B. It was intended to be sung as well as read.
    C. It was given its noblest musical expression in Handel's setting.
    D. Handel's setting was written some fifty years earlier than the poem.
63. When did Daniel Defoe write his best-known fiction?
    A. In his fifty's   B. In his sixty's
    C. In his thirty's   D. In his forty's
64. Which of the following novels didn't appear in 1720?
    A. *Captain Singleton*   B. *Duncan Campbel*
    C. *Journal of the Plague Year*   D. *Memoirs of Cavalier*
65. What made Robinson Crusoe want to return home when he first

came out?

A. A huge storm B. A shark
C. A group of pirates D. A rover

66. Which writer was flattered and courted by both Tories and Whigs?

A. John Dryden B. Danial Defoe
C. Johnathan Swift D. Alexander Pope

67. Which writer joined the army?

A. Richard Steele B. Joseph Addison
C. Henry Fielding D. Oliver Goldsmith

68. In the early 18th century, English writers of the neo-classic school were the following except _____.

A. Alexander Pope B. Joseph Addison
C. Richard Steele D. Oliver Goldsmith

69. The following novels were written by Daniel Defoe except _____.

A. *Robison Crusoe* B. *Hymn to the Pillory*
C. *Moll Flanders* D. *Captain Singleton*

70. The following are William Blake's collections of poems except _____.

A. *Poetical Sketches* B. *Songs of Innocence*
C. *Songs of Experience* D. *Prophecies*

71. "In seed time learn, in harvest teach, in winter enjoy." This proverb is cited from William Blake's _____.

A. *Songs of Experience*
B. *Songs of Innocence*
C. *The Marriage of Heaven and Hell*
D. *Poetical Sketches*

72. _____'s *Reliques of Ancient English Poetry* marks an epoch in the history of English poetry. It did much to hasten the coming of the new Romantic Movement.

A. Walter Scott B. Thomas Gray
C. Robert Burns D. Thomas Percy

73. _____ is a master satirist, and his irony is deadly. But his satire is masked by an outward gravity, and an apparent calmness conceals

his bitter irony. This makes his satire all the more powerful, as shown in his *A Modest Proposal*.

A. Alexander Pope   B. Henry Fielding
C. Daniel Defoe   D. Jonathan Swift

74. Which play is a fine example of sentimentalism in the 18th century literature?

A. *Night Thoughts*   B. *The Rivals*
C. *The Vicar of Wakefield*   D. *Tristram Shandy*

III. Match-Making

Group One

Column A   Column B

1. Henry Fielding   a. *The Tale of a Tub*
2. John Dryden   b. *The Dunciad*
3. Jonathan Swift   c. *Joseph Andrews*
4. Joseph Addison   d. *A Song for St. Cecilia's Day*
5. Alexander Pope   e. *The Campaign*
6. Richard Brinsley Sheridan   f. *She Stoops to Conquer*
7. William Blake   g. *The School for Scandal*
8. Oliver Goldsmith   h. *Songs of Experience*

Group Two

Column A   Column B

1. John Dryden   a. *The History of Tom Jones, a Foundling*
2. Daniel Defoe   b. *Elegy Written in a Country Churchyard*
3. Jonathan Swift   c. *The Traveler*
4. Alexander Pope   d. *My Heart's in the Highlands*
5. Henry Fielding   e. *An Essay of Dramatic Poesy*

6. Thomas Gray   f. *London*
7. Oliver Goldsmith   g. *Captain Singleton*
8. Richard Brinsley Sheridan   h. *An Essay on Man*
9. William Blake   i. *The Critic*
10. Robert Burns   j. *Gulliver's Travels*

IV. Define the Literary Terms.

1. The Enlightenment
2. Sentimentalism
3. Neo-classicism
4. Elegy
5. Archaism
6. Romanticism

V. Answer the Following Questions Briefly.

1. What are the features of Enlighteners?
2. Why can we call John Dryden a many-sided talent?
3. Make an outline of *Robinson Crusoe*.
4. What is the significance of *Robinson Crusoe*? What do you think is the value of *Robinson Crusoe*?
5. Why is *Gulliver's Travels* called a satirical novel?
6. What are the features of Henry Fielding's novels?
7. What is Richard Steele's and Joseph Addison's contribution to English literature?
8. What are the features of Daniel Defoe's novels?
9. What are Jonathan Swift's writing features?
10. What are the features of Henry Fielding's novels?
11. What is William Blake's position in English literature?

12. What are the three stages of the Enlightenment?
13. What is Alexander Pope's position in English literature?
14. Are there any differences in William Blake's two collections of lyrics *Songs of Innocence* and *Songs of Experience*? Why?
15. Do you know other Chinese sarcastic writers like Johnathan Swift? What's the representative work of him/her?

Part VII

The 19th Century (First Half): The Romantic Period

I. Fill in the Blanks.

1. _____ is an era that criticizes the feudal system or capitalist system from a humanitarian standpoint, emphasizes creative freedom, opposes classicism and pays attention to expressing people's inner feelings.
2. The so-called Romantic Period extends from the _____ to the third decade of the _____.
3. The publication of _____ marks the real rise of British Romantic literature.
4. _____ is a pioneer of the era of British romanticism.
5. The Lake Poets refer to an early school in the English Romantic Movement in the 19th century, represented by _____, _____ and _____.
6. George Gordon Byron's poetic novel _____ shows the real life in Europe in the early 19th century through the protagonist's life experience in different countries such as Spain, Greece, Turkey, Russia and Britain.
7. In _____, Samuel Taylor Coleridge employs a superficially loose and disjointed construction which is actually carefully designed to trigger associations of imagery that produce mental echoes of juxtaposed impressions.
8. Some social and intellectual events give rise to the Romantic Peri-

od, such as _____, _____ and _____.
9. There were two pre-romanticists, who were _____ and _____.
10. In addition to the Lake Poets, there were _____ poets in the Romantic Period, such as George Gordon Byron, Percy Bysshe Shelley, and John Keats.
11. The Preface to the _____ serves as the manifesto of Romantic Movement in poetry.
12. The publication in 1812 of the first two cantos of _____, a poem narrating his travels between 1809 and 1811 in Europe, brought George Gordon Byron fame.
13. _____ is regarded as the most wonderful lyricist England has ever produced mainly for his poems on nature, on love, and on politics.
14. The founder and great master of historical novel is _____.
15. As one of the greatest female writers of the 19th century, _____ brought something new to the readers of the 19th century when they got tired of the vulgar and boring sentimental novels and Gothic novels.
16. _____ is a love story which was the first of Jane Austen's novels to be published.
17. In 1796, _____ contributed four sonnets to Samuel Taylor Coleridge's *Poems on Various Subjects* (1796). This was followed by *Blank Verse* (1798) and *Pride's Cure* (1802).
18. Walter Scott's _____ represents the conflicts between Anglo-Saxon and Norman Conquerors in the 12th century.
19. The Romantic Age began in 1798 when the joint work _____ was published by William Wordsworth and Samuel Taylor Coleridge.
20. Jane Austen was a one of famous women _____ who appeared in the Romantic Age.
21. Living in the Lake District in the northwestern part of England, William Wordsworth, _____ are famously known as the "Lake Poets".

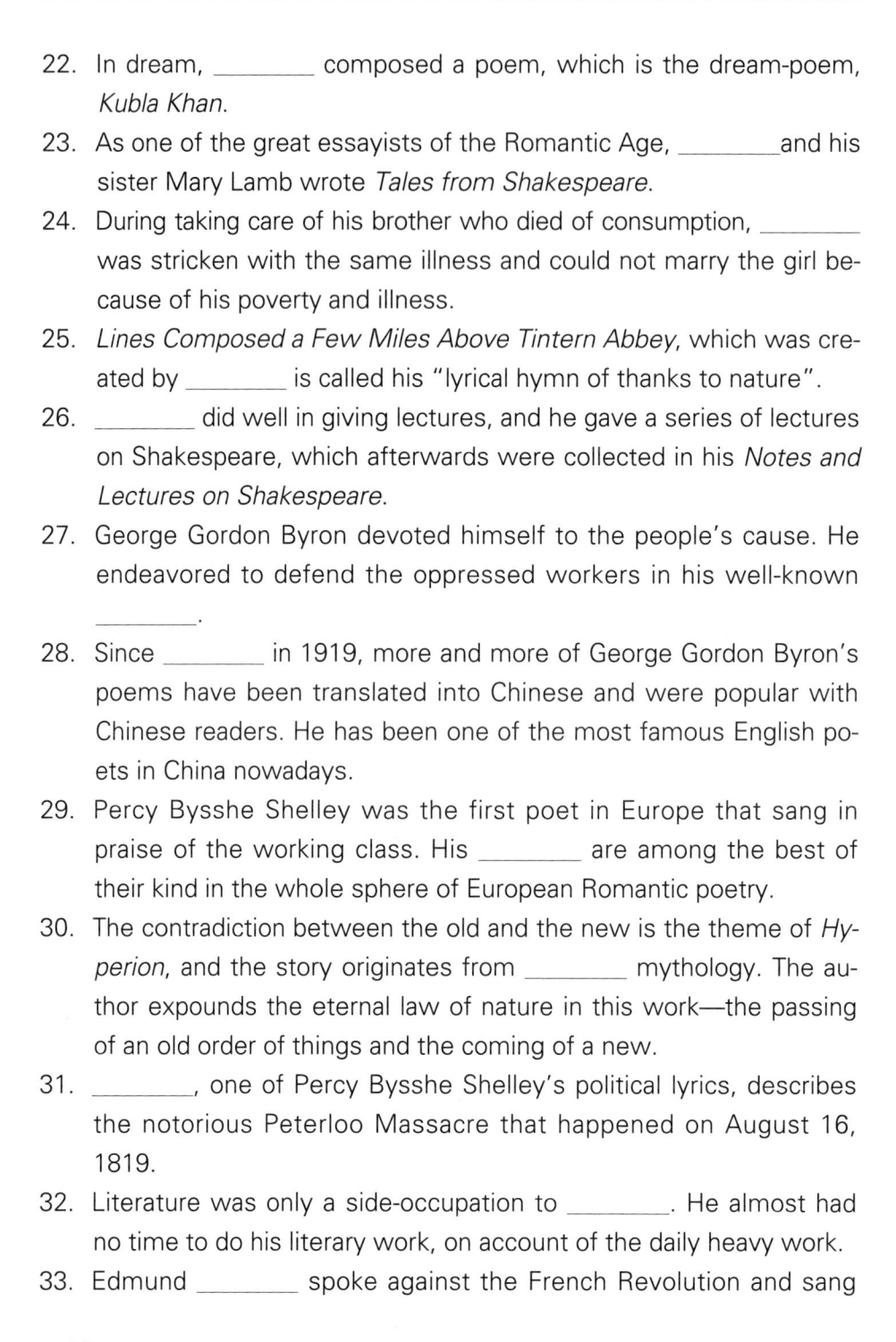

22. In dream, _____ composed a poem, which is the dream-poem, *Kubla Khan*.
23. As one of the great essayists of the Romantic Age, _____ and his sister Mary Lamb wrote *Tales from Shakespeare*.
24. During taking care of his brother who died of consumption, _____ was stricken with the same illness and could not marry the girl because of his poverty and illness.
25. *Lines Composed a Few Miles Above Tintern Abbey*, which was created by _____ is called his "lyrical hymn of thanks to nature".
26. _____ did well in giving lectures, and he gave a series of lectures on Shakespeare, which afterwards were collected in his *Notes and Lectures on Shakespeare*.
27. George Gordon Byron devoted himself to the people's cause. He endeavored to defend the oppressed workers in his well-known _____.
28. Since _____ in 1919, more and more of George Gordon Byron's poems have been translated into Chinese and were popular with Chinese readers. He has been one of the most famous English poets in China nowadays.
29. Percy Bysshe Shelley was the first poet in Europe that sang in praise of the working class. His _____ are among the best of their kind in the whole sphere of European Romantic poetry.
30. The contradiction between the old and the new is the theme of *Hyperion*, and the story originates from _____ mythology. The author expounds the eternal law of nature in this work—the passing of an old order of things and the coming of a new.
31. _____, one of Percy Bysshe Shelley's political lyrics, describes the notorious Peterloo Massacre that happened on August 16, 1819.
32. Literature was only a side-occupation to _____. He almost had no time to do his literary work, on account of the daily heavy work.
33. Edmund _____ spoke against the French Revolution and sang

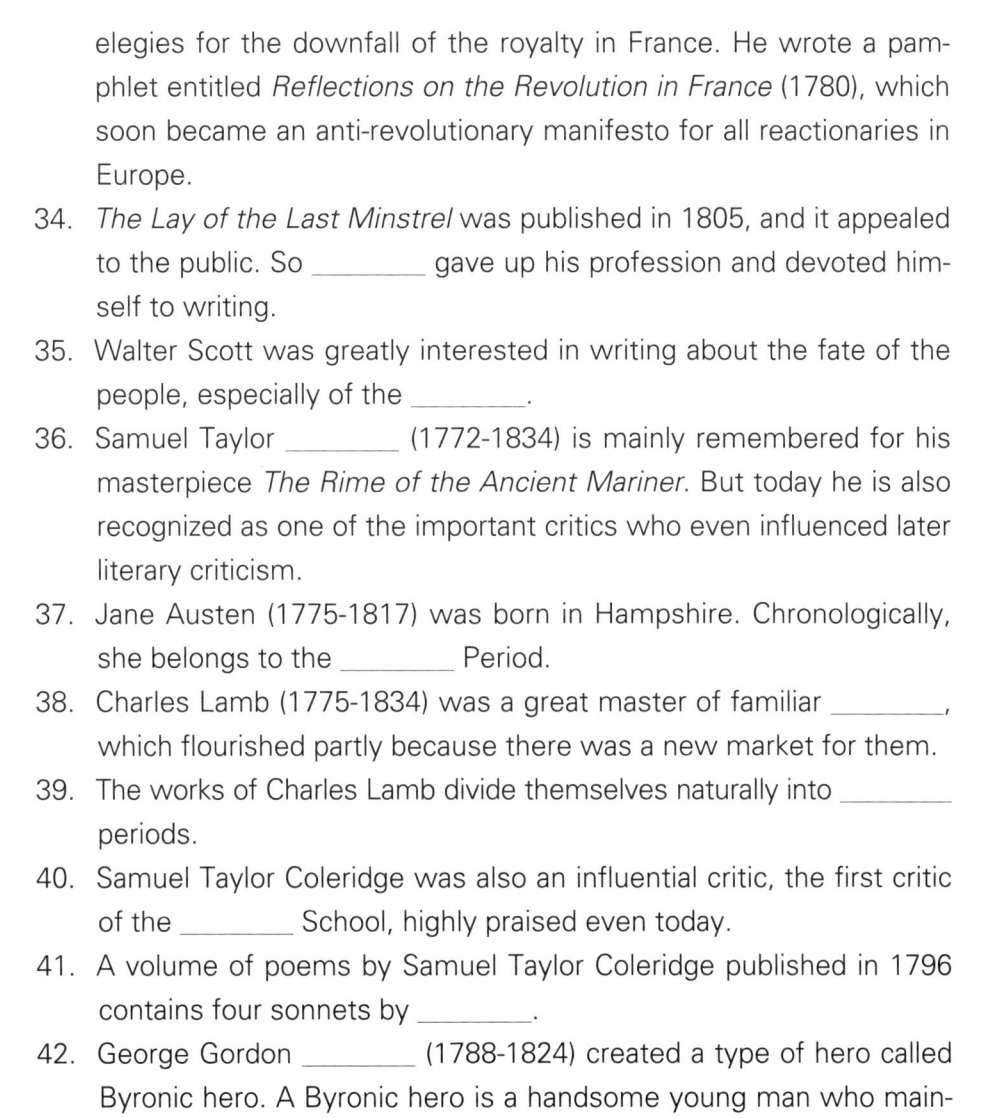

elegies for the downfall of the royalty in France. He wrote a pamphlet entitled *Reflections on the Revolution in France* (1780), which soon became an anti-revolutionary manifesto for all reactionaries in Europe.

34. *The Lay of the Last Minstrel* was published in 1805, and it appealed to the public. So _____ gave up his profession and devoted himself to writing.

35. Walter Scott was greatly interested in writing about the fate of the people, especially of the _____.

36. Samuel Taylor _____ (1772-1834) is mainly remembered for his masterpiece *The Rime of the Ancient Mariner*. But today he is also recognized as one of the important critics who even influenced later literary criticism.

37. Jane Austen (1775-1817) was born in Hampshire. Chronologically, she belongs to the _____ Period.

38. Charles Lamb (1775-1834) was a great master of familiar _____, which flourished partly because there was a new market for them.

39. The works of Charles Lamb divide themselves naturally into _____ periods.

40. Samuel Taylor Coleridge was also an influential critic, the first critic of the _____ School, highly praised even today.

41. A volume of poems by Samuel Taylor Coleridge published in 1796 contains four sonnets by _____.

42. George Gordon _____ (1788-1824) created a type of hero called Byronic hero. A Byronic hero is a handsome young man who maintains an attitude of pride and cynicism. The Byronic hero conceals his inner misery behind a careless façade.

43. *Don Juan* is a long _____ epic, because George Gordon Byron makes the hero see a lot of the world, comment on, criticize and satirize the world.

44. George Gordon Byron was one of the most excellent representatives of English _____, and he was one of the most influential

poets of his time.

45. At Oxford, Percy Bysshe _____ published a pamphlet entitled *The Necessity of Atheism*, in which he thought that God's being could not be proved. For this he was expelled after only six months at Oxford.

46. John Keats learned the art of poetry mainly from the poets of the English _____, such as Spenser, Shakespeare and Milton.

47. John Keats has often been regarded as a _____ poet because his poetry is distinguished by sensuousness and the perfection of form.

48. During his lifetime, the most widely known work of _____ was a poem entitled *The Song of the Shirt*, which was a lament for a poor London seamstress.

II. Choose the Best Answer for Each Question.

1. Which of the following poems embodies the great power of nature that may influence our life deeply as revealed in the poem?
   A. *Kubla Khan*　　　　　　　B. *I wandered lonely as a cloud*
   C. *The Prelude*　　　　　　　D. *Intimations of Immortality*

2. Which of the following poets is not a representative of the Lake Poets?
   A. William Wordsworth　　　　B. Samuel Taylor Coleridge
   C. Robert Southey　　　　　　D. Percy Bysshe Shelley

3. This 625-line ballad is among his essential works. It tells of a sailor who kills an albatross and for that crime against nature endures terrible punishments. Which of the following poems is described above?
   A. *Rime of the Ancient Mariner*　B. *Biographia Literaria*
   C. *London*　　　　　　　　　　D. *Childe Harold*

4. The chant-like, musical incantations of _____ result from Samuel

Taylor Coleridge's masterful use of iambic tetrameter and alternating rhyme schemes.

    A. *Kubla Khan*   B. *Childe Harold's Pilgrimage*

    C. *Don Juan*   D. *She Walks in Beauty*

5. Romantic literature originated in _____.

    A. the late of the 16th century   B. the 17th century

    C. the end of the 18th century   D. the 19th century

6. The most important work of Walter Scott is _____.

    A. *Ivanhoe*

    B. *Essays of Elia*

    C. *On an Infant Dying as Soon as Born*

    D. *The Eve of St. Agnes*

7. Which of the following poets is the founder of European historical novels?

    A. William Makepeace Thackeray

    B. Charles Dickens

    C. Charlotte Brontë

    D. Walter Scott

8. Which of the following author's interests are in the small world of rural gentry and clergy?

    A. George Eliot   B. Jane Austen

    C. Alfred Tennyson   D. Walter Scott

9. Which of the following works contains five different love patterns?

    A. *Pride and Prejudice*   B. *Emma*

    C. *Persuasion*   D. *Northanger Abbey*

10. When we talk about British socialist poets, the first name that comes into our minds is _____.

    A. Jane Austen   B. Percy Bysshe Shelley

    C. William Wordsworth   D. John Keats

11. Which of the following is NOT the feature of *Pride and Prejudice*?

    A. Irony   B. Dramatic irony

    C. Alliteration   D. Satire

12. Which of the following is George Gordon Byron's earliest work?
    A. *Childe Harold's Pilgrimage*   B. Verse drama *Manfred*
    C. *Don Juan*   D. *Song for the Luddites*
13. "The trumpet of a prophecy! O, wind, if winter comes, can spring be far behind?" Which poet said the above sentence?
    A. Jane Austen   B. Percy Bysshe Shelley
    C. John Keats   D. Bingleys
14. Which of the following is Not the characteristic of Charles Lamb's prose?
    A. Humors   B. Archaism
    C. Satire   D. Intensely personal
15. Walter Scott was one of the most important British writers in the first 30 years of the 19th century. His death in 1833 marked _____.
    A. the beginning of the Romantic Age
    B. the end of the Romantic Age
    C. the beginning of British realism
    D. the end of British realism
16. _____ were two important novelists in the English Romantic Age.
    A. George Gordon Byron and John Keats
    B. Bingleys and Samuel Taylor Coleridge
    C. Walter Scott and Jane Austen
    D. George Eliot and William Hazlitt
17. The first critic of the _____ School was Samuel Taylor Coleridge.
    A. Romantic   B. Realistic
    C. Classical   D. Idealistic
18. _____ was a long poem written by George Gordon Byron?
    A. *She Walks in Beauty* B. *Don Juan*
    C. *A Red, Red Rose*   D. *The Isle of Greece*
19. Which work was written by Samuel Taylor Coleridge himself?
    A. *Lyrical Ballads*   B. *Kubla Khan*
    C. *Childe Harold's Pilgrimage* D. *Hebrew Melodies*

20. _____ wrote *Adonais* because of the death of John Keats?
   A. George Gordon Byron   B. Samuel Taylor Coleridge
   C. Geoffrey Chaucer   D. Percy Bysshe Shelley
21. _____ is considered to be the most wonderful lyricist in England owing to his poems mainly on nature, on love, and on politics.
   A. Percy Bysshe Shelley   B. George Gordon Byron
   C. Charles Lamb   D. Jane Austen
22. _____ has been regarded as the highest achievement of John Keats although the long epic was unfinished.
   A. *The Lost Love*
   B. *Hyperion*
   C. *The Rime of the Ancient Mariner*
   D. *When I Have Fear*
23. Which of the following is Percy Bysshe Shelley's famous poetic plays?
   A. *Prometheus Unbound*   B. *Ode to the Nightingale*
   C. *The Revolt of Islam*   D. *Queen Mab*
24. Which famous work was seen as a symbol of the break with classicism and the beginning of the Romantic Age?
   A. *Bright Star*
   B. *Lyrical Ballads*
   C. *Tales from Shakespeare*
   D. *Lines Composed a Few Miles Above Tintern Abbey*
25. Whose masterpiece is *Pride and Prejudice*?
   A. Walter Scott   B. Charles Dickens
   C. Jane Austen   D. Robert Southey
26. Which literary criticism did Samuel Taylor Coleridge finish in 1817?
   A. *The Eve of St. Agnes*   B. *Queen Mab*
   C. *Childe Harold's Pilgrimage* D. *Biographia Literaria*
27. Which is George Gordon Byron's first volume of poems?
   A. *Hours of Idleness*   B. *Don Juan*
   C. *Manfred*   D. *Cain*

28. Who completed *The Prelude*, containing all together 14 books in 1805?
    A. William Wordsworth   B. Robert Southey
    C. George Gordon Byron   D. William Hazlitt
29. Which novel is the last of Walter Scott's that again deals with the time of the Crusaders of the 12th century?
    A. *Count Robert of Paris*   B. *Rob Roy*
    C. *Ivanhoe*   D. *Don Juan*
30. We may say that Walter Scott's historical novel paved the path for the development of the realistic novel of the _____ century.
    A. 18th   B. 19th   C. 20th   D. 21st
31. Samuel Taylor Coleridge's works can be divided into three classes except _____.
    A. poetic   B. critical   C. natural   D. philosophical
32. The aesthetic theory of _____ was influenced by Samuel Taylor Coleridge's ideas on poetry writing and John Keats's ideas.
    A. T. S. Eliot   B. Jane Austen
    C. Walter Scott   D. Charles Lamb
33. Which of the following novels is not written by Jane Austen?
    A. *Emma*   B. *Persuasion*
    C. *Pride and Prejudice*   D. *Lovel the Widower*
34. It may be noted that the first decades of the _____ centuries also witnessed new births in the essay as a form of literature.
    A. 16th and 17th   B. 17th and 18th
    C. 18th and 19th   D. 19th and 20th
35. George Gordon Byron's condemnation on the unjust society and his sympathy for the _____ people was easily seen in his poems such as *Ode to the Framers of the Frame Bill* (1812), *Song for the Luddites* (1816).
    A. oppressed   B. ruling   C. capitalist   D. exploiting
36. *Don Juan* is one of George Gordon Byron's _____ works.
    A. satirical   B. didactic   C. descriptive   D. eulogizing

37. *Childe Harold's Pilgrimage* consists of _____ cantos written in various periods of the Byron's life.

    A. one   B. two   C. three   D. four

38. George Gordon Byron's _____ was translated into Chinese by Ma Junwu, Su Manshu, Hu Shi and others by the end of the 19th century.

    A. *The Isles of Greece*   B. *When We Two Parted*
    C. *She Walks in Beauty*   D. *Manfred*

39. Among Percy Bysshe Shelley's lyrics, the greatest political lyric is _____.

    A. *Song to the Men of England*   B. *Ode to the West Wind*
    C. *Queen Mab*   D. *To a Skylark*

40. _____ leading principle is: "Beauty is truth, truth beauty".

    A. John Keats's   B. William Wordsworth's
    C. Samuel Taylor Coleridge's D. Charles Lamb's

41. Thomas Hood's famous works include _____ which is a satirical poem holding up to ridicule the worship of gold by the bourgeoisie.

    A. *Miss Kilmansegg*   B. *The Song of the Shirt*
    C. *The Bridge of Sighs*   D. *The Song of the Lower Classes*

42. The following poets belong to the Active Romantic group except _____.

    A. George Gordon Byron   B. Samuel Taylor Coleridge
    C. Percy Bysshe Shelley   D. John Keats

43. The following poets belong to the Passive Romantic group except _____.

    A. William Wordsworth   B. Samuel Taylor Coleridge
    C. Percy Bysshe Shelley   D. Robert Southey

44. Who was called "the best and least selfish man I ever know" by George Gordon Byron?

    A. Percy Bysshe Shelley   B. William Wordsworth
    C. Charles Lamb   D. Jane Austen

45. Which of the following is not written by George Gordon Byron?

  A. *She Walks in Beauty* B. *The Isles of Greece*
  C. *When We Two Parted* D. *Prometheus Unbound*
46. Which of the following historical novel is not written by Walter Scott?
  A. *Rob Roy* B. *Ivanhoe*
  C. *The Lady of the Lake* D. *Waverly*
47. _____ is the first important woman novelist in English literature.
  A. Jane Austen B. Emily Dickinson
  C. Anne Brontë D. Mary Shelley

III. Match-Making

Group One

	Column A		Column B
1.	William Wordsworth	a.	*The Lost Love*
2.	Samuel Taylor Coleridge	b.	*The Isles of Greece*
3.	Charles Lamb	c.	*The Tragedies of Shakespeare*
4.	George Gordon Byron	d.	*The Rime of the Ancient Mariner*
5.	Jane Austen	e.	*Mansfield Park*

Group Two

	Column A		Column B
1.	Thomas Hood	a.	*Tales from Shakespeare*
2.	John Keats	b.	*Isabella*
3.	George Gordon Byron	c.	*Punch*
4.	Charles Lamb	d.	*The Characters of Shakespeare's Plays*
5.	William Hazlitt	e.	*Ode to the Framers of the Frame Bill*

上编　英国文学史练习

Group Three

Column A   Column B
1. Samuel Taylor Coleridge   a. *The Prelude*
2. Walter Scott   b. *Kubla Khan*
3. William Wordsworth   c. *On the Knocking at the Gate in Macbeth*
4. Robert Southey   d. *Ivanhoe*
5. Thomas De Quincey   e. *Joan of Arc*

Group Four

Column A   Column B
1. William Wordsworth   a. *Wit and Humor*
2. Jane Austen   b. *Lamia*
3. Percy Bysshe Shelley   c. *Ode to Duty*
4. John Keats   d. *Ode to the West Wind*
5. Leigh Hunt   e. *Pride and Prejudice*

Group Five

Column A   Column B
1. Thomas Hood   a. *The Excursion*
2. John Keats   b. *To Autumn*
3. Walter Scott   c. *Northanger Abbey*
4. William Wordsworth   d. *The Black Dwarf*
5. Jane Austen   e. *Miss Kilmansegg*

IV. Define the Literary Terms.

1. Romanticism
2. The Lake Poets
3. Byronic hero

V. Answer the Following Questions Briefly.

1. Briefly describe the characteristics of romanticism.
2. What are the differences between romanticism and realism?
3. Why is Jane Austen a representative of female writers?
4. Please briefly describe Samuel Taylor Coleridge.
5. Make a brief comment on *Pride and Prejudice*.

Part VIII

The 19th Century (Second Half): The Victorian Age and Critical Realism

I. Fill in the Blanks.

1. The Victorian Period is from _____ to _____ when Queen Victoria ruled over England.
2. _____ is the predominant theme in Early Victorian literature.
3. The two major parties, _____ and _____, kept office in quick turn during the Victorian Period.
4. In order to solve the problem of _____, the Poor-Law Amendment Act of 1834 abolished outdoor relief and parochial responsibility which were often corrupt and insufficient in administration.
5. The pictures of the London slums described in Charles Dickens's novel _____ and of the cemetery described in _____ are not romantic exaggerations of a Gothic imagination but true pictures of actuality that can be verified and proved.
6. During the years after 1832, the major contradiction on the political stage became more definitely that between labor and capital. The years between 1832 and the early 1850s saw an important series of events known as the _____.
7. Though it failed, _____ signified the first great political movement of the proletariat in English history.
8. The critical realists of the 19th century first set themselves the task of criticizing the capitalist society from a _____ viewpoint and delineated the crying contradictions of reality.

9. The greatest English realist of the Victorian Age was _____. With a striking force and truthfulness, he created pictures of bourgeois civilization and described the misery and sufferings of common people.
10. The English working class created a literature of its own which can be called the _____ literature, for it developed among the participants of the Chartist movement before and after the revolutionary events of 1848.
11. The Chartist writers introduced a new theme into English literature—the struggle of the _____ for its rights.
12. Charles Robert Darwin's _____ (1859) and *The Decent of Man* (1871) shook the theoretical basis of the traditional faith.
13. Elizabeth Barrett Browning's most perfect work is the _____, which contains the record of courtship and marriage.
14. Elizabeth Barrett Browning's poem *Lady Geraldine's Courtship* works under the influence of _____'s idylls.
15. The themes of Elizabeth Barrett Browning's poems center on life, _____ and liberation of women.
16. In the poem _____, Elizabeth Barrett Browning voices the humanitarian protest against the practice of employing child labor in mines and factories.
17. Elizabeth Barrett Browning's poems attracted _____ who was 6 years her junior, and they later fell in love and got married.
18. The themes of Elizabeth Barrett Browning's poems center on life, love and _____ of women. She was against slavery and employment of _____.
19. _____ was considered to deserve the laureateship, but which eventually was awarded to Alfred Tennyson in 1850. Her greatest work, *Sonnets from the Portuguese* (1850), is a sequence of love sonnets addressing to her husband.
20. _____ can be called Sappho of England and idol of Emily Dickinson of America.

21. Alfred Tennyson is the most representative _____ in the Victorian Period.
22. _____ became the poet-laureate after the death of William Wordsworth in 1850.
23. In the _____, Alfred Tennyson painted the character of the first English national hero, King Arthur, and gave a new meaning to the legends which had grown up in the Middle Ages about the Knights of the Round Table.
24. _____ was written by Alfred Tennyson in memory of A. H. Hallam, his closest friend and the fiancé of his sister.
25. Alfred Tennyson's use of _____ is worth noticing. He and Robert Browning brought this form to an independent type, though it was already used by Renaissance poets such as John Donne and others.
26. *Break, Break, Break* was written by _____.
27. _____ is a serio-comic blank verse narrative poem, written by Alfred Tennyson, published in 1847. It is Alfred Tennyson's contribution to the question of the higher education of women.
28. T. S. Eliot called _____ "the great master of metric as well as of melancholia." He excelled in the use of the musical qualities of words to emphasize his rhythm and meaning.
29. _____ was born in Calcutta on July 18, 1811, the only child of an Englishman in the Indian Civil Service.
30. *Vanity Fair* presents a panorama of the society of the English upper-middle class of the first half of the _____ century.
31. _____ is William Makepeace Thackeray's masterpiece, taking the title from the fair in Bunyan's *The Pilgrim's Progress,* where all sorts of cheats are displayed for sale.
32. *Vanity Fair*, written by _____ was published in 1847-1848 in monthly installments, showing a picture of the life of the English upper-middle class of the first half of the 19th century.
33. The subtitle of the novel *Vanity Fair* is _____, points to the au-

thor's intention to portray not individuals singly but the whole of the notorious "Vanity Fair", a name William Makepeace Thackeray gave English bourgeois and aristocratic society.

34. The central figure in *Vanity Fair* is _____, she is a perfect embodiment of the spirit of Vanity Fair as her only aspiration in life is to gain wealth and position by any means.

35. In *Vanity Fair*, with biting irony, William Makepeace Thackeray exposes the vices of this society: _____, _____, and moral degradation.

36. _____ was one of the greatest critical realist writers of the Victorian Age. His representative works in the early period include *Oliver Twist, David Copperfield* and so on.

37. The Victorian Age is an age of _____ rather than of romanticism. In this period, to be true to life becomes the first requirement for literary writing.

38. Charles Dickens's novel _____ is a powerful exposure of bourgeois society and tells the story of a poor child. It shows the extreme brutality and corruption of the oppressors and their agents under the mask of philanthropy.

39. Charles Dickens's success with the comic _____ (1836) established Dickens as a popular humorist.

40. _____ is Charles Dickens's first true novel.

41. *Barnaby Rudge*, Charles Dickens's first _____ novel, is set in the period of the Gordon antipoverty riots of 1780.

42. *Hard Times* (1854) is an earnest attack on the vulgarity and materialism of the rising _____ class industrialists.

43. _____ is Charles Dickens's first and most classic Christmas book published in 1843.

44. Charles Dickens's novel _____ is a satire on the abuses of the Court of Chancery, which shows Dickens at his best in handling complex narrative and interlocking plots.

45. *Oliver Twist* is a novel worth reading many times if one wants to

know the conditions of life in the then England, Dickens's humanitarian thought and his viewpoint on _____.

46. Many critics have called _____ the best of Charles Dickens's novels.

47. *Great Expectations* (1860-1861) is told in the first person by _____, a young man who learns through adversity to discard his own superficial snobbishness.

48. Of Charles Dickens's fictional art, the most distinguished feature is his successful _____.

49. Charles Dickens always tried to soften the problems and wished for _____ rather than revolution.

50. The Marshalsea Prison in *Little* _____ is more than a prison; it is a microcosm of the capitalist world.

51. In the basic plot of *A Tale of Two Cities*, the fate of Dr. Manette is closely interwoven with the development of the _____ Revolution.

52. The most important poet of the Victorian Age was Alfred Tennyson. Next to him were _____ and his wife.

53. Robert Browning is an English poet, and noted for his mastery of _____.

54. *My Last Duchess*, which was published in 1842, is written by _____.

55. Charles Dickens liked to use _____ technique in his novels, with which he usually ended his novels with relative happy scenes.

56. In *Oliver Twist*, Charles Dickens gave a sympathetic description of even a street girl named Nancy, which shows Dickens's _____ viewpoint.

57. Robert Browning's dramatic monologue is an objective form of drama with a purpose of _____ rather than expressing the poet's feeling or sentiment.

58. _____ is Robert Browning's masterpiece which tells a horrible story of a man's murder of his beautiful young wife.

59. *Adam Bede* is a novel of moral conflicts, showing the contest of

personal desires, passions, temperament, human weaknesses and the claims of moral duty. The writer of this novel is _____.

60. George _____ (1819-1881) is the penname of Mary Ann Evans.
61. George Eliot published her first story "_____" in *Blackwood's Magazine*.
62. Some critics have called *Middlemarch* written by George _____ the greatest of Victorian novels.
63. George Eliot is often called the most intellectual of the _____ novelists.
64. *Middlemarch* is a novel of English _____ life in the early 19th century, just before the Reform Bill of 1832.
65. In *The Mill on the Floss*, there is fusion of traditional tragedy and _____.
66. In many of George Eliot's novels, one can find that she was always concerned with virtue and _____. Her novels are good examples of moral criticism.
67. After the publication of *Adam Bede*, George Eliot's identity as a _____ was gradually known though she tried to conceal her real name.
68. _____ on the Floss (1859-1860) tells of the love, estrangement, and eventual reconciliation of the daughter and son of a country miller.
69. _____ was regarded as George Eliot's greatest novel, probably inspired by her life at Coventry.
70. The novel _____ was called by the famous American writer Henry James a "treasure-house of detail."
71. *Silas* _____ (1861) is set in the period before the Industrial Revolution.
72. _____, _____ and their sister _____ are collectively referred to as Brontë Sisters.
73. The novel _____ successfully created the first woman character who takes an independent and freedom-seeking attitude toward

love, life and society.
74. Emily Brontë's only novel is _____.
75. *Wuthering Heights* is a symbolic novel combining the techniques of _____, _____, and _____.
76. The description of _____ is very important in *Wuthering Heights* in that the exterior nature expressed the inner nature of humanity.
77. The novel _____ is a good example of the Gothic novel. The description of the natural scenes and the human passions are both scaring and terrifying.
78. Charlotte Brontë's novel, _____, based on her Brussels experiences, was refused by a publisher and was not published until after her death.
79. What one can know from the novel *Jane Eyre* is that the ideal life is _____ and _____. Though it is rare, it is more precious.
80. Both *Jane Eyre* and the still greater *Wuthering Heights* brought to the novel an introspection and an intense concentration on the _____ which before them had been the province of poetry alone.
81. The reason *Jane Eyre* has great appeal to readers is that it successfully created the first woman character who takes an independent and freedom-seeking attitude toward _____, life and society.
82. Heathcliff and Catherine are the characters in the novel _____.
83. Mr. _____ became disabled in the novel *Jane Eyre*.
84. In 1865 the first series of _____'s *Essays in Criticism* was published, and in 1869, *Culture and Anarchy*, a fierce attack on middle-class materialism and narrow-mindedness, considered by many to be his finest work.
85. Matthew Arnold is important both as a _____ and as a critic.
86. *Culture and* _____, a fierce attack on middle-class materialism and narrow-mindedness, is Matthew Arnold's best work.
87. _____'s works range from poems for children to love lyrics, sonnets and religious poetry. Her poetry is remarkable for its simplicity and singing quality. But her poetry was often melancholy and con-

cerned with thoughts of death.

88. Gerard Manley _____ is a remarkable experimenter and innovator in the rhythm, vocabulary, and formal arrangements of English verse.

89. Of the six "points" in the Chartists' program, four, namely, manhood suffrage, the removal of property qualifications for membership in the House of Commons, the payment of members and the _____, have long since become part of English law, while the two others—annual Parliaments and equal electoral districts—remain to this day unrealized.

90. All the important events of the Chartist Movement, esp. the class contradictions underlying these events, found their expression in the novels of the critical realists like Charles Dickens (*Hard Times*), Charlotte _____ (*Shirley*) and Mrs. _____ (*Mary Barton, North and South*) etc.

91. Elizabeth Gaskell, in her novel *Mary* _____ (1848), described the inhuman conditions of life of English workers and the birth of Chartist movement as the inevitable result of the monstrous exploitation.

92. The greatness of the English realists lies not only in their satirical portrayal of bourgeoisie and in the exposure of the greed and hypocrisy of the ruling classes, but also in their profound humanism which is revealed in their sympathy for the _____ people.

93. In the fifties and sixties of 19th century, the critical realistic novel began to _____.

94. _____ is Robert Browning's first long poem.

95. Robert Browning's interest lay, not in universal law, but in individual _____.

96. The greatest contribution of Robert Browning to English poetry is his skillful and unmatched use of dramatic _____.

97. As a poet, Ernest Jones followed the tradition of the revolutionary romanticism of George Gordon _____ and Percy Bysshe _____.

98. William Makepeace Thackeray's novels mainly contain a satirical portrayal of the _____ strata of society.
99. The main butt of satire in *Bleak House* is aimed at the abuses of the English _____.
100. William _____ was the first writer who voiced the ideal of socialism in his poetry and prose in the 19th century.
101. The last of William Makepeace Thackeray's great novels, _____, is in a setting divided between the fast and fashionable society of England and America of the Revolution.

II. Choose the Best Answer for Each Question.

1. Which of the following is NOT a Victorian writer?
   A. Emily Brontë
   B. Charles Dickens
   C. Gerard Manley Hopkins
   D. William Wordsworth
2. English critical realism found its expression chiefly in the form of _____.
   A. novel   B. poetry   C. drama   D. essay
3. In which of the following poems, Elizabeth Barrett Browning expressed her deep interest in the struggle of Italy to shake off her bondage to Austria?
   A. *Casa Guidi Windows*
   B. *The Cry of the Children*
   C. *The Runaway Slave at Pilgrim's Poiny*
   D. *Poems Before Congress*
4. Which of the following works is the work of Charles Dickens in the first period?
   A. *Sketches by Boz*
   B. *American Notes*
   C. *The Cricket on the Hearth*
   D. *Hard Times*
5. In _____, Dickens takes the French Revolution as the background of his novel, and the two cities are Paris and London in the

time of that revolution.

A. *Edwin Drood*   B. *A Tale of Two Cities*
C. Brontë Sisters   D. *A Christmas Carol*

6. Charlotte Brontë, Emily Brontë, and their gifted sister Anne Brontë came from a large family of _____.

A. Austria   B. America   C. Irish origin   D. England

7. Both *Jane Eyre* and the still greater _____ brought to the novel an introspection and an intense concentration on the inner life of emotion which before them had been the province of poetry alone.

A. *Wuthering Heights*   B. *The Tenant of Wildfell Hall*
C. *Shirley*   D. *The Professor*

8. Which of the following novels does Mrs. Reed appear in?

A. *Jane Eyre*   B. *I Wandered Lonely as a Cloud*
C. *The Prelude*   D. *Edwin Drood*

9. Which of the following is NOT Charlotte Brontë's work?

A. *The Professor*   B. *Shirley*
C. *Villette*   D. *Rime of the Ancient Mariner*

10. This novel is a riddle which means different things to different people. From the social point of view, it is a story about a poor man abused, betrayed and distorted by his social betters because he is a poor nobody. As a love story, this is one of the most moving. Which novel is described above?

A. *Vanity Fair*   B. *Childe Harold*
C. *Wuthering Heights*   D. Becky Sharp

11. Which of the following authors studied at Cambridge and left it without taking a degree?

A. Gerard Manley Hopkins   B. William Makepeace Thackeray
C. Walter Scott   D. Jane Austen

12. _____, the title was taken form Bunyan's *The Pilgrim's Progress*, and the sub-title of the book is *A Novel Without a Hero*.

A. *Vanity Fair*   B. *The Book of Snobs*
C. *Adam Bede*   D. *Biographia Literaria*

13. Which of the following is NOT George Eliot's writing style?
    A. Psychological realism   B. Soul
    C. Moral teaching   D. Dramatic irony
14. _____ is known as the father of Western European historical novels.
    A. Percy Bysshe Shelley   B. Charles Dickens
    C. Alfred Tennyson   D. Walter Scott
15. Which of the following poems is in Alfred Tennyson's *Anthology*?
    A. *The Bridge of Sighs*   B. *Ulysses*
    C. *Far from the Madding Crowd* D. *Wessex Tales*
16. T. S. Eliot has called _____ "the great master of metric as well as of melancholia."
    A. Alfred Tennyson   B. Robert Browning
    C. John Keats   D. Bingleys
17. Which of the following is NOT Robert Browning's work?
    A. *Pauline*   B. *My Last Duchess*
    C. *Beowulf*   D. *Bells and Pomeganates*
18. It is Robert Browning's best-known dramatic monologue. The poem takes its sources from the life of Alfonso II, duke of Ferrara of the 16th century Italy, whose young wife died suspiciously after three years of marriage. The work's name is _____.
    A. *The Song of the Shirt*   B. *The Ring and the Book*
    C. *How Do I Love Thee?*   D. *My Last Duchess*
19. Who wrote *Pied Beauty*?
    A. Christina Georgina Rossetti   B. Gerard Manley Hopkins
    C. George Eliot   D. William Makepeace Thackeray
20. The Victorian Period refers to the years between the Queen Victoria's accession in _____ and her death in 1901.
    A. 1837   B. 1847   C. 1857   D. 1867
21. The awakened social conscience is the predominant theme in _____ Victorian literature.
    A. Early   B. Middle   C. Late   D. Final

22. _____ (1838) is of the typical workhouse in the years before experience and protests introduced ameliorating modifications in the administration of the law.
    A. *Jane Eyre*   B. *Ulysses*
    C. *Oliver Twist*   D. *The Book of Snobs*
23. The years between 1832 and the early 1850s saw an important series of events known as the _____ Movement.
    A. Luddite   B. Swing
    C. May Fourth   D. Chartist
24. All the important events of the Chartist Movement, esp. the class contradictions underlying these events, found their expression in the novels of the _____ like Dickens (*Hard Times*), Charlotte Brontë (*Shirley*) and Mrs. Gaskell (*Mary Barton*, *North and South*) etc.
    A. realists   B. Romantic writers
    C. naturalistic writers D. critical realists
25. Though it failed, Chartism signified the first great political movement of the proletariat in _____ history.
    A. French   B. English   C. American   D. Russian
26. The critical realism of the _____ century flourished in the forties and in the beginning of fifties.
    A. 18th   B. 19th   C. 20th   D. 17th
27. The critical realists first set themselves the task of criticizing the capitalist society from a _____ viewpoint and delineated the crying contradictions of reality.
    A. democratic   B. republic   C. colonialist   D. populist
28. The greatest English realist of the Victorian Age was _____.
    A. Charlotte Brontë   B. Alfred Tennyson
    C. George Eliot   D. Charles Dickens
29. William Makepeace Thackeray's novels mainly contain a satirical portrayal of the _____ strata of society.
    A. middle   B. poor   C. upper   D. bourgeois

30. Elizabeth Gaskell, in her novel _____, described the inhuman conditions of life of English workers and the birth of Chartist Movement as the inevitable result of the monstrous exploitation.
    A. *Mary Barton*　　　　　　　B. *North and South*
    C. *Wives and Daughters*　　　D. *Oliver Twist*
31. Who is the greatest poet in the second half of the 19th century in England?
    A. Alfred Tennyson　　　　　　B. Robert Browning
    C. Charles Algernon Swinburne　D. Charles Dickens
32. Elizabeth Barrett Browning's most perfect work is the _____, which contains the record of courtship and marriage.
    A. *The Seraphim*　　　　　　　B. *Poems Before Congress*
    C. *Sonnets from the Portuguese*　D. *Last Poems*
33. Who can be called Sappho of England and idol of Emily Dickinson of America?
    A. Elizabeth Barrett Browning　B. Thomas Hardy
    C. Jonathan Swift　　　　　　　D. John Milton
34. Which of the following poets is not the main Chartist poet _____?
    A. Thomas Cooper　　　　　　B. William James Linton
    C. Ernest Jones　　　　　　　　D. John Milton
35. _____ has been called "the supreme epic of English life".
    A. *A Tale of Two Cities*　　　B. *David Copperfield*
    C. *Pickwick Papers*　　　　　D. *Oliver Twist*
36. Which of all books does Charles Dickens like best?
    A. *The Old Curiosity Shop*　　B. *David Copperfield*
    C. *Hard Times*　　　　　　　　D. *Oliver Twist*
37. Which is not the theme of Elizabeth Barrett Browning's poems?
    A. Life　　　　　　　　　　　　B. Love
    C. Liberation of women　　　　D. Work
38. _____ was written in memory of Arthur Hallam, a beloved friend and college-mate of Alfred Tennyson's, who had died in 1833.
    A. *In Memoriam*　　　　　　　B. *Queen Mary*

C. *Harold*   D. *Becket*

39. In 1850 William Wordsworth, who had been poet-laureate after Southey, died; and _____ became the poet-laureate.

    A. William Makepeace Thackeray

    B. William Shakespeare

    C. Walter Scott

    D. Alfred Tennyson

40. In the _____ Alfred Tennyson painted the character of the first English national hero, King Arthur, and gave a new meaning to the legends which had grown up in the Middle Ages about the Knights of the Round Table.

    A. *Idylls of the King*   B. *Demeter*

    C. *The Death of Enone*   D. *Merlin and the Gleam*

41. Which is the last of William Makepeace Thackeray's great novel?

    A. *The Virginians*   B. *The Rose and the Ring*

    C. *Vanity Fair*   D. *The Adventures of Philip*

42. _____ presents a panorama of the society of the English upper-middle class of the first half of the 19th century. What is more important, none of William Makepeace Thackeray's other novels can rival it in width of social life, and in depth of social criticism.

    A. *The Virginians*   B. *Little Dorrit*

    C. *Vanity Fair*   D. *Lovel the Widower*

43. Which is not the style of William Makepeace Thackeray's works?

    A. Ease   B. Refinement

    C. An exquisite naturalness   D. Romance

44. Which novel exposes the terrible conditions of English private schools?

    A. *Nicholas Nickleby*   B. *Oliver Twist*

    C. *Tale of Two Cities*   D. *David Copperfield*

45. _____ makes a fierce attack on the bourgeois system of education and bourgeois utilitarianism.

    A. *Great Expectations*   B. *Hard Times*

C. *Martin Chuzzlewit*   D. *Dombey and Son*

46. _____ is often regarded as the semi-autobiography of the author Charles Dickens in which the early life of the hero is largely based on the author's early life.
   A. *Tom Jones*   B. *David Copperfield*
   C. *Oliver Twist*   D. *Great Expectations*

47. _____ is Charles Dickens's first true novel and has a carefully worked-out plot.
   A. *Oliver Twist*   B. *David Copperfield*
   C. *Ulysses*   D. *Great Expectations*

48. _____, Charles Dickens's first historical novel, is set in the period of the Gordon antipoverty riots of 1780.
   A. *The Old Curiosity Shop*   B. *Dombey and Son*
   C. *Barnaby Rudge*   D. *Martin Chuzzlewit*

49. _____ is an earnest attack on the vulgarity and materialism of the rising middle-class industrialists.
   A. *The Old Curiosity Shop*   B. *Little Dorrit*
   C. *Bleak House*   D. *Hard Times*

50. *Great Expectations* (1860-1861) is told in the _____ person by Pip, a young man who learns through adversity to discard his own superficial snobbishness.
   A. first   B. second   C. third   D. fourth

51. _____ is a novel worth reading many times if one wants to know Charles Dickens's humanitarian thought and his viewpoint on virtue.
   A. *Hard Times*   B. *Great Expectations*
   C. *Oliver Twist*   D. *Bleak House*

52. Dramatic monologue was already much used by the poets in the _____ century. John Donne and other poets are some of the best examples.
   A. 15th and 16th   B. 16th and 17th
   C. 17th and 18th   D. 18th and 19th

53. George Eliot's poetical work, *The Spanish Gypsy* (1868), a blank

verse drama, showed that her real talent lay in _____.

A. prose   B. novel   C. poem   D. drama

54. In 1859, George Eliot published her first novel, _____, a rural tragedy among the non-conformists in country scenes remembered from her Warwickshire childhood.

A. *The Mill on the Floss*   B. *Felix Holt*
C. *Adam Bede*   D. *Silas Marner*

55. A trip to Italy, where George Eliot worked diligently at research in Renaissance politics, preceded the writing of her _____ novel, *Romola*, set in the time of Savonarola.

A. rustic   B. historical   C. Romantic   D. realistic

56. _____ combined a humorous and affectionate treatment of rural and small town characters with a deep analysis of major characters who aspire to more than the mediocre roles that society offers. Her novels are also called didactic novels.

A. William Wordsworth   B. Percy Bysshe Shelley
C. Robert Louis Stevenson   D. George Eliot

57. Among George Eliot's many novels, most critics agree that _____ is required reading in university English courses. This novel was regarded as her greatest novel, probably inspired by her life at Coventry.

A. *The Mill on the Floss*   B. *Middlemarch*
C. *Adam Bede*   D. *Silas Marner*

58. _____ was called by the famous American writer Henry James a "treasure-house of detail."

A. *The Book of Snobs*   B. *Middlemarch*
C. *Adam Bede*   D. *The Western Canon*

59. In George Eliot's novels, especially in *The Mill on the Floss*, there is fusion of traditional tragedy and _____. This fusion was recognized as one of the greatest phenomena in the 19th century.

A. realism   B. romanticism   C. classicism   D. colonialism

60. Charlotte Brontë set to work on a new novel, _____, which was published in August, 1847. This poetic, imaginative story of the love

of a young governess for her married employer also has undoubted connections with her experiences in Brussels.

A. *Jane Eyre*   B. *Agnes Grey*

C. *Wuthering Heights*   D. *The Tenant of Wildfell Hall*

61. Among the friendships Charlotte Brontë formed there was one with _____, to whom she had dedicated *Jane Eyre*.

    A. William Makepeace Thackeray

    B. Charles Dickens

    C. George Eliot

    D. Alfred Tennyson

62. _____ is Emily Brontë's only novel. This novel alone has attracted one generation of readers after another because it touched upon the utmost intensity of human feeling and sentiment.

    A. *Jane Eyre*   B. *Treasure Island*

    C. *Wuthering Heights*   D. *Kidnapped*

63. _____ written by Emily Brontë is a symbolic novel combining the techniques of realism, romanticism and symbolism.

    A. *Wuthering Heights*   B. *Life of Charlotte Brontë*

    C. *Emma*   D. *Mary Barton*

64. As a friend of Charlotte Brontë, *Life of Charlotte Brontë* written by _____ is one of the best biographies in English Literature.

    A. Mrs. Elizabeth Gaskell   B. Elizabeth Barrett Browning

    C. Harriet Beecher Stowe   D. Robert Burns

65. George Eliot was the pseudonym of _____.

    A. Galsworthy   B. Charles Dickens

    C. Mary Ann Evans   D. Emily Charlotte

66. _____ and *Middlemarch* were George Eliot's last novels.

    A. *Felix Holt the Radical*   B. *The Mill on the Floss*

    C. *Daniel Deronda*   D. *Adam Bede*

67. _____ written by George Eliot is largely autobiographical in its early chapters.

    A. *The Mill on the Floss*   B. *Silas Marner*

C. *Past and Present* D. *Life of Schiller*

68. _____ written by Charlotte Brontë is a realistic description of her experiences at the boarding school in Brussels.

   A. *Past and Present* B. *Villette*
   C. *Wuthering Heights* D. *Jane Eyre*

69. Matthew Arnold's career as a writer may be divided roughly into _____ phases.

   A. two   B. four   C. six   D. seven

70. In 1865 the first series of Matthew Arnold's *Essays in Criticism* was published, and in 1869, _____, a fierce attack on middle-class materialism and narrow-mindedness, considered by many to be his finest work.

   A. *The Strayed Reveller and Other Poems*
   B. *Dover Beach*
   C. *Nicholas Nickleby*
   D. *Culture and Anarchy*

71. Many of Matthew Arnold's best poems convey a melancholy, _____ sense of the dilemmas of modern life.

   A. pessimistic   B. optimistic   C. happy   D. hopeful

72. Christina Georgina Rossetti's later works in prose and verse are mostly _____.

   A. religious   B. political   C. ethnic   D. educational

73. Christina Georgina Rossetti's poetry is remarkable for its _____ and singing quality.

   A. imagination   B. simplicity   C. fancy   D. liveliness

74. The keynote of _____ love poems is the union of the body and the soul.

   A. Dante Gabriel Rossetti's   B. George Eliot's
   C. Charlotte Brontë's   D. William Makepeace Thackeray's

75. *Goblin Market* is Christina Georgina Rossetti's chief _____ poem.

   A. lyrical   B. free   C. narrative   D. blank

76. Mrs. _____ is also regarded as one of the two greatest English poetesses besides Christina Georgina Rossetti.
    A. Browning   B. Alfred Tennyson
    C. Emily Dickenson   D. Richard Wright
77. _____ has been criticized for his obscurity.
    A. Robert Browning   B. William Morris
    C. Algernon Charles   D. Oscar Wilde
78. Oscar Wilde is the representative among the writers of aestheticism and decadence. _____ is a typical decadent novel written by him.
    A. *Idylls of the King*   B. *The Picture of Dorian Gray*
    C. *Cry of the Children*   D. *Men and Women*
79. Although not widely read or appreciated until the _____ century, Gerard Manley Hopkins is in many respects a deeply characteristic Victorian writer.
    A. 17th   B. 18th   C. 19th   D. 20th
80. Heathcliff is a rebel against the _____ matrimonial system.
    A. bourgeois   B. proletarian
    C. working class   D. peasantry
81. _____ is one of the novels written by Thomas Hardy.
    A. *Jude the Obscure*   B. *Pied Beauty*
    C. *In Memoriam*   D. *Goblin Market*
82. *A Dream of John Ball* written by _____ deals with the peasant rising of 1381.
    A. Robert Browning   B. George Meredith
    C. William Morris   D. Elizabeth Cleghorn Gaskell
83. _____ is regarded as Charles Dickens's masterpiece.
    A. *David Copperfield*   B. *Wuthering Heights*
    C. *Vanity Fair*   D. *The Mill on the Floss*
84. _____ put forward the theory of "art for art's sake" for the first time.
    A. Theophile Gautier   B. Oscar Wilde

C. William Morris　　　　　D. Alfred Tennyson
85. Most of _____'s important works, including *Men and Women* and *Dramatic Lyrics*, are written in the form of dramatic monologue.
   A. Robert Browning　　　B. Oscar Wilde
   C. George Eliot　　　　　D. Algernon Charles
86. Alfred Tennyson wrote the following short poems except _____.
   A. *Break, Break, Break*　　B. *Crossing the Bar*
   C. *The Eagle*　　　　　　D. *The Cry of the Children*
87. Robert Browning produced the following remarkable short poems except _____.
   A. *Pauline*　　　　　　　B. *Home Thoughts, from Sea*
   C. *Meeting at Night*　　　D. *Home Thoughts, from Abroad*
88. Which of the following novels was not written by George Eliot?
   A. *Adam Bede*　　　　　B. *Ulysses*
   C. *Silas Marner*　　　　　D. *The Mill on the Floss*
89. *My Last Duchess* is the representative of _____.
   A. novels　　　　　　　　B. short lyrics
   C. dramatic monologues　　D. essays
90. *Sartor Resartus* is _____'s first original work.
   A. Robert Browning　　　B. Thomas Carlyle
   C. Charles Dickens　　　　D. Algernon Charles
91. Which of the following is Thomas Babington Macaulay's masterpiece?
   A. *Critical and Historical Essays*　B. *History of England*
   C. *The Book of Snobs*　　D. *Oliver Twist*

III. Match-Making

Group One

Column A	Column B
1. Charles Dickens	a. *Jane Eyre*

上编　英国文学史练习

2. Charlotte Brontë   b. *Oliver Twist*
3. William Makepeace Thackeray c. *Middlemarch, a Study of Provincial Life*
4. George Eliot   d. *The Book of Snobs*
5. Alfred Tennyson   e. *Ulysses*
6. William J. Linton   f. *Modern Painters*
7. Thomas Carlyle   g. *History of the French Revolution*
8. Algernon Charles Swinburne h. *Songs Before Sunrise*
9. John Ruskin   i. *Blade-Time Will Come*
10. Matthew Arnold   j. *Culture and Anarchy*

Group Two
Column A   Column B
1. Thomas Cooper   a. *The Shakespearean Chartist Hymn*
2. William Makepeace Thackeray b. *Lady Windermere's Fan*
3. Robert Browning   c. *Bleak House*
4. Alfred Tennyson   d. *The Eagle*
5. Christina Georgina Rossetti e. *New Grub Street*
6. Oscar Wild   f. *Pendennis*
7. George Meredith   g. *The Ring and the Book*
8. George Gissing   h. *Goblin Market*
9. William Morris   i. *A Dream of John Ball*
10. Charles Dickens   j. *The Egoist*

Group Three
Column A   Column B
1. Ernest Jones   a. *The Song of the Shirt*
2. Charlotte Brontë   b. *The House of Life*
3. Thomas Hood   c. *Treasure Island*
4. George Eliot   d. *The Song of the Lower Classes*
5. Thomas Hardy   e. *The Return of the Native*

· 89 ·

6. Walter Pater   f. *History of England*
7. Dante Gabriel Rossetti   g. *Rubaiyat of Omar Khayyam*
8. Thomas Babington Macaulay   h. *The Renaissance*
9. Robert Louis Stevenson   i. *Adam Bede*
10. Edward Fitzgerald   j. *Professor*

Group Four

Column A   Column B
1. Alec and Angel   a. *Jane Eyre*
2. Amelia and Becky   b. *Adam Bede*
3. Rochester and Jane   c. *David Copperfield*
4. Trent and Nell   d. *Tess of the D'Urbervilles*
5. Elizabeth and Darcy   e. *Wuthering Heights*
6. Tom and Maggie   f. *Pride and Prejudice*
7. Heathcliff and Catherine   g. *The Mill on the Floss*
8. Henry Carson   h. *Vanity Fair*
9. Hetty and Arthur   i. *The Old Curiosity Shop*
10. Mr. Peggotty and Steerforth   j. *Mary Barton*

IV. Define the Literary Terms.

1. English critical realism
2. Dramatic monologue
3. Characterization

V. Answer the Following Questions Briefly.

1. Please briefly describe the historical background of the Victorian period.
2. What are the greatness and weakness of English critical realists?

3. Compare the features of William Makepeace Thackeray's works with those of Charles Dickens's.
4. Make a comment of the 19th century's critical realists' major contribution.
5. Charlotte Brontë is a writer of realism combined with romanticism. Why is *Jane Eyre* written by her a successful novel?
6. Based on *Jane Eyre* by Charlotte Brontë, discuss the theme of her works and the image of women protagonists.
7. Make a comment on the plot of *Adam Bede*.
8. Summarize the plot of *Vanity Fair*.
9. Make a comment on William Makepeace Thackeray's masterpiece *Vanity Fair*.
10. Make a brief comment on Rebecca Sharp, the central figure of the novel *Vanity Fair*.
11. Summarize the three periods of Charles Dickens's literary career.
12. Make a brief comment on Charles Dickens's fictional art.
13. Based on *Oliver Twist*, how does Charles Dickens express his humanitarian thought?
14. What contribution does Robert Browning make to the English poetry?
15. What are the characteristics of George Eliot's novels?
16. Make a brief comment on *Wuthering Heights*.
17. Why is Jane Eyre one of the most popular characters for the contemporary readers? Make a brief comment on her.
18. Make a brief comment on the characteristics of Alfred Tennyson's poetry.
19. Summarize the four phrases of Matthew Arnold's career as a writer.
20. What are the characteristics of William Makepeace Thackeray's novels?
21. Summarize the plot of *Adam Bede*.

22. Summarize the plot of *Wuthering Heights*.
23. Make a brief comment on the Chartist literature.
24. Make a brief comment on Christina Rossetti's works.

Part IX

The 20th Century: Transition from the 19th to the 20th Century Before 1945

I. Fill in the Blanks.

1. _____, the bard and advocate of imperialism, glorified the colonial expansion of Great Britain in his short stories, poems and novels.
2. The end of the 19th century was a period of struggle between _____ and _____ trends in art and literature.
3. Oscar Wilde expounded the theory of "_____" in his critical essays.
4. In the works of Samuel Butler and his follower George Bernard Shaw, the narrow-mindedness, the hypocrisy and the greed of the _____ classes were mercilessly scourged.
5. In the 1920s, James Joyce, David Herbert Lawrence, Virginia Woolf and others made the _____ breakthrough in fiction writing and it affected poetry writing.
6. Thomas Hardy's _____ was published anonymously in 1874.
7. Thomas Hardy's novels culminated with the two greatest works, _____ and _____.
8. Jude in *Jude the Obscure* shows the horrible decline of a man and woman drawn together by _____.
9. _____ is a gigantic epic drama that was published in three parts in 1903, 1906, and 1908.
10. The subtitle of *Tess of the D'Urbervilles* is _____.

11. In the preface to *The Portrait of Dorian Gray*, Oscar Wilde emphasized that art and morality are totally _____.
12. In 1884, George Bernard Shaw became one of the founders of the _____ that spread the socialist ideas.
13. George Bernard Shaw was a master of _____.
14. In George Bernard Shaw's later published plays, he included long _____ to talk about his characters, their social background and the problems they had.
15. *The Man of Destiny* is a mock-heroic skit on _____.
16. George Bernard Shaw's *Pygmalion* was later adapted into musical comedy entitled _____, which is a satire on dramatic criticism.
17. *Mrs. Warren's Profession* does have the conventional comic ending, for example, the _____ of the lovers and the _____ between generations.
18. William Butler Yeats was an Irishman of _____ descent.
19. Maud Gonne drew William Butler Yeats into the _____ movement.
20. William Butler Yeats worked to simplify his style, to rid it of _____ vagueness, and to bring it close to the _____ of everyday speech.
21. In William Butler Yeats's aims and practice, and rejection of late Victorian poetic modes, he gave impetus to the _____ movement in poetry.
22. *The Man of Property* was the highest point of social _____ ever attained by John Galsworthy.
23. Forsytism is the specifically English type of _____ morality and social attitudes.
24. John Galsworthy was moved throughout life by an acute sense of social _____ but his emotions were always engaged on the side of the _____ and the _____.
25. The "Bloomsbury group" was criticized not only for the _____ of their personal life, but also for the _____ and sometimes for the _____ of their works.

26. The "stream of consciousness" technique is a means of exploring the _____ of Virginia Woolf's characters.
27. *Jacob's Room* is an _____ and _____ treatment of the death of a young man during the first world war.
28. In *A Room of One's Own*, Virginia Woolf created an imaginary figure, Judith Shakespeare, sister of the playwright William Shakespeare, in order to make a _____.
29. Virginia Woolf's greatest contribution to English literature is her use of the "_____" technique.
30. Virginia Woolf's concern with the position of women ushered the approach of _____ in literary criticism.
31. Narrow-minded Dubliners became the main characters in _____'s writing, as objects either to be exposed or to be ridiculed.
32. _____ is a book about man's fate as well as a series of sketches of Dublin.
33. *A Portrait of the Artist as a Young Man* has many autobiographical elements. It is representatively true not only of James Joyce but of the relation between the _____ and _____ in modern world.
34. The innovation in form of *A Portrait of the Artist as a Young Man* was James Joyce's use of Stephen Dedalus's _____ at different stages of his life.
35. In *Ulysses*, a character presents an unbroken stream of thoughts, feelings, memories and reactions to the current action, with no description or explanation by a separate _____.
36. *Sons and Lovers* is about the effect of the love of a _____ upon the development of a son. It also shows the _____ love of a mother and the unhappiness of a woman who misplaced her love.
37. Almost all writers who wrote boldly about _____ in their works had to choose to exile themselves in other countries for the freedom of writing.
38. Rupert Brooke's poems were the last of that period to express idealistic _____ in the face of war.

39. Thomas Stearns Eliot's classic expression of the temper of his age is _____.
40. *The Waste Land* is obscure and hard to understand for its absence of _____.
41. In the latter part of Thomas Stearns Eliot's life, he aimed to revitalize _____ and wrote plays that would seem perfectly natural to audiences although the characters were speaking poetic language.
42. *The Love Song of J. Alfred Prufrock* is a sort of _____ in lines of varying lengths and occasional rhymes.
43. *The White Goddess* written by Robert Graves is a study of the poetic _____.
44. Wystan Hugh Auden's early poems were concerned with _____ of his native country and were intended to shock their readers; while his later poetry, though often as satirical as the early poems had been, became increasingly concerned with _____.
45. Wystan Hugh Auden's most important contribution to 20th century poetry is his experimentation in many verse _____ and _____, combining an off-hand informality with remarkable technical skill.
46. Dylan Thomas was influenced by the modern _____ and _____.
47. *Do Not Go Gentle into That Good Night* uses intense mood to create the emotion of raging resistance to _____.
48. Tess in *Tess of the D'Urbervilles* is seduced by a squire named Alec before she married the clergyman's son named _____.
49. A strong influence was exercised on George Bernard Shaw by the _____, the English reformist organization.
50. _____ is the founder of the "stream of consciousness" school of novel writing.
51. *Sons and Lovers* is _____'s novel.
52. _____ is Oscar Wilde's only novel describing the author's aesthetical view.
53. Both of Oscar Wilde's _____ and *Salome* are typical unwholesome products of the decadent literary trend.

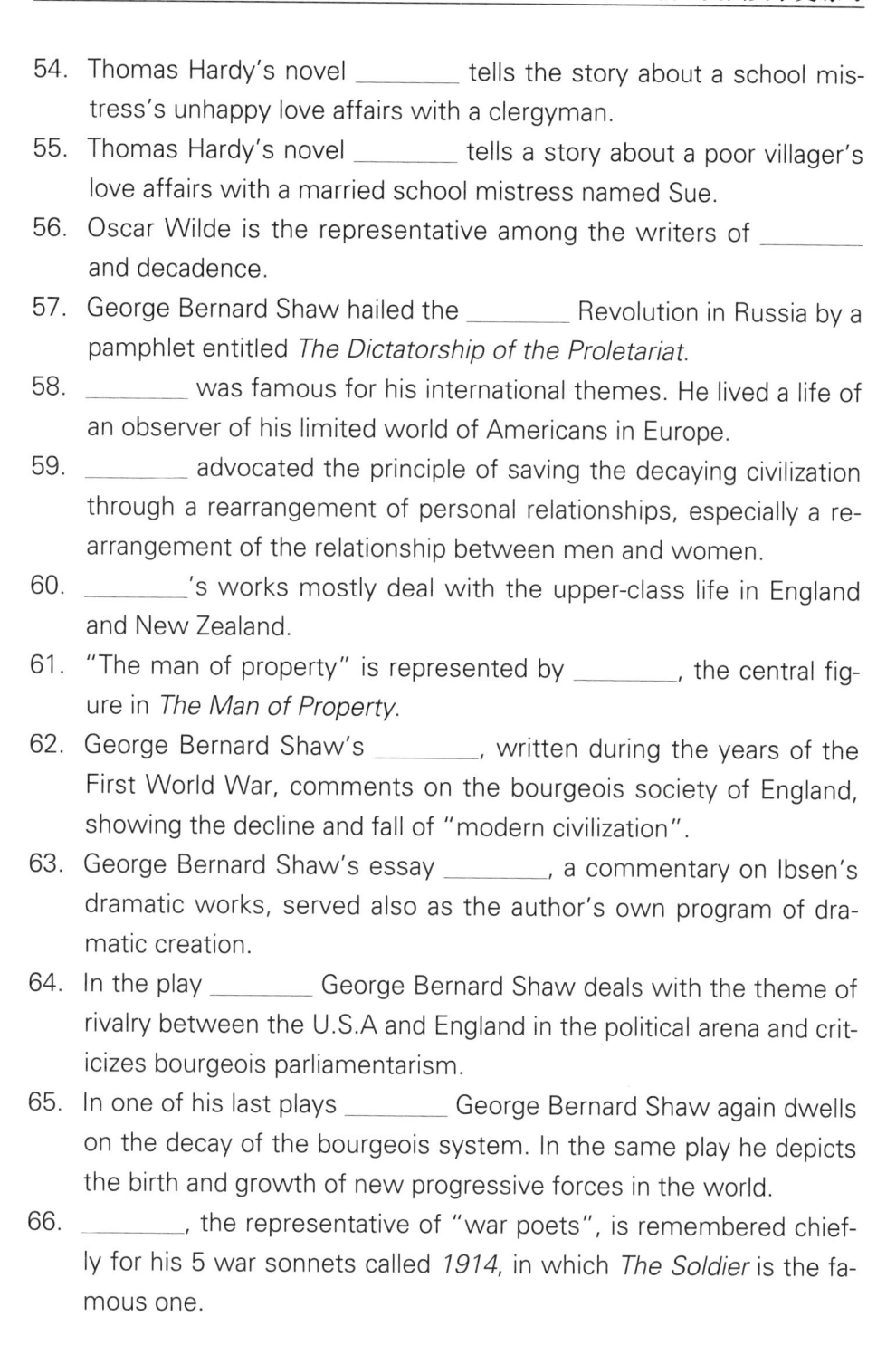

54. Thomas Hardy's novel _____ tells the story about a school mistress's unhappy love affairs with a clergyman.
55. Thomas Hardy's novel _____ tells a story about a poor villager's love affairs with a married school mistress named Sue.
56. Oscar Wilde is the representative among the writers of _____ and decadence.
57. George Bernard Shaw hailed the _____ Revolution in Russia by a pamphlet entitled *The Dictatorship of the Proletariat*.
58. _____ was famous for his international themes. He lived a life of an observer of his limited world of Americans in Europe.
59. _____ advocated the principle of saving the decaying civilization through a rearrangement of personal relationships, especially a rearrangement of the relationship between men and women.
60. _____'s works mostly deal with the upper-class life in England and New Zealand.
61. "The man of property" is represented by _____, the central figure in *The Man of Property*.
62. George Bernard Shaw's _____, written during the years of the First World War, comments on the bourgeois society of England, showing the decline and fall of "modern civilization".
63. George Bernard Shaw's essay _____, a commentary on Ibsen's dramatic works, served also as the author's own program of dramatic creation.
64. In the play _____ George Bernard Shaw deals with the theme of rivalry between the U.S.A and England in the political arena and criticizes bourgeois parliamentarism.
65. In one of his last plays _____ George Bernard Shaw again dwells on the decay of the bourgeois system. In the same play he depicts the birth and growth of new progressive forces in the world.
66. _____, the representative of "war poets", is remembered chiefly for his 5 war sonnets called *1914*, in which *The Soldier* is the famous one.

67. In English literature, James Joyce and _____ are the two best-known novelists of the "stream of consciousness" school.
68. _____'s admirers have praised him as "second only to Shakespeare in his mastery of English language."
69. _____ was the biographer, critic and editor of the *Dictionary of National Biography*.
70. _____ is the climax of Virginia Woolf's experiments in novel form.
71. John Galsworthy also distinguished himself as a playwright. His two important plays include *The Silver Box* and _____.
72. _____ was a landmark in the development of John Galsworthy's art. The novel established his place in literature as representative of bourgeois realism in the 20th-century English novel.
73. The novel _____ describes the mental activities of two Dubliners in a single day. This formless, plotless novel records the thoughts, shades and fleeting flashes of the mind.
74. _____ concerns Thomas Stearns Eliot's faith and emotional satisfaction in the church.
75. In _____, George Bernard Shaw satirizes the liberal talks and preaches Christian socialism.
76. The play _____ is a historical play dealing with the struggle of an illiterate peasant girl for liberating France from the English.

II. Choose the Best Answer for Each Question.

1. Which of the following is NOT the realistic writer?
   A. Thomas Hardy   B. Oscar Wilde
   C. George Bernard Shaw   D. Samuel Butler
2. Who is the last Victorian novelist?
   A. Oscar Wilde   B. Alfred Tennyson
   C. Thomas Hardy   D. Charlotte Brontë

3. Thomas Hardy's first masterpiece is _____.
   A. *Far from the Madding Crowd* B. *Desperate Remedies*
   C. *Jude the Obscure* D. *Tess of the D'Urbervilles*
4. Which of the following is NOT Oscar Wilde's comedy?
   A. *The Importance of Being Earnest*
   B. *Lady Windermere's Fan*
   C. *The Decay of Lying*
   D. *An Ideal Husband*
5. *Mrs. Warren's Profession*, a treatment of commercialized vice, was about the economic bias of _____.
   A. drugs   B. prostitution
   C. fraud   D. theft
6. George Bernard Shaw reached dramatic maturity in _____, a brilliant satire on military glory and antiwar statement.
   A. *Arms and the Man*   B. *The Man of Destiny*
   C. *Man and Superman*   D. *Major Barbara*
7. *Mrs. Warren's Profession* is a comedy for its witty _____ and surprising turns of plot.
   A. dialogue   B. story   C. style   D. expression
8. Which of the following is NOT the place that influenced William Butler Yeats?
   A. Sligo   B. Bristol   C. London   D. Dublin
9. William Butler Yeats's first book of poetry published in 1889, and *The Celtic Twilight*, published in 1893 drew on ancient _____ legend.
   A. English   B. Celtic   C. Irish   D. French
10. After returning to Ireland in 1896, William Butler Yeats gave less attention to _____ and devoted himself largely to _____.
    A. drama; poetry   B. poetry; novel
    C. novel; poetry   D. poetry; drama
11. Maud Gonne's _____ in 1903 marked an important change in William Butler Yeats's life.

A. death   B. marriage   C. departure   D. divorce

12. William Butler Yeats won the Nobel Prize for literature in _____.
    A. 1922   B. 1923   C. 1924   D. 1925

13. John Sinjohn is the pseudonym of _____.
    A. John Galsworthy   B. Matthew Arnold
    C. Oscar Wilde   D. Rupert Brooke

14. Which of the following is NOT the work of John Galsworthy?
    A. *The Man of Property*   B. *From the Four Winds*
    C. *Mrs. Dalloway*   D. *A Man of Devon*

15. Which of the following is NOT the profession of John Galsworthy?
    A. Dramatist   B. Novelist   C. Poet   D. Literary critic

16. _____ became the center of activity of group of writers, painters and intellectuals in the early twentieth century.
    A. Yorkshire   B. Manchester
    C. Sheffield   D. Bloomsbury

17. Which of the following is one of the founder of the Hogarth Press?
    A. Virginia Woolf   B. James Joyce
    C. John Galsworthy   D. Robert Graves

18. Virginia Woolf was much concerned with the position of women and the constrictions they suffered under so she wrote several essays on the subject EXCEPT _____.
    A. *A Room of One's Own*   B. *Mrs. Dalloway*
    C. *The Years*   D. *Three Guineas*

19. In James Joyce's last year, he began to reject his _____ faith in favor of a literary mission.
    A. Catholic   B. Christian   C. Puritan   D. Orthodox

20. James Joyce displayed the liberating effect of _____.
    A. modernism   B. realism   C. aestheticism   D. romanticism

21. In the third of the fifteen stories in *Dubliners*, Joyce drew on his own childhood recollections, and the uncle in the story is a reminiscence of Joyce's _____.
    A. uncle   B. teacher   C. old friend   D. father

22. Rupert Brooke was an English poet best known for his idealistic _____ sonnets.
    A. love   B. memorial   C. war   D. nostalgia
23. *The Soldier* was written by _____.
    A. Rupert Brooke   B. Dylan Thomas
    C. William Butler Yeats   D. Robert Graves
24. *The Waste Land*'s noticeable characteristics are varied _____ and _____ to harmonize with the changing subject matter.
    A. length; rhythm   B. image; length
    C. image; rhythm   D. length; metaphor
25. *The Waste Land* is broadly acknowledged as one of the most recognizable landmarks of _____.
    A. romanticism   B. realism
    C. modernism   D. Victorian Age
26. _____ made the greatest contribution to rediscover the charms of the metaphysical poetry and the drama of the early 17th century.
    A. John Donne   B. John Milton
    C. John Bunyan   D. Thomas Stearns Eliot
27. Thomas Stearns Eliot was awarded the Nobel Prize in Literature in _____.
    A. 1947   B. 1948   C. 1949   D. 1950
28. Robert Graves thought of himself as a _____ but his fame rests on his _____.
    A. novelist; poems   B. poet; dramas
    C. poet; novels   D. dramatist; novels
29. Thomas Hardy's novel _____ describes a poor shepherd's love affairs with a rich young lady.
    A. *Under the Greenwood Tree*   B. *The Poor Man and the Lady*
    C. *The Trumpet-Major*   D. *Far from the Madding Crowd*
30. Thomas Hardy is one of the representatives of English _____ at the turn of the 19th century.
    A. pre-romanticism   B. critical realism

C. new romanticism D. neo-classicism

31. _____ was one of the most prominent of the 20th century English realistic writers. *The Man of Property* is one of his works.
   A. James Joyce B. John Galsworthy
   C. Oscar Wilde D. Rupert Brooke

32. It took John Galsworthy 22 years to accomplish the monumental work, his masterpiece _____.
   A. *From the Four Winds* B. *Caravan*
   C. *The Forsyte Saga* D. *The Man of Property*

33. Besides poetry and short stories, James Joyce wrote two novels, _____ and *Finnegans Wake*.
   A. *Dubliners* B. *The Portrait*
   C. *Ulysses* D. *The Soldier*

34. Virginia Woolf's novel _____, published in 1925, made her reputation as an important psychological writer.
   A. *Room of One's Own* B. *Mrs. Dalloway*
   C. *The Years* D. *Three Guineas*

35. David Herbert Lawrence's novel _____ was taken as a typical example of Oedipus Complex in fiction.
   A. *Sons and Lovers* B. *The White Peacock*
   C. *Lady Chatterley's Lover* D. *The Rainbow*

36. According to Thomas Hardy's own classification, his novels divide themselves into three groups. They are the following except _____.
   A. novels of character and environment
   B. romances and fantasies
   C. novels of ingenuity
   D. working class literature

37. John _____ was one of the most prominent of the 20th century English realistic writers. *The Man of Property* is one of his works.
   A. Galsworthy B. Smith
   C. Keats D. Suckling

38. The trilogy *The Forsyte Saga* consists of *The Man of Property*, *In Chancery* and _____.
    A. *Mrs. Dalloway*   B. *To Let*
    C. *Araby*   D. *Mrs. Warren's Profession*
39. _____ represents the much more readable novelists of the stream of consciousness school. She is a fine artist, a woman of sharp sensitivity who, in one of her frequent mental depressions, committed suicide.
    A. Virginia Woolf   B. Doris Lessing
    C. Christina Georgina Rossetti   D. Charlotte Brontë
40. _____ is generally regarded as Virginia Woolf's most remarkable work. The autobiographical elements in the novel are obvious. Mr. and Mrs. Ramsay are apparently drawn from the author's parents.
    A. *Mrs. Dalloway*   B. *To the Lighthouse*
    C. *The Waves*   D. *The Lake of Innisfree*
41. *The Rainbow* and *Women in Love* are the two distinguished novels written by _____.
    A. James Joyce   B. Thomas Hardy
    C. David Herbert Lawrence   D. Oscar Wilde
42. The judgment of _____ as "a good man fallen among the Fabians" has been, and still remains, the guiding idea in our estimation of his life and career.
    A. George Bernard Shaw   B. William Butler Yeats
    C. John Galsworthy   D. James Joyce
43. On a world tour made in 1931, George Bernard Shaw visited _____.
    A. China   B. Japan   C. Russia   D. the USA
44. In 1913, Thomas Stearns Eliot published his first volume of verse, _____ *and Other Observations* in which the influence of some French symbolists can be seen.
    A. *The Love Song of J. Alfred Prufrock*
    B. *Prufrock*
    C. *The Waste Land*

D. *She Tells Her Love While Half Asleep*
45. _____ made experiments in reviving verse drama which had flourished in Shakespeare's time.
   A. George Bernard Shaw   B. John Galsworthy
   C. Thomas Stearns Eliot   D. Wystan Hugh Auden
46. The following novels belong to the "stream of consciousness" school of novel writing except _____.
   A. *Ulysses*   B. *Finnegans Wake*
   C. *The Good Companions*   D. *The Waves*
47. Which of the following works was not written by George Bernard Shaw?
   A. *Mrs. Warren's Profession*   B. *The Man of Property*
   C. *Major Barbara*   D. *Pygmalion*
48. In 1923, _____ was awarded the Nobel Prize in Literature.
   A. William Butler Yeats   B. Samuel Butler
   C. Thomas Stearns Eliot   D. David Herbert Lawrence
49. William Butler Yeats is the following except _____.
   A. an Irish poet   B. a dramatist
   C. a critic   D. a novelist

III. Match-Making

Group One

Column A   Column B
1. *The Isle Lake of Innisfree*   a. George Bernard Shaw
2. *Mrs. Dalloway*   b. William Butler Yeats
3. *Mrs. Warren's Profession*   c. John Galsworthy
4. *The Man of Property*   d. Virginia Woolf
5. *The Soldier*   e. Thomas Hardy
6. *The Darkling Thrush*   f. Rupert Brooke

Group Two

	Column A		Column B
1.	*The Return of the Native*	a.	Virginia Woolf
2.	*The Man of Destiny*	b.	David Herbert Lawrence
3.	*Orlando: A Biography*	c.	George Bernard Shaw
4.	*The Lost Girl*	d.	Thomas Stearns Eliot
5.	*The Love Song of J. Alfred Prufrock*	e.	Thomas Hardy
6.	*Count Belisarius*	f.	Wystan Hugh Auden
7.	*Spain*	g.	Dylan Thomas
8.	*In Country Sleep*	h.	Robert Graves

Group Three

	Column A		Column B
1.	*Jude the Obscure*	a.	George Bernard Shaw
2.	*The Portrait of Dorian Gray*	b.	William Butler Yeats
3.	*Pygmalion*	c.	Thomas Hardy
4.	*From the Four Winds*	d.	James Joyce
5.	*When You Are Old*	e.	Oscar Wilde
6.	*A Room of One's Own*	f.	David Herbert Lawrence
7.	*Ulysses*	g.	Virginia Woolf
8.	*Sons and Lovers*	h.	John Galsworthy

Group Four

	Column A		Column B
1.	*The Importance of Being Earnest*	a.	Thomas Stearns Eliot
2.	*Saint Joan*	b.	Robert Graves
3.	*The Waste Land*	c.	George Bernard Shaw
4.	*I, Claudius*	d.	Dylan Thomas
5.	*Do Not Go Gentle into That Good Night*	e.	Wystan Hugh Auden

6. *Finnegans Wake*   f.   Oscar Wilde
7. *Lady Chatterley's Lover* g.   James Joyce
8. *The Age of Anxiety*   h.   David Herbert Lawrence

IV. Define the Literary Terms.

1. Stream of consciousness
2. Aestheticism
3. Modernism
4. Naturalism
5. Imagism

V. Answer the Following Questions Briefly.

1. What are William Butler Yeats's four phases of his literature career?
2. Talk about the content and theme of *The Waste Land*.
3. Talk about your opinion about heroine Tess in *Tess of the D'Urbervilles*.
4. Tell the story of *Jude the Obscure*.
5. Tell the story of *The Man of Property*.
6. Make a comment on John Galsworthy.
7. Make a comment on George Bernard Shaw.
8. Make a brief comment on *Sons and Lovers*.
9. What are the characteristics of Thomas Hardy's novels?
10. What do you know about George Bernard Shaw's literary ideas?
11. Make a comparison between Tess in *Tess of the D'Urbervilles* and Lu Sifeng in *Thunderstorm* (雷雨).
12. Make a comment on Oscar Wilde.
13. Make a comment on Thomas Stearns Eliot.
14. Make a comment on David Herbert Lawrence.

15. Make a comment on Virginia Woolf.
16. Make a comment on James Joyce.
17. Make an introduction of and a comment on *Mrs. Warren's Profession*.
18. Make an introduction of and a comment on *A Room of One's Own*.
19. Make a comment on *Ulysses*.

Part X

The 20th Century: Contemporary Literature Since 1945

I. Fill in the Blanks.

1. Doris Lessing wrote about the violence of the _____ while Ted Hughes wrote mainly about the violence of _____.
2. The story in *The Grass Is Singing* takes place in _____ in southern Africa during the 1940s. It deals with the _____ between whites and blacks in that country.
3. Philip Arthur Larkin tried to seek the quiet, rational restraint of _____ and escaped from the threats and chaos of modern _____ and society.
4. Philip Arthur Larkin's poems are highly _____ but have _____ verse forms.
5. In Ted Hughes's poems, he often uses a _____ to symbolize the wild and predatory nature.
6. Seamus Heaney's work was deeply associated with the lessons of _____.
7. *The Grass Is Singing* delves into the question between _____ and _____.
8. In *The Grass Is Singing*, Mary Turner's _____ brought her freedom from depression and pain.
9. At the beginning of Doris Lessing's writing, she attempted to solve the _____ faced in Southern Rhodesia.
10. Doris Lessing's perception and strong mind was closely associated

· 108 ·

with her _____ life in her childhood.

11. Doris Lessing wrote five autobiographical novels known collectively as _____.

12. *The Golden Notebook* (1962) explores the lives of _____ in England.

13. Philip Arthur Larkin's early poetry was influenced by _____ and when he grew mature he was influenced by _____.

14. Philip Arthur Larkin began his career as a _____.

15. Philip Arthur Larkin's poems are marked by an accuracy about _____, _____, and _____.

16. In *The Whitsun Weddings*, Whitsun is the _____ festival of Pentecost in the UK.

17. In Ted Hughes's early works he questioned man's _____ in the universal scheme.

18. In Ted Hughes's work, he looked for an understanding of human life and its mysterious bonds with _____.

19. Ted Hughes's work is marked by a mythical framework, using the lyric and dramatic _____ to illustrate intense subject matter.

20. In Seamus Heaney's early works, he writes about the disappearing world of unspoiled rural _____.

21. Many of Seamus Heaney's works concern his own family history and focus on _____ in his own family.

22. _____ is the first poem in the collection *Death of a Naturalist*.

II. Choose the Best Answer for Each Question.

1. A group of experimental playwrights such as Samuel Becket were influenced by _____.
   A. existentialism   B. modernism
   C. surrealism   D. transcendentalism

2. Doris Lessing was the _____ female writer who was awarded

the Nobel Prize in Literature.

   A. 10th   B. 11th   C. 12th   D. 13th

3. Which of the following is NOT the work of Doris Lessing?

   A. *The Grass Is Singing*   B. *The Golden Notebook*
   C. *European Literature*   D. *The Whitsun Weddings*

4. Ted Hughes's works contain various forms EXCEPT _____.

   A. poem   B. drama   C. criticism   D. essay

5. The most famous of Ted Hughes's subjects is "Crow", a mixture of different images EXCEPT _____.

   A. sin   B. god   C. bird   D. man

6. In _____, Seamus Heaney was awarded the Nobel Prize in Literature.

   A. 1992   B. 1993   C. 1994   D. 1995

7. *The Haw Lantern* contains a brilliant sonnet sequence in memory of Seamus Heaney's _____.

   A. lover   B. wife   C. mother   D. sister

8. Which of the following is NOT the work of Doris Lessing?

   A. *Martha Quest*
   B. *This Was the Old Chief's Country*
   C. *The Golden Notebook*
   D. *The North Ship*

9. Which of the following is NOT the work of Philip Arthur Larkin?

   A. *A Girl in Winter*   B. *The Less Deceived*
   C. *Hawk Roosting*   D. *The Whitsun Weddings*

10. Which of the following is NOT the work of Ted Hughes?

    A. *Wolfwatching*   B. *Snowdrop*
    C. *Flowers and Insects*   D. *Going*

11. Ted Hughes examined the themes of survival and the mystery and destructiveness of the _____ in his animal poems.

    A. human-being   B. cosmos
    C. creature   D. nature

12. Which of the following is NOT the work of Seamus Heaney?

A. *Death of a Naturalist* B. *Hawk Roosting*
C. *Door into the Dark* D. *Station Island*

13. Seamus Heaney's collection entitled *Seeing Things* contains many poems for his _____.
    A. father B. mother C. wife D. brother

III. Match-Making

Group One
Column A   Column B
1. *The Grass Is Singing*   a. Seamus Heaney
2. *The Whitsun Weddings*   b. Doris Lessing
3. *Hawk Roosting*   c. Philip Arthur Larkin
4. *Exposure*   d. Ted Hughes

Group Two
Column A   Column B
1. *The Golden Notebook*   a. Seamus Heaney
2. *Snowdrop*   b. Doris Lessing
3. *The Less Deceived*   c. Ted Hughes
4. *Digging*   d. Philip Arthur Larkin

Group Three
Column A   Column B
1. *Children of Violence*   a. Ted Hughes
2. *High Window*   b. Seamus Heaney
3. *Lupercalia*   c. Philip Arthur Larkin
4. *Death of a Naturalist*   d. Doris Lessing

IV. Define the Literary Term.

1. Surrealism

V. Answer the Following Questions Briefly.

1. Make a comment on *The Grass Is Singing*.
2. Make a comment on Seamus Heaney.
3. The 20th-century English writers fall into three groups. What are they?
4. Make a comment on Doris Lessing.
5. Make a comment on Philip Arthur Larkin.
6. Make a comment on Ted Hughes.

下 编
英国文学选段练习

Part Two
Exercises on Selected Readings of English Literature

下编　英国文学选段练习

Exercise 1

Of men was the mildest and most beloved,
To his kin the kindest, keenest for praise.
Then the Goth's people reared a mighty pile
With shields and armour hung, as he had asked,
And in the midst the warriors laid their lord,
Lamenting. Then the warriors on the mound
Kindled a mighty bale fire; the smoke rose
Black from the Swedish pine, the sound of flame.

QUESTIONS:
1. These lines are taken from a(n) _____.
   A. sonnet				B. epic
   C. ballad				D. play
2. The man concerned in the excerpt is _____.
3. What does this excerpt mainly talk about?
4. Make a brief comment on this national epic.

Exercise 2

When Little John went into the quire,
The people began for to laugh;
He askt them seven times in the church,
Least three times should not be enough.

"Who gives me this maid?" said Little John;
Quoth Robin Hood, "That do I,
And he that takes her from Allin-a-Dale
Full dearly he shall her buy."

· 115 ·

And thus having end of this merry wedding,
The bride looked like a queen;
And so they returned to the merry greenwood,
Amongst the leaves so green."

QUESTIONS:
1. The genre of this excerpt is _____.
2. These lines are taken from _____.
3. Ballad is a story told in _____, usually in _____ stanzas, with the second and fourth lines _____. There is a _____ by the audience, which usually follows each stanza.
4. Can you describe Robin Hood's character?
5. What are the features of English ballads?
6. What are the themes of English ballads?

Exercise 3

As soon as April pierces to the root
The drought of March, and bathes each bud and shoot
Through every vein of sap with gentle showers
From whose engendering liquor spring the flowers;
When zephyrs have breathed softly all about
Inspiring every wood and field to sprout,
And in the zodiac the youthful sun
His journey halfway through the Ram has run;
When little birds are busy with their song
Who sleep with open eyes the whole night long
Life stirs their hearts and tingles in them so,
Then off as pilgrims people long to go,
And palmers to set out for distant strands
And foreign shrines renowned in many lands.

And specially in England people ride
To Canterbury from every countryside
To visit there the blessed martyred saint
Who gave them strength when they were sick and faint.

QUESTIONS:
1. This excerpt is taken from _____, the opening passage of the Prologue.
2. This is _____'s masterpiece.
3. _____ provides a framework of this poem, and it includes vivid sketches of typical medieval figures.
4. How much do you know about this masterpiece?
5. What is the social significance of this poem?

Exercise 4

I find no peace and all my war is done,
I fear and hope, I burn and freeze like ice
I fly above the wind, yet can I not arise,
And naught I have and all the world I seize on
That loseth nor locketh holdeth me in prison,
And holdeth me not; yet can I 'scape nowise;
Nor letteth me live nor die at my devise.
And yet of death it giveth me occasion.
Without eyen I see; and without tongue I plain
I desire to perish, and yet I ask health;
I love another, and thus I hate myself;
I feed me in sorrow, and laugh in all my pain.
Likewise displeaseth me both death and life,
And my delight is causer of this strife.

QUESTIONS:
1. The title of this poem is _____.
2. The author of this poem is _____ who introduced into England the _____, a 14-line poem with a complicated rhyme scheme, rhyming abba abba cde cde or abba abba cdcd ee.
3. The whole poem is a series of _____, representing a popular Petrarchan convention.
4. Give a possible and reasonable explanation of the following line:
   That loseth nor locketh holdeth me in prison

Exercise 5

The soote season, that bud and bloom forth brings,
With green hath clad the hill and eke the vale;
The nightingale with feathers new she sings;
The turtle to her make hath told her tale.
Summer is come, for every spray now springs
The hart hath hung his old head on the pale;
The buck in brake his winter coat he flings,
The fishes float with new repaired scale;
The adder all her slough away she slings,
The swift swallow pursueth the flies small;
The busy bee her honey now she mings.
Winter is worn, that was the flowers' bale.
And thus I see among these pleasant thins,
Each care decays, and yet my sorrow springs.

QUESTIONS:
1. The title of this poem is _____.
2. The poet who wrote this poem is _____.
3. The rhyme scheme of this poem is _____.

4. This poem is one of the best lyrics on _____.
   A. spring   B. summer
   C. autumn   D. winter
5. Give a possible and reasonable explanation of the following line:
   Winter is worn, that was the flowers' bale.
6. Translate the last two lines, and try to explain why the speaker's sorrow springs while each care decays among the pleasant things.
7. In Chinese literature there are countless poems on the same topic. Collect as many such Chinese poems as possible, and compare the ways in which spring is sung of.

Exercise 6

Lyke as a ship that through the ocean wyde,
By conduct of some star doth make her way,
Whenas a storme hath dimd her trusty guyde,
Out of her course doth wander far astray.
So I whose star, that wont with her bright ray
Me to direct, with clouds is overcast,
Doe wander now in darknesse and dismay,
Through hidden perils round about me plast.
Yet hope I well, that when this storme is past
My Helice the lodestar of my lyfe
Will shine again, and looke on me at last,
With lovely light to cleare my cloudy grief.
Till then I wander carefull comfortlesse,
In secret sorrow and pensiveness.

QUESTIONS:
1. This poem is taken from _____.
2. The poet who wrote this poem is _____.

3. The rhyme scheme of this sonnet is _____.
4. The sonnet based on an intricate pattern of interlocking rhymes is called _____.
5. What does the poet compare his love to? How important is her love to him?

Exercise 7

One day I wrote her name upon the strand,
But came the waves and washed it away:
Agayne I wrote it with a second hand,
But came the tyde, and made my paynes his pray.
"Vayne man," said she, "that doest in vaine assay,
A mortall thing so to immortalize,
For I myselve shall lyke to this decay,
And eek my name bee wyped out lykewize.
"Not so," quod I, "let baser things devize
To dy in dust, but you shall live by fame:
My verse your virtues rare shall eternize,
And in the heavens wryte your glorious name.
Where whenas death shall all the world subdew,
Out love shall live, and later life renew."

QUESTIONS:
1. This poem is a _____ sonnet with the rhyme scheme _____.
2. Give a possible and reasonable explanation of the words and phrases:
    strand: _____.
    with a second hand: _____.
    to dy in dust: _____.

3. Illustrate three representative works of the writer: _____, _____, _____.

Exercise 8

If all the world and love were young,
And truth in every shepherd's tongue,
These pretty pleasures might me move
To live with thee and be thy love.

Time drives the flocks from field to fold
When rivers rage and rocks grow cold,
And Philomel becometh dumb
The rest complains of cares to come.

The flowers do fade, and wanton fields
To wayward winter reckoning yields;
A honey tongue, a heart of gall,
Is fancy's spring, but sorrow's fall.

Thy gowns, thy shoes, thy beds of roses,
Thy cap, thy kirtle, and thy posies
Soon break, soon wither, soon forgotten—
In folly ripe, in reason rotten.

Thy belt of straw and ivy buds,
Thy coral clasps and amber studs,
All these in me no means can move
To come to thee and be thy love.

But could youth last and love still breed,
Had joys no date nor age no need,

Then these delights my mind might move
To live with thee and be thy love.

QUESTIONS:
1. The title of this poem is _____.
2. This is a reply written by _____ to Christopher Marlowe's _____.
3. This poem consists of six _____, each having the rhyme scheme of _____.
4. Did the girl accept the shepherd's invitation of being his love? Find the related lines to prove your idea.
5. Translate the last stanza into Chinese.

Exercise 9

Leave me, O love which reachest but to dust;
And thou, my mind, aspire to higher things;
Grow rich in that which never taketh rust'
Whatever fades but fading pleasure brings.
Draw in thy beams, and humble all thy might
To that sweet yoke where lasting freedoms be;
Which breaks the clouds and opens forth the light,
That doth both shine and give us sight to see.
O take fast hold; let that light be thy guide
In this small course which birth draws out to death'
And think how evil becometh him to slide'
Who seeketh heav'n, and comes of heav'nly breath.
Then farewell, world; thy uttermost I see;
Eternal Love, maintain thy life in me.

QUESTIONS:
1. The rhyme scheme of this poem is _____.

2. This is one of _____'s best sonnets.
3. Why do you think the poet refuses the "love"? What kind of love does he refuse?

Exercise 10

A Gentle Knight was pricking on the plaine,
Ycladd in mightie armes and silver shielde,
Wherein old dints of deepe wounds did remaine
The cruell marks of many a bloudy fielde;
Yet armes till that time did he never wield:
His angry steede did chide his foming bitt,
As much disdayning to the curbe to yield:
Full jolly knight he seemd, and faire did sitt,
As one for knightly giusts and fierce encounters fitt.

QUESTIONS:
1. These lines are taken from _____ written by _____.
2. This 9-line stanza form is called _____, the first eight lines are _____ lines, and the last line is an _____ line.
3. The knight's name in this stanza is _____.
4. The knight stands for _____.
5. The knight set out on his quest to rescue the parents of Una, a beautiful lady. What does she symbolize?

Exercise 11

Studies serve for delight, for ornament, and for ability. Their chief use for delight is in privateness and retiring; for ornament, is in discourse; and for ability, is in the judgment and disposition of business. ... To spend too much time in studies is sloth; to use them too much for ornament is affectation; to make judgment wholly by their rules is the humor of a scholar. ... Crafty men contemn studies, simple men admire them, and wise men use them, for they teach not their own use; but that is a wisdom without them, and above them, won by observation...

QUESTIONS:
1. These words are taken from an essay written by _____.
2. What is the title of this essay?
3. What do you think about the language of this essay?

Exercise 12

Reading maketh a full man, conference a ready man, and writing an exact man. And therefore, if a man write little, he had need have a great memory; if he confer little, he had need have a present wit; and if he read little, he had need have more cunning, to seem to know that he doth not. Histories make men wise; poets, witty; the mathematics, subtle; natural philosophy, deep; moral, grave; logic and rhetoric, able to contend.

QUESTIONS:
1. This passage is taken from an essay written by _____.
2. What is the title of the essay?
3. Translate this passage into Chinese.

Exercise 13

Come live with me and be my love,
And we will all the pleasures prove
That valleys, groves, hills, and fields,

Woods or steepy mountain yields.

And we will sit upon the rocks,
Seeing the shepherds feed their flocks
By shallow rivers to whose falls
Melodious birds sing madrigals.

And I will make thee beds of roses
And a thousand fragrant posies,
A cap of flowers, and a kirtle
Embroidered all with leaves of myrtle;

A gown made of the finest wool
Which from our pretty lambs we pull;
Fair lined slippers for the cold,
With buckles of the purest gold;

A belt of straw and ivy buds,
With coral clasps and amber studs:
And if these pleasures may thee move,
Come live with me, and be my love.

Thy silver dishes for thy meat
As precious as the gods do eat,
Shall on an ivory table be
Prepared each day for thee and me.

The shepherds' swains shall dance and sing
For the delight each May morning.
If these delights thy mind may move,
Then live with me and be my love.

QUESTIONS:
1. The title of this poem is _____.
2. This is a _____ lyric of invitation to love written by _____.
3. Many poets have written replies to it. The finest reply is _____ written by the great Elizabethan Romantic poet _____.
4. What writing feature did the writer use in the first stanza?
5. What is the theme of this poem?
6. What kind of life is idealized in this poem?

Exercise 14

To be, or not to be—that is the question:
Whether 'tis nobler in the mind to suffer
The slings and arrows of outrageous fortune
Or to take arms against a sea of troubles
And by opposing end them. To die, to sleep—
No more—and by a sleep to say we end
The heartache, and the thousand natural shocks
That flesh is heir to, 'Tis a consummation
Devoutly to be wished. To die, to sleep—
To sleep—perchance to dream: ay, there's the rub,
For in that sleep of death what dreams may come
When we have shuffled off this mortal coil,
Must give us pause. There's the respect
That makes calamity of so long life.
For who would bear the whips and scorns of time,
Th' oppressor's wrong, the proud man's contumely
The pangs of despised love, the law's delay,
The insolence of office, and the spurns
That patient merit of th' unworthly-takes,
When he himself might his quietus make

With a bare bodkin? Who would fardels bear,
To grunt and sweat under a weary life,
But that the dread of something after death,
The undiscovered country, from whose bourn
No traveller returns, puzzles the will,
And makes us rather bear those ills we have
Than fly to others that we know not of?
Thus conscience does make cowards of us all,
And thus the native hue of resolution
Is sicklied o'er with the pale cast of thought,
And enterprises of great pitch and moment
With this regard their currents turn awry
And lose the name of action.

QUESTIONS:
1. These lines are taken from a play entitled _____.
2. The playwright of the play is _____.
3. In the play these lines are uttered by _____.
4. Give an explanation of "to be or not to be".
5. About the utterer, what does this speech show?

Exercise 15

Shall I compare thee to a summer's day?
Thou art more lovely and more temperate.
Rough winds do shake the darling buds of May,
And summer's lease hath all too short a date:
Sometimes too hot the eye of heaven shines,
And often is his gold complexion dimmed;
And every fair from fair sometime declines,
By chance, or nature's changing course, untrimmed:

But thy eternal summer shall not fade,
Nor lose possession of that fair thou owest;
Nor shall Death brag thou wanderest in his shade
When in eternal lines to time thou growest.
So long as men can breathe or eyes can see,
So long lives this, and this gives life to thee.

QUESTIONS:
1. This is one of William Shakespeare's best known _____.
    A. sonnets
    B. ballads
    C. songs
2. It runs in iambic pentameter rhymed _____.
3. Explain the logical structure of this poem.
4. What's the theme of this poem?

Exercise 16

When, in disgrace with fortune and man's eyes,
I all alone beweep my outcast state,
And trouble deaf heaven with my bootless cries,
And look upon myself and curse my fate,
Wishing me like to one more rich in hope,
Featured like him, like him with friends possessed,
Desiring this man's art and that man's scope,
With what I most enjoy contented least,
Yet in these thought myself almost despising,
Haply I think on thee, and then my state,
Like to the lark at break of day arising,
From sullen earth, sings hymns at heaven's gate,
For thy sweet love rememb'red such wealth brings,

That then I scorn to change my state with kings.

QUESTIONS:
1. This is an _____ sonnet.
2. In this poem, the poet praises the power of _____ and shows his admiration for the young man in the poem.
3. Find out the meaning of the word "state" in Lines 2, 10 and 14.
4. The lark symbolizes the _____.
5. Make a brief comment on this sonnet.

Exercise 17

Drink to me only with thine eyes,
And I will pledge with mine;
O leave a kiss but in the cup,
And I'll not look for wine.
The thirst that from the soul doth rise,
Doth ask a drink divine:
But might I of Jove's nectar sup,
I would not change for thine.

I sent thee late a rosy wreath,
Not so much honoring thee,
As giving it a hope, that there
It could not withered be.
But thou thereon did'st only breathe,
And sent'st it back to me;
Since when it grows and smells, I swear,
Not of itself, but thee.

QUESTIONS:
1. The title of this poem is _____.

2. This is a classic lyric in the _____ meter—alternate 8-syllable lines and 6-syllable lines of _____ meter and with alternate rhymes.
3. This is a poem by one of the most outstanding figures in the literary world of the early 17th century, _____. In his later years he became the "literary king" of his time. A group of young poets gathered around him, and were proud to call themselves "Sons of _____".
4. Make a comment on the poem.

Exercise 18

Had I as many souls as there be stars
I'd give them all for Mephistophilis!
By him I'll be great emperor of the world,
And make a bridge through the mobbing air
To pass he ocean with a band of men;
I'll join the hills that country continent to Spain,
And both contributory to my crown;
The emperor shall not live but by my leave,
Not any potentate of Germany.
Now that I have obtained what I desire
I'll live in speculation of this art
Till Mephistophilis return again.

QUESTIONS:
1. These lines are taken from the play _____ written by _____.
2. The speaker of the passage quoted above is _____.
3. Briefly comment on the theme of this play.

Exercise 19

And though it in the center sit,
Yet when the other far doth roam,
It leans and hearkens after it,
And grows erect, as that comes home.

Such wilt thou be to me, who must
Like th' other foot, obliquely run;
Thy firmness makes my circle just,
And makes me end where I begun.

QUESTIONS:
1. The type of this poem is _____.
   A. poetry
   B. play
   C. ballad
2. Its title is _____ and its author is _____.
3. The tone of this poem is _____, it's because of _____.
4. How do you understand this sentence, "Thy firmness makes my circle just, And makes me end where I begun."?

Exercise 20

Gather ye rosebuds while ye may,
Old time is still a-flying;
And this same flower that smiles today
Tomorrow will be dying.

The glorious lamp of heaven, the sun,
The higher he's a-getting,

The sooner will his race be run,
And nearer he's to setting.

That age is best which is the first,
When youth and blood are warmer;
But being spent, the worse, and worst,
Times still succeed the former.

Then be not coy, but use your time,
And while ye may, go marry:
For having lost but once your prime,
You may forever tarry.

QUESTIONS:
1. The title of this poem is _____ and its author is _____.
2. The theme of the poem is _____, meaning "_____" or _____.
3. How do you understand "Cavalier poetry"?
4. Translate the poem into Chinese.

Exercise 21

Sweet day, so cool, so calm, so bright,
The bridal of the earth and sky:
The dew shall weep thy fall tonight;
For thou must die.

Sweet rose, whose hue, angry and brave,
Bids the rash gazer wipe his eye:
Thy root is ever in its grave,
And thou must die.

Sweet spring, full of sweet days and roses,
A box where sweets compacted lie;
My music shows ye have your closes,
And all must die.

Only a sweet and virtuous soul.
Like seasoned timber, never gives
But though the whole world turn to coal,
Then chiefly lives.

QUESTIONS:
1. The title of this poem is _____ and its author is _____.
2. The first two stanzas are devoted to the "_____" and the "_____", which uses the technique of _____ and _____.
3. What belief does this poem convey?

Exercise 22

Nine times the space that measures day and night
To mortal men, he with his horrid crew,
Lay vanquished, rolling in the fiery gulf,
Confounded though immortal. But his doom
Reserved him to more wrath; for now the thought
Both of lost happiness and lasting pain
Torments him; round he throws his baleful eyes,
That witnessed huge affliction and dismay,
Mixed with obdurate pride and steadfast hate.
At once, as far as angels ken, he views
The dismal situation waste and wild;

QUESTIONS:
1. The title of this poem is _____ and its author is _____.
2. The main characters in this poem are _____, _____ and _____.
3. The war in this poem reveals the war between _____ and _____ headed by _____ in England.
4. How do you understand "blank verse"? Why is it used in this poem?

Exercise 23

Out upon it! I have loved
   Three whole days together!
And am like to love three more,
If it prove fair weather.

Time shall molt away his wings
Ere he shall discover
In the whole wide world again
Such a constant lover.

QUESTIONS:
1. The title of this poem is _____ and its writer is _____, regarded as a _____.
2. The tone of this poem is _____.
   A. complimentary
   B. classic
   C. ironic

Exercise 24

Tell me not, Sweet, I am unkind

That from the nunnery
Of thy chaste breast and quiet mind,
To war and arms I fly.

True, a new mistress now I chase
The first foe in the field;
And with a stronger faith embrace
A sword, a horse, a shield.

QUESTIONS:
1. The title of this poem is _____ and its writer is _____, who once studied in _____ University.
2. This poem was printed when he was _____.
   A. at home
   B. in prison
   C. with his brother

Exercise 25

Had we but world enough, and time,
This coyness, lady, were no crime.
We would sit down, and think which way
To walk, and pass our long love's day.
Thou by the Indian Ganges' side
Shouldst rubies find; I by the tide
Of Humber would complain. I would
Love you ten years before the flood,
And you should, if you please, refuse
Till the conversion of the Jews.

QUESTIONS:
1. These lines are chosen from _____, whose writer is _____.

2. At first it looks like a dozen other poems on the _____ theme. But soon the _____ is made to sound deep and hollow, reverberating like a bell.
3. How can you describe the author's characteristic from this poem?

Exercise 26

Almost five thousand years ago, there were pilgrims walking to the Celestial City, as these two honest persons are; and Beelzebub, Apollyon, and Legion, with their companions, perceiving by the path that the pilgrims made, that their way to the city lay through this town of Vanity, they contrived here to set up a fair; a fair wherein should be sold all sorts of vanity, and that is should last all the year long. Therefore at this fair are all such merchandise sold, as houses, lands, trades, places, honors, preferments, titles, countries, kingdoms, lusts, pleasures, and delights of all sorts, as whores, bawds, wives, husbands, children, masters, servants, lives, blood, bodies, souls, silver, gold, pearls, precious stones, and what not.

QUESTIONS:
1. These sentences are chosen from _____ written by _____.
2. The novel begins with a man named _____, he comes from city of _____. He has two objects, one is to get rid of his _____, the other is to make his way to _____. He has a journey of _____ stages. Most famous is _____, where the leading character and _____ are thrown into a dungeon by Giant Despair. And then at last the _____, the deep river that the leading character must cross, and the city of _____ and the glorious company of angels that come singing down the streets. At last, the author wakes up and it turns out to be a dream!
3. How do you understand this novel?

Exercise 27

The trumpet's loud clangor
Excites us to arms,
With shrill notes of anger
And mortal alarms.
The double double double beat
Of the thundering drum
Cries: "Hark! the foes come;
Charge, charge, 'tis too late retreat."

The soft complaining flute
In dying notes discovers
The woes of hopeless lovers,
Whose dirge is whispered by the warbling lute.

QUESTIONS:
1. These sentences are chosen from _____, whose writer is _____ and these two sections are the _____ section.
2. The writer was _____ for about twenty years but had to resign in _____ when James II was expelled.

Exercise 28

I was dreadfully frightened (that I must acknowledge) when I perceived him to run my way; and especially, when, as I thought, I saw him pursued by the whole body; and now I expected that part of my dream was coming to pass, and that he would certainly take shelter in my grove; but I could not depend by any means upon my dream for the rest of it, viz., that the other savages would not pursue him thither, and find him there. However, I kept my station, and my spirits began to recover when I found that there was not above three men that followed him; and still more was I encouraged when I found that he outstripped them exceedingly in running and gained ground of them; so that, if he could but hold it for half an hour, I saw easily he would fairly get away from them all.

There was between them and my castle the creek, which I mentioned often at the first part of my story, where I landed my cargoes out of the ship; and this I saw plainly he must necessarily swim over, or the poor wretch would be taken there. But when the savage escaping came thither, he made nothing of it, though the tide was then up; but plunging in, swam through in about thirty strokes or thereabouts, landed, and ran on with exceeding strength and swiftness; when the three persons came to the creek, I found that two of them could swim, but the third could not, and that standing on the other side, he looked at the other, but went no farther; and soon after went softly back again, which, as it happened, was very well for him in the end.

QUESTIONS:
1. This passage is chosen from the novel _____ written by _____.
2. This excerpt describes the story when _____.
3. What do you think of the writer from this novel?

Exercise 29

It seems that upon the first moment I was discovered sleeping on the ground after my landing, the Emperor had early notice of it by an express; and determined in council that I should be tied in the manner I have related (which was done in the night while I slept), that plenty of meat and drink should be sent me, and a machine prepared to carry me to the capital city.

This resolution perhaps may appear very bold and dangerous, and I am confident would not be imitated by any prince in Europe on the like occasion; however, in my opinion it was extremely prudent as well as generous. For supposing these people had endeavored to kill me with their spears and arrows while I was asleep; I should certainly have awaked with the first sense of smart, which might so far have roused my rage and strength, as to enable me to break the strings wherewith I was tied; after which, as they were not able to make resistance, so they could expect no mercy.

QUESTIONS:
1. This excerpt is from the novel _____ and its writer is _____.
2. This excerpt describes the voyage to _____.
3. How many islands did the leading role travel?
   A. 2   B. 3   C. 4   D. 5
4. Why did the author use the first-person narrative?

Exercise 30

My friend Sir Roger, being a good churchman, has beautified the inside of his church with several texts of his own choosing; he has likewise given a handsome pulpit cloth, and railed in the communion table at his own expense. He has often told me that, at his coming to his estate, he found his parishioners very irregular; and that, in order to make them kneel and join in the responses, he gave every one of them a hassock and a Common Prayer book, and at the same time employed an itinerant singing master, who goes about the country for that purpose, to instruct them rightly in the tunes of the Psalms; upon which they now very much value themselves, and indeed outdo most of the country churches that I have ever heard.

QUESTIONS:
1. This excerpt is chosen from the article "_____", an article from _____.
2. What do you think of the Sir Roger mentioned in the passage?

Exercise 31

Some to conceit alone their taste confine,
And glitt'ring thoughts struck out at ev'ry line;
Pleas'd with a work where nothing's just or fit,
One glaring chaos and wild heap of wit:
Poets, like painters, thus unskill'd to trace
The naked nature and the living grace,
With gold and jewels cover ev'ry part,
And hide with ornaments their want of art.

QUESTIONS:
1. These sentences are chosen from _____ written by _____.
2. Which of the following is not true about this excerpt?
   A. It is the author's first famous work.
   B. It contains 744 lines and is divided into three parts.
   C. The "want of art" in the excerpt means "the lack of logistic technique".
   D. The whole poem was written in heroic couplets.
3. What is the peculiar style of the author's poem?

Exercise 32

Mr. Western grew every day fonder and fonder of Sophia, insomuch that his beloved dogs themselves almost gave place to her in his affections; but as he could not prevail on himself to abandon these, he contrived very cunningly to enjoy their company, together with that of his daughter, by insisting on her riding a hunting with him.

Sophia, to whom her father's word was a law, readily complied with his desires, though she had not the least delight in a sport, which was of too rough and masculine a nature to suit with her disposition. She had however another motive, beside her obedience, to accompany the old gentleman in the chase; for by her presence she hoped in some measure to restrain his impetuosity, and to prevent him from so frequently exposing his neck to the utmost hazard.

QUESTIONS:
1. This excerpt is chosen from the novel _____ written by _____.
2. What does this novel mainly talk about?

Exercise 33

For who to dumb Forgetfulness a prey,
　This pleasing anxious being e'er resigned,
Left the warm precincts of the cheerful day,
　Nor cast one longing lingering look behind?

On some fond breast the parting soul relies,
　Some pious drops the closing eye requires;
Even from the tomb the voice of Nature cries,
　Even in our ashes live their wonted fires.

QUESTIONS:
1. These lines are chosen from _____ written by _____.
2. This poem is full of the gentle _____ which marks all the characteristics of early _____ poetry.
3. How do you evaluate the author's poems?

Exercise 34

　　The place of our retreat was in a little neighborhood, consisting of farmers, who tilled their own grounds, and were equal strangers to opulence and poverty. As they had almost all the conveniences of life within themselves, they seldom visited towns or cities in search of superfluities. Remote from the polite, they still retained the primeval simplicity of manners; and frugal by habit, they scarcely knew that temperance was a virtue. They wrought with cheerfulness on days of labor; but observed festivals as intervals of idleness and pleasure. They kept up the Christmas carol, sent true-love knots on Valentine morning, ate pancakes on Shrovetide, showed their wit on the first of April, and religiously cracked nuts on Michaelmas Eve. Being apprised of our approach, the whole neighborhood came out to meet their minister, dressed in their finest clothes, and preceded by a pipe and tabor; a feast was also provided for our reception, at which we sat cheerfully down; and what the conversation wanted in wit was made up in laughter.

QUESTIONS:

1. The excerpt is chosen from the novel _____ written by _____.
2. The novel tells a story about _____ and his family. They used to live in prosperity and content, however, misfortune came upon them one day. He and his family have to move to another village, living under the patronage of a _____ called Thornhill. Thornhill turns out to be a wicked ruffian who seduces the vicar's _____ Olivia and then deserts her. Then their house was burnt into ash. The vicar was put into prison because of _____, whose eldest son George challenges the Squire to a duel to _____, but he is overpowered by ruffians and also thrown into prison. In the end, they were saved by _____.
3. What does the author want to convey by writing this novel?

Exercise 35

Lady Sneer. The paragraphs, you say, Mr. Snake, were all inserted?
Snake. They were, madam; and, as I copied them myself in a feigned hand, there

can be no suspicion whence they came.

Lady Sneer. Did you circulate the report of Lady Britle's in trigue with Captain Boastall?

Snake. That's in as fine a train as your ladyship could wish. In the common course of things, I think it must reach Mrs. Clackitt's ears within four-and-twenty hours; and then, you know, the business is as good as done.

QUESTIONS:
1. This excerpt is chosen from a famous _____ called _____ written by _____.
2. By the conclusion of the play, it is clear that only the _____ have no true honor, which shows that the society is like a _____.
3. Which of the following is true about this excerpt?
   A. Its author is from Germany.
   B. Its author's second play is *The Rivals*.
   C. The author wrote this excerpt in 1774.
   D. The vanity, greed and hypocrisy of the high class are criticized.

Exercise 36

Tyger! Tyger! burning bright
In the forests of the night,
What immortal hand or eye
Could frame thy fearful symmetry?

In what distant deeps or skies
Burnt the fire of thine eyes?
On what wings dare he aspire?
What the hand dare seize the fire?

And what shoulder, and what art,

Could twist the sinews of thy heart?
And when thy heart began to beat,
What dread hand? And what dread feet?

What the hammer? what the chain?
In what furnace was thy brain?
What the anvil? What dread grasp
Dare its deadly terrors clasp?

When the stars threw down their spears,
And water'd heaven with their tears,
Did he smile his work to see?
Did he who made the Lamb make thee?

Tyger! Tyger! burning bright
In the forests of the night,
What immortal hand or eye
Dare frame thy fearful symmetry?

QUESTIONS:

1. This poem is entitled _____ written by _____.
2. Which of the following is not the author's work?
   A. *London*   B. *The Deserted Village*
   C. *The Chimney Sweeper*   D. *The Sick Rose*
3. This poem is written in _____ quatrains rhyming "aabb".
4. Which of the following figure of speeches is frequently used in this poem.
   A. rhetorical question   B. metaphor
   C. alliteration   D. analogy
5. How do you understand the word "Tyger" in this poem?
6. Try to translate the first section.

Exercise 37

O, Mary, at thy window be!
It is the wish'd, the trysted hour.
Those smiles and glances let me see,
That make the miser's treasure poor.
How blithely wad I bide the stoure,
A weary slave frae sun to sun.
Could I the rich reward secure—
The lovely Mary Morrison!

QUESTIONS:
1. The title of this poem is _____ written by _____.
2. Which of the following is not the author's work?
    A. *John Anderson, My Jo*   B. *A Red, Red Rose*
    C. *The Epitaph*   D. *Auld Lang Syne*

Exercise 38

Now's the day, and now's the hour:
See the front o' battle lour,
See approach proud Edward's power—
Chains and Slaverie!

Wha will be a traitor knave?
Wha can fill a coward's grave?
Wha sae base as be a slave?
Let him turn and flee!

QUESTIONS:
1. The excerpt above is chosen from _____ written by _____.

2. Can you translate the second stanza of this excerpt into Chinese?

Exercise 39

Mark but this flea, and mark in this,
How little that which thou deniest me is;
It sucked me first, and now sucks thee,
And in this flea, our two bloods mingled bee;
Thou know'st that this cannot be said
A sin, nor shame, nor loss of maidenhead,
Yet this enjoys before it woo,
And pampered swells with one blood made of two,
And this, alas, is more then wee would doe.

Oh stay, three lives in one flea spare,
Where wee almost, yea more then married are.
<u>This flea is you and I, and this</u>
<u>Our marriage bed, and marriage temple is;</u>
Though parents grudge, and you, we are met,
And cloistered in these living walls of Jet.
Though use make you apt to kill me,
Let not to that, self-murder added bee,
And sacrilege, three sins in killing three.

Cruel and sudden, hast thou since
Purpled thy nail, in blood of innocence?
Wherein could this flea guilty bee,
Except in that drop which it sucked from thee?
Yet thou triumph'st, and say'st that thou
Find'st not thy self, nor me the weaker now;
'Tis true, then learn how false fears bee;

Just so much honor, when thou yield'st to me,
Will waste, as this flea's death took life from thee.

QUESTIONS:
1. The title of this poem is _____.
2. This is _____'s representative poem.
   A. Robert Herrick
   B. John Donne
   C. John Milton
3. The rhetorical device of the underlined sentence is _____.
4. One conspicuous feature of this poem is _____. A love poem in metaphysical poetry is not _____, but analytical through _____.
5. The speaker compares the flea to a performer of love and attempts to persuade the young girl to accept his love. The theme of this poem, _____, was a popular at that time.

Exercise 40

Methought I saw my late espoused saint
Brought to me like Alcestis, from the grave,
Whom Jove's great son to her glad husband gave,
Rescued from death by force, though pale and faint.
Mine, as whom washed from spot of childbed taint
Purification in the old Law did save,
And such, as yet once more I trust to have
Full sight of her in Heaven without restraint,
Came vested all in white, pure as her mind.
Her face was veil'd; yet to my fancied sight
Love, sweetness, goodness, in her person shined
So clear, as in no face with more delight.

But O, as to embrace me she inclined.
I waked, she fled, and day brought back my night.

QUESTIONS:
1. The title of this poem is _____.
2. This poem was written by _____ in a dream vision in memory of his wife, Katherine Woodcock in 1658.
3. This poem is written in Italian sonnet form with the rhyme scheme of _____.
4. Make a brief comment on the last two lines of the poem.
5. Su Shi has a poem in memory of his deceased wife Wang Fu. Try to write down this poem.

Exercise 41

O my luve's like a red, red rose,
That's newly sprung in June;
O my luve's like the melodie
That's sweetly play'd in tune.

As fair art thou, my bonie lass,
So deep in luve am I.
And I will luve thee still, my dear,
Till a' the seas gang dry.

Till a'the seas gang dry, my dear,
And the rocks melt wi' the sun.
O I will luve thee still, my dear,
While the sands o' life shall run.

And fare-thee-weel, my only luve!

And fare-thee-weel, a while!

And I will come again, my luve,

Tho' it were ten thousand mile!

QUESTIONS:
1. This is one of the most famous poems of _____, written in the form of _____.
2. What are the symbolic meanings of "a red, red rose"?
3. Make a brief comment on this poem.

Exercise 42

I wandered lonely as a cloud

That floats on high o'er vales and hills,

When all at once I saw a crowd,

A host, of golden daffodils;

Beside the lake, beneath the trees,

Fluttering and dancing in the breeze.

Continuous as the stars that shine

And twinkle on the Milky Way,

They stretched in never-ending line

Along the margin of a bay;

Ten thousand say I at a glance,

Tossing their heads in sprightly dance.

The waves beside them danced; but they

Outdid the sparkling waves in glee;

A poet could not but be gay,

In such a jocund company;

I gazed—and gazed—but little thought

What wealth the show to me had brought:

For oft, when on my couch I lie
In vacant or in pensive mood,
They flash upon that inward eye
Which is the bliss of solitude;
And then my heart with pleasure fills,
And dances with the daffodils.

QUESTIONS:
1. The poet who wrote poem is _____.
2. The title of this poem is _____.
3. This poem best represents the poet's central idea of his creative process— "_____".
4. In this poem, the image of cloud is outstanding and important. So is the image of daffodils. In some sense, they form a contrast: the _____ is lonely and the _____ are happy.
5. What is the theme of this poem?

Exercise 43

Behold her, single in the field,
You solitary Highland Lass!
Reaping and singing by herself;
Stop here, or gently pass!
Alone she cuts and binds the grain,
And sings a melancholy strain;
O listen! for the Vale profound
Is overflowing with the sound.

No Nightingale did ever chaunt

More welcome notes to weary bands
Of travellers in some shady haunt,
Among Arabian sands;
A voice so thrilling ne'er was heard
In springtime from the Cuckoo bird,
Breaking the silence of the seas
Among the farthest Hebrides.

QUESTIONS:
1. The poet who wrote this poem is _____.
2. This poem is entitled _____.
3. What does this poem mainly talk about?
4. What's the rhyme scheme of each stanza?

Exercise 44

She dwelt among the untrodden ways
Beside the springs of Dove.
A Maid whom there were none to praise
And very few to love;

A violet by a mossy stone
Half hidden from the eye!
—Fair as a star, when only one
Is shining in the sky.

She lived unknown, and few could know
When Lucy ceased to be;
But she is in her grave, and, oh,
The difference to me!

QUESTIONS:
1. The poet who wrote this poem is _____.
2. In the second stanza, the poet compares the girl to a _____.
3. Appreciate the first two lines of the second stanza "A violet by a mossy stone / Half hidden from the eye!" It may reminds one of an image of a girl in Bai Juyi's poem "琵琶行" in which there are such two lines "_____".

Exercise 45

In Xanadu did Kubla Khan
A stately pleasure-dome decree:
Where Alph, the sacred river, ran
Through caverns measureless to man
Down to a sunless sea.
So twice five miles of fertile ground
With walls and towers were girdled round:
And there were gardens bright with sinuous rills,
Where blossom'd many an incense-bearing tree;
And here were forests ancient as the hills,
Enfolding sunny sports of greenery.

QUESTIONS:
1. The title of this poem is _____. The poet who wrote this poem is _____.
2. The writer completed a joint work with William Wordsworth entitled _____.
3. This poem is said to have been composed in a _____.

Exercise 46

It is an ancient Mariner,
And he stoppeth one of three.
'By thy long grey beard and glittering eye,
Now wherefore stopp'st thou me?

The Bridegroom's doors are opened wide,
And I am next of kin;
The guests are met, the feast is set:
May'st hear the merry din.'

He holds him with his skinny hand,
'There was a ship,' quoth he.
'Hold off! unhand me, grey-beard loon!'
Eftsoons his hand dropt he.

He holds him with his glittering eye—
The Wedding-Guest stood still,
And listens like a three years' child:
The Mariner hath his will.

The Wedding-Guest sat on a stone:
He cannot choose but hear;
And thus spake on that ancient man,
The bright-eyed Mariner.

'The ship was cheered, the harbour cleared,
Merrily did we drop
Below the kirk, below the hill,
Below the lighthouse top.

The Sun came up upon the left,
Out of the sea came he!
And he shone bright, and on the right
Went down into the sea.

Higher and higher every day,
Till over the mast at noon—
The Wedding-Guest here beat his breast,
For he heard the loud bassoon.

The bride hath paced into the hall,
Red as a rose is she;
Nodding their heads before her goes
The merry minstrelsy.

The Wedding-Guest he beat his breast,
Yet he cannot choose but hear;
And thus spake on that ancient man,
The bright-eyed Mariner.

And now the STORM-BLAST came, and he
Was tyrannous and strong:
He struck with his o'ertaking wings,
And chased us south along.

With sloping masts and dipping prow,
As who pursued with yell and blow
Still treads the shadow of his foe,
And forward bends his head,
The ship drove fast, loud roared the blast,
And southward aye we fled.

And now there came both mist and snow,
And it grew wondrous cold:
And ice, mast-high, came floating by,
As green as emerald.

And through the drifts the snowy clifts
Did send a dismal sheen:
Nor shapes of men nor beasts we ken—
The ice was all between.

The ice was here, the ice was there,
The ice was all around:
It cracked and growled, and roared and howled,
Like noises in a swound!

At length did cross an Albatross,
Thorough the fog it came;
As if it had been a Christian soul,
We hailed it in God's name.

It ate the food it ne'er had eat,
And round and round it flew.
The ice did split with a thunder-fit;
The helmsman steered us through!

And a good south wind sprung up behind;
The Albatross did follow,
And every day, for food or play,
Came to the mariner's hollo!

In mist or cloud, on mast or shroud,
It perched for vespers nine;

Whiles all the night, through fog-smoke white,
Glimmered the white Moon-shine.'

'God save thee, ancient Mariner!
From the fiends, that plague thee thus!—
Why look'st thou so?'—With my cross-bow
I shot the ALBATROSS.

QUESTIONS:
1. The form of this poem is a _____.
2. The title of this poem is _____.
3. This poem was written by _____.
   A. Samuel Taylor Coleridge   B. William Wordsworth
   C. George Gordon Byron   D. Percy Bysshe Shelley
4. Please comment on the poem briefly.

Exercise 47

Eternal Spirit of the chainless Mind!
Brightest in dungeons, Liberty! thou art:
For there thy habitation is the heart—
The heart which love of thee alone can bind;
And when thy sons to fetters are consign'd—
To fetters, and the damp vault's dayless gloom,
Their country conquers with their martyrdom.
And Freedom's fame finds wings on every wind.
Chillon! thy prison is a holy place,
And thy sad floor an altar—for 't was trod,
Until his very steps have left a trace
Worn, as if thy cold pavement were a sod,
By Bornnivard!—May none those marks efface!

For they appeal from tyranny to God.

QUESTIONS:
1. This poem is a _____ written by _____.
2. The title of this poem is _____.
3. What does the poem describe?

Exercise 48

The Isles of Greece

1
The isles of Greece, the isles of Greece!
Where burning Sappho loved and sung.
Where grew the arts of war and peace,
Where Delos rose, and Phoebus sprung!
Eternal summer gilds them yet,
But all, except their sun, is set.

2
The Scian and the Teian muse,
The hero's harp, the lover's lute,
Have found the fame your shores refuse:
Their place of birth alone is mute
To sounds which echo further west
Than your sires' "Islands of the Blest".

3
The mountains look on Marathon—
And Marathon looks on the sea;
And musing there an hour alone,
I dream'd that Greece might still be free;
For standing on the Persians' grave,

I could not deem myself a slave.

4

A king sate on the rocky brow
Which looks o'er sea-born Salamis;
And ships, by thousands, lay below,
And men in nations; —all were his!
He counted them at break of day—
And, when the sun set, where were they?

5

And where are they? and where art thou,
My country? On thy voiceless shore
The heroic lay is tuneless now—
The heroic bosom beats no more!
And must thy lyre, so long divine,
Degenerate into hands like mine?

6

'Tis something, in the dearth of fame,
Though link'd among a fetter'd race,
To feel at least a patriot's shame,
Even as I sing, suffuse my face;
For what is left the poet here?
For Greeks a blush—for Greece a tear.

7

Must we but weep o'er days more blest?
Must we but blush? —Our fathers bled.
Earth! render back from out thy breast
A remnant of our Spartan dead!
Of the three hundred grant but three,
To make a new Thermopylae!

8

What, silent still? and silent all?
Ah! no; —the voices of the dead

Sound like a distant torrent's fall,

And answer, "Let one living head,

But one arise. —we come, we come!"

'Tis but the living who are dumb.

9

In vain—in vain: strike other chords;

Fill high the cup with Samian wine!

Leave battles to the Turkish hordes,

And shed the blood of Scio's vine!

Hark! rising to the ignoble call—

How answers each bold Bacchanal!

10

You have the Pyrrhic dance as yet;

Where is the Pyrrhic phalanx gone?

Of two such lessons, why forget

The nobler and the manlier one?

You have the letters Cadmus gave—

Think ye he meant them for a slave?

11

Fill high the bowl with Samian wine!

We will not think of themes like these!

It made Anacreon's song divine:

He served—but served Polycrates—

A tyrant; but our masters then

Were still, at least, our countrymen.

12

The tyrant of the Chersonese

Was freedom's best and bravest friend;

That tyrant was Miltiades!

Oh! that the present hour would lend

Another despot of the kind!

Such chains as his were sure to bind.

13
Fill high the bowl with Samian wine!
On Suli's rock, and Parga's shore,
Exists the remnant of a line
Such as the Doric mothers bore;
And there, perhaps, some seed is sown,
The Heracleidan blood might own.
14
Trust not for freedom to the Franks—
They have a king who buys and sells;
In native swords, and native ranks,
The only hope of courage dwells;
But Turkish force, and Latin fraud,
Would break your shield, however broad.
15
Fill high the bowl with Samian wine!
Our virgins dance beneath the shade—
I see their glorious black eyes shine;
But gazing on each glowing maid,
My own the burning tear-drop laves,
To think such breasts must suckle slaves.
16
Place me on Sunium's marbled steep,
Where nothing, save the waves and I,
May hear our mutual murmurs sweep;
There, swan-like, let me sing and die:
A land of slaves shall ne'er be mine—
Dash down yon cup of Samian wine!

QUESTIONS:
1. These lines were written by _____.
2. This excerpt is taken from the writer's masterpiece _____.

3. Who is "Sappho" in Line 2 and who is "Phoebus" in Line 4?
4. In this song poem, the writer talks about the past glory of the ancient _____.
   A. England   B. Italy
   C. Greece   D. France
5. Lu Xun talked about the relationship between Byron and Greece in this way: "裴伦平时，又至有情愫于希腊，思想所趣，如磁指南。特希腊时自由悉丧，入突厥版图，受其羁縻，不敢抗拒。诗人惋惜悲愤，往往见于篇章，怀前古之光荣，哀后人之零落，或与斥责，或加激励，思使之攘突厥而复兴，更睹往日庄严之希腊。" Can you justify why Lu Xun said this with what you can find in this poem?

Exercise 49

When we two parted
In silence and tears,
Half broken-hearted
To sever for years,
Pale grew thy cheek and cold,
Colder thy kiss;
Truly that hour foretold
Sorrow to this!

The dew of the morning
Sunk chill on my brow—
It felt like the warning
Of what I feel now.
Thy vows are all broken,
And light is thy fame:
I hear thy name spoken,
And share in its shame.

They name thee before me,
A knell to mine ear;
A shudder comes o'er me—
Why wert thou so dear?
They know not I knew thee
Who knew thee too well:
long, long shall I rue thee,
Too deeply to tell.

In secret we met—
In silence I grieve,
That thy heart could forget,
Thy spirit deceive.
If I should meet thee
After long years,
How should I greet thee?
With silence and tears.

QUESTIONS:

1. This poem is entitled _____ written by _____.
2. This poem follows the time order to tell a story of two lovers, where one has intentionally left the other. The three narrative pictures in the poem are _____, _____ and _____.
3. Make a brief comment on this poem.

Exercise 50

She walks in beauty, like the night
Of cloudless climes and starry skies;
And all that's best of dark and bright

Meet in her aspect and her eyes;
Thus mellowed to that tender light
Which heaven to gaudy day denies.

One shade the more, one ray the less,
Had half impaired the nameless grace
Which waves in every raven tress,
Or softly lightens o'er her face;
Where thoughts serenely sweet express
How pure, how dear their dwelling place.

And on that cheek, and o'er that brow,
So soft, so calm, yet eloquent
The smiles that win, the tints that glow.
But tell of days in goodness spent,
A mind at peace with all below,
A heart whose love is innocent!

QUESTIONS:

1. This poem is entitled _____ written by _____ in 1813.
2. This poem is written in three _____ stanzas of _____ rhyming "ababab".
3. Traditional love poems often compare beautiful women to flowers, but in this poem, the poet compares this beautiful lady to _____.

Exercise 51

Men of England, wherefore plough
For the lords who lay ye low?
Wherefore weave with toil and care

The rich robes your tyrants wear?

Wherefore feed and clothe and save
From the cradle to the grave
Those ungrateful drones who would
Drain your sweat—nay, drink your blood?

Wherefore, Bees of England, forge
Many a weapon, chain, and scourge,
That these stingless drones may spoil
The forced produce of your toil?

Have ye leisure, comfort, calm
Shelter, food, love's gentle balm?
Or what is it ye buy so dear
With your pain and with your fear?

The seed ye sow, another reaps;
The wealth ye find, another keeps;
The robes ye weave, another wears;
The arms ye forge, another bears.

Sow seed—but let no tyrant reap;
Find wealth—let no impostor heap;
Weave robes—let not the idle wear;
Forge arms—in your defence to bear.

QUESTIONS:

1. The rhyme scheme for each stanza is _____.
2. The author of this poem is _____.
3. The title of this poem is _____.
4. The figures of speech used in this selection are _____, _____,

_____, _____ and _____.

Exercise 52

Ode to the West Wind

I

O, wild West Wind, thou breath of Autumn's being,
Thou, from whose unseen presence the leaves dead
Are driven, like ghosts from an enchanter fleeing,

Yellow, and black, and pale, and hectic red,
Pestilence-stricken multitudes: O, thou,
Who chariotest to their dark wintry bed

The winged seeds, where they lie cold and low,
Each like a corpse within its grave, until
Thine azure sister of the spring shall blow

Her clarion o'er the dreaming earth, and fill
(Driving sweet buds like flocks to feed in air)
With living hues and odours plain and hill:

Wild Spirit, which art moving everywhere;
Destroyer and preserver; hear, O, hear!

II
Thou on whose stream, mid the steep sky's commotion.
Loose clouds like earth's decaying leaves are shed,
Shook from the tangled boughs of Heaven and Ocean,

Angels of rain and lightning: there are spread
On the blue surface of thine airy surge,
Like the bright hair uplifted from the head

Of some fierce Maenad, even from the dim verge
Of the horizon to the zenith's height
The locks of the approaching storm, Thou dirge

Of the dying year, to which this closing night
Will be the dome of a vast sepulcher,
Vaulted with all thy congregated might

Of vapors, from whose solid atmosphere
Black rain, and fire and hail will hurst: O, hear!

III
Thou who didst waken from his summer dreams
The blue Mediterranean, where he lay,
Lulled by the coil of his crystalline streams,

Beside a pumice isle in Bai's bay,
And saw in sleep old palaces and towers
Quivering within the wave's intenser day,

All overgrown with azure moss and flowers
So sweet, the sense faints picturing them! Thou
For whose path the Atlantic's level powers

Cleave themselves into chasms, while far below
The sea blooms and the oozy woods which wear
The sapless foliage of the ocean, know

Thy voice, and suddenly grow grey with fear,
And tremble and despoil themselves: O, hear!

IV
If I were a dead leaf thou mightest bear;
If I were a swift cloud to fly with thee;
A wave to pant beneath thy power, and share

The impulse of thy strength. only less free
Than thou, O uncontrollable! If even
I were as in my boyhood, and could be

The comrade of thy wanderings over heaven,
As then, when to outstrip thy skiey speed
Scarce seemed a vision; I would ne'er have striven

As thus with thee in prayer in my sore need.
Oh! lift me as a wave, a leaf, a cloud!
I fall upon the thorns of life! I bleed!

A heavy weight of hours has chained and bowed
One too like thee tameless, and swift, and proud.

V
Make me thy lyre, even as the forest is:
What if my leaves are falling like its own!
The tumult of thy mighty harmonies

Will take from both a deep, autumnal tone,
Sweet though in sadness. Be thou, spirit fierce,
My spirit! Be thou me, impetuous one!

Drive my dead thoughts over the universe
Like withered leaves to quicken a new birth!
And, by the incantation of this verse,

Scatter, as from an unextinguished hearth
Ashes and sparks, my words among mankind!
Be through my lips to unawakened earth

The trumpet of a prophecy! O, wind,
If Winter comes, can Spring be far behind?

QUESTIONS:
1. This poem is one of _____'s great lyrics.
2. What does west wind in this poem symbolize?
3. Briefly comment on the poem.

Exercise 53

A Song

A widow bird sat mourning for her love
Upon a wintry bough;
The frozen wind crept on above
The freezing stream below.

There was no leaf upon the forest bare,
No flower upon her ground,
And little motion in the air
Except the mill-wheel's sound.

QUESTIONS:
1. This short poem was written by _____.
2. The meaning of "a widow bird" in the first line means:
3. This short poem is famous for its _____. Compare this poem with the famous Chinese poem "天净沙·秋思".

Exercise 54

Much have I travell'd in the realms of gold,
And many goodly states and kingdoms seen;
Round many western islands have I been
Which bards in fealty to Apollo hold.
Oft of one wide expanse had I been told
That deep-brow'd Homer ruled as his demesne;
Yet did I never breathe its pure serene
Till I heard Chapman speak out loud and bold:
Then felt I like some watcher of the skies
When a new planet swims into his ken;
Or like stout Cortez when with eagle eyes
He star'd at the Pacific—and all his men
Look'd at each other with a wild surmise—
Silent, upon a peak in Darien.

QUESTIONS:
1. The title of this poem is _____.
2. The poet who wrote this poem is _____.
3. The form of this poem is a(n) _____.
4. The rhyme scheme of this poem is _____.
   A. abba, abba, cdcdcd   B. aaab, bbba, cdcdcd
   C. baaa, abba, ccddcc   D. abba, abba, ccccdd
5. What does the poem describe?

Exercise 55

Away! away! for I will fly to thee,
Not charioted by Bacchus and his pards,
But on the viewless wings of Poesy,
Though the dull brain perplexes and retards:
Already with thee! tender is the night,
And haply, the Queen-Moon is on her throne,
Cluster'd around by all her starry Fays;
But here there is no light.
Save what from heaven is with the breezes blown
Through verdurous glooms and winding mossy ways.

I cannot see what flowers are at my feet,
Nor what soft incense hangs upon the boughs,
But, in embalmed darkness, guess each sweet
Wherewith the seasonable month endows
The grass, the thicket, and the furit-tree wild;
White hawthorn, and the pastoral eglantine;
Fast fading violets cover'd up in leaves;
And mid-May's eldest child,
The coming musk-rose, full of dewy wine,
The murmurous haunt of flies on summer eves.

QUESTIONS:
1. The poet who wrote these lines is _____.
2. The title of this poem is _____.
3. All the lines in each stanza are in iambic pentameter, with the exception of the eighth line which has only _____ feet.
4. Briefly comment on the poem.

Exercise 56

Season of mists and mellow fruitfulness,
Close bosom-friend of the maturing sun;
Conspiring with him how to load and bless
With fruit the vines that round the thatch-eves run;
To bend with apples the moss'd cottage-trees,
And fill all fruit with ripeness to the core;
To swell the gourd, and plump the hazel shells
With a sweet kernel; to set budding more,
And still more, later flowers for the bees,
Until they think warm days will never cease,
For Summer has o'er-brimm'd their clammy cells.

Who hath not seen thee oft amid thy store?
Sometimes whoever seeks abroad may find
Thee sitting careless on a granary floor,
Thy hair soft-lifted by the winnowing wind;
Or on a half-reap'd furrow sound asleep,
Drows'd with the fume of poppies, while thy hook
Spares the next swath and all its twined flowers
And sometimes like a gleaner thou dost keep
Steady thy laden head across a brook;
Or by a cyder-press, with patient look,
Thou watchest the last oozings hours by hours.

Where are the songs of Spring? Ay, where are they?
Think not of them, thou hast thy music too,
While barred clouds bloom the soft-dying day,
And touch the stubble plains with rosy hue;
Then in a wailful choir the small gnats mourn
Among the river sallows, borne aloft

Or sinking as the light wind lives or dies;
And full-grown lambs loud bleat from hilly bourn;
Hedge-crickets sing; and now with treble soft
The red-breast whistles from a garden-croft;
And gathering swallows twitter in the skies.

QUESTIONS:
1. This poem is entitled _____, considered to be one of John Keats's best odes.
2. The poem is written in three 11-line stanzas of iambic pentameter lines rhyming "_____".
3. In these three stanzas, the poet respectively describes the _____, _____, and _____. The poet shows his deep love for _____, the season of ripeness and warmth.

Exercise 57

The poetry of earth is never dead:
When all the birds are faint with the hot sun,
And hide in cooling trees, a voice will run
From hedge to hedge about the new-mown mead;
That is the Grasshopper's—he takes the lead
In summer luxury, he has never done
With his delights; for when tired out with fun
He rests at ease beneath some pleasant weed.
The poetry of earth is ceasing never:
On a lone winter evening, when the frost
Has wrought a silence, from the stove there shrills
The Cricket's song, in warmth increasing ever,
And seems to one in drowsiness half lost,
The Grasshopper's among some grassy hills.

QUESTIONS:

1. This poem was written by _____, entitled _____.
2. The poem is filled with a _____, _____, and _____ atmosphere.
3. This poem is divided into two parts. In the first part, the poet expresses his main idea: _____. In the second part, the poet repeats and stresses the idea that _____.

Exercise 58

The name of Ivanhoe was no sooner pronounced than it flew from mouth to mouth with all the celerity with which eagerness could convey and curiosity receive it. It was no long ere it reached the circle of the prince, whose brow darkened as he heard the news. Looking around him, however, with an air of scorn, "My lords," said he, "and especially you, Sir Prior, what think ye of the doctrine the learned tell us concerning innate attractions and antipathies? Methinks that I felt the presence of my brother's minion, even when I least guessed whom yonder suit of armour inclosed."

"Front-de-Boeuf must prepare to restore his fief of Ivanhoe," said De Bracy, who, having discharged his part honourably in the tournament, had laid his shield and helmet aside, and again mingled with the Prince's retinue.

"Ay," answered Waldemar Fitzurse, "this gallant is likely to reclaim the castle and manor which Richard assigned to him, and which your Highness's generosity has since given to Front-de-Boeuf.

(from Chapter XIII)

QUESTIONS:

1. This excerpt is taken from the novel _____.
2. _____ is the author of this novel.
3. This novel is the first of the author's _____ novel.

Exercise 59

"I bide tryste" was the reply; "and so I think do you, Mr. Osbaldistone."

"You are then the person who requested to meet me here at this unusual hour?"

"I am," he replied. "Follow me, and you shall know my reasons."

"Before following you, I must know your name and purpose," I answered.

"I am a man," was the reply; "and my purpose is friendly to you."

"A man!" I repeated. "That is a very brief description."

"It will serve for one who has no other to give," said the stranger. "He that is without name, without friends, without coin, without country, is still at least a man; and he that has all these is no more."

"Yet this is still too general an account of yourself, to say the least of it, to establish your credit with a stranger."

QUESTIONS:
1. This selection is taken from a novel entitled _____.
2. The author of this novel is _____.
3. The conversation is a talk between _____ and _____.

Exercise 60

It is a truth universally acknowledged that a single man in possession of a good fortune must be in want of a wife.

However little known the feelings or views of such a man may be on his first entering a neighbourhood, this truth is so well fixed in the minds of the surrounding families, that he is considered as the rightful property of some one or other of their daughters.

"My dear Mr. Bennet," said his lady to him one day, "have you heard that Netherfield Park is let at last?"

Mr. Bennet replied that he had not.

"But it is," returned she; "for Mrs. Long has just been here, and she told me all about it."

Mr. Bennet made no answer.

"Do you not want to know who has taken it?" cried his wife impatiently.

"You want to tell me, and I have no objection to hearing it."

This was invitation enough.

"Why, my dear, you must know, Mrs. Long says that Netherfield is taken by a young man of large fortune from the north of England; that he came down on Monday in a chaise and four to see the place, and was so much delighted with it that he agreed with Mr. Morris immediately; that he is to take possession before Michaelmas, and some of his servants are to be in the house by the end of next week."

"What is his name?"

"Bingley."

"Is he married or single?"

"Oh! single, my dear, to be sure! A single man of large fortune; four or five thousand a year. What a fine thing for our girls!"

"How so? how can it affect them?"

"My dear Mr. Bennet," replied his wife, "how can you be so tiresome! You must know that I am thinking of his marrying one of them."

"Is that his design in setting here?"

"Design! Nonsense, how can you talk so! But it is very likely that he may fall in love with one of them, and therefore you must visit him as soon as he comes."

QUESTIONS:

1. This selection is taken from the novel _____.
2. The author of this novel is _____.
3. Please comment on the style of this selection.
4. What is the author's attitude towards marriage in this novel?

Exercise 61

On nothing per annum, then, and during a course of some two or three years, of which we can afford to give but a very brief history, Crawley and his wife lived very happily and comfortably at Paris. It was in this period that he quitted the Guards, and sold out of the army. When we find him again, his mustachios and the title of Colonel on his card are the only relics of his military profession.

It has been mentioned that Rebecca, soon after her arrival in Paris, took a very smart and leading position in the society of that capital, and was welcomed at some of the most distinguished houses of the restored French nobility. The English men of fashion in Paris courted her, too, to the disgust of the ladies their wives, who could not bear the parvenue. For some months the salons of the Faubourg St. Germain, in which her place was secured, and the splendours of the new Court, where she was received with much distinction, delighted, and perhaps a little intoxicated Mrs. Crawley, who may have been disposed during this period of elation to slight the people—honest young military men mostly—who formed her husband's chief society.

But the Colonel yawned sadly among the Duchesses and great ladies of the Court. The old women who played ecarte made such a noise about a five-franc piece, that it was not worth Colonel Crawley's while to sit down at a card-table. The wit of their conversation he could not appreciate, being ignorant of their language. And what good could his wife get, he urged, by making curtsies every night to a whole circle of Princesses? He left Rebecca presently to frequent these parties alone; resuming his own simple pursuits and amusements amongst the amiable friends of his own choice.

The truth is, when we say of a gentleman that he lives elegantly on nothing a year, we use the word "nothing" to signify something unknown, meaning, simply, that we don't know how the gentleman in question defrays the expenses of his establishment.

QUESTIONS:
1. This selection is taken from a novel entitled _____.

2. The novel takes its title from that fair described in John Bunyan's work entitled _____, where all sorts of cheats are displayed for sale.
3. _____ wrote this novel.
4. There have a subtitle of the novel, that is _____. Why?

Exercise 62

"This," said Mr. Quinion, in allusion to myself, "is he."

"This," said the stranger, with a certain condescending roll in his voice, and a certain indescribable air of doing something genteel, which impressed me very much, "is Master Copperfield. I hope I see you well, sir?"

I said I was very well, and hoped he was. I was sufficiently ill at ease, Heaven knows; but it was not in my nature to complain much at that time of my life, so I said I was very well, and hoped he was.

"I am," said the stranger, "thank Heaven, quite well. I have received a letter from Mr. Murdstone, in which he mentions that he would desire me to receive into an apartment in the rear of my house, which is at present unoccupied—and is, in short, to be let as a—in short," said the stranger with a smile, and in a burst of confidence, "as a bedroom—the young beginner whom I have now the pleasure to—" and the stranger waved his hand, and settled his chin in his shirtcollar.

QUESTIONS:
1. This passage is taken from a novel entitled _____.
2. The author who wrote this novel is _____.
3. In this passage, what do "he" and "I" in the underlined sentences refer to?
4. Why do we say this is the author's autobiographical novel?

· 177 ·

Exercise 63

He remained as motionless as a statue, and turned almost as pale. The two figures were standing opposite to each other, with clasped hands, about to part; and while they were bending to kiss, Gyp, who had been running among the brushwood, came out, caught sight of them, and gave a sharp bark. They separated with a start—one hurried through the gate out of the Grove, and the other, turning round, walked slowly, with a sort of saunter, towards Adam, who still stood transfixed and pale, clutching tighter the stick with which he held the basket of tools over his shoulder, and looking at the approaching figure with eyes in which amazement was fast turning to fierceness.

Arthur Donnithorne looked flushed and excited; he had tried to make unpleasant feelings more bearable by drinking a little more wine than usual at dinner today, and was still enough under its flattering influence to think more lightly of this unwished—for rencontre with Adam than he would otherwise have done. After all, Adam was the best person who could have happened to see him and Hetty together; he was a sensible fellow, and would not babble about it to other people. Arthur felt confident that he could laugh the thing off, and explained away.

QUESTIONS:
1. What is the title of this novel?
2. Who is the author of this novel?
3. The "he" in the first sentence is _____.
4. What is the relationship between Arthur and Hetty?

Exercise 64

Hitherto, while gathering up the discourse of Mr. Brocklehurst and Miss Temple, I had not, at the same time, neglected precautions to secure my personal safety; which I thought would be effected, if I could only elude observation. To this end, I had sat well back on the form, and while seeming to be busy with my sum, had held my slate in such a manner as to conceal my face: I might have escaped notice, had not my treacherous slate somehow happened to slip from my hand, and falling with an obtrusive crash, directly drawn every eye upon me; I knew it was all over now, and, as I stooped to pick up the two fragments of slate, I rallied my forces for the worst. It came.

"A careless girl!" said Mr. Brocklehurst, and immediately after—"It is the new pupil, I perceive." And before I could draw breath, "I must not forget I have a word to say respecting her." Then aloud: how loud it seemed to me! "Let the child who broke her slate, come forward!"

Of my own accord, I could not have stirred; I was paralyzed: but the two great girls who sat on each side of me, set me on my legs and pushed me towards the dread judge, and then Miss Temple gently assisted me to his very feet, and I caught her whispered counsel.

"Don't be afraid, Jane. I saw it was an accident; you shall not be punished."

The kind whisper went to my heart like a dagger.

"Another minute, and she will despise me for a hypocrite," thought I; and an impulse of fury against Reed, Brocklehurst, and Co., bounded in my pulses at the conviction. I was no Helen Burns.

"Fetch that stool," said Mr. Brocklehurst, pointing to a very high one from which a monitor had just risen: it was brought.

"Place the child upon it."

And I was placed there, by whom I don't know: I was in no condition to note particulars.

QUESTIONS:
1. This selection is taken from a novel entitled _____.
2. The author of the novel is _____.
3. Please briefly comment on this passage.

Exercise 65

Do you think, because I am poor, obscure, plain, and little, I am soulless and heartless? You think wrong!—I have as much soul as you—and full as much heart! And if God had gifted me with some beauty and much wealth, I should have made it as hard for you to leave me, as it is now for me to leave you.

QUESTIONS:
1. This passage is taken from a novel entitled _____.
2. What does the work mainly talk about?
3. Comment on the heroine of this work.

Exercise 66

"There's a letter for you, Mrs. Linton," I said, gently inserting it in one hand that rested on her knee." You must read it immediately, because it wants an answer. Shall I break the seal?" "Yes," she answered, without altering the direction of her eyes. I opened it—it was very short. "Now," I continued, "read it." She drew away her hand, and let it fall. I replaced it in her lap, and stood waiting till it should please her to glance down; but that movement was so long delayed that at last I resumed:

"Must I read it, ma'am? It is from Mr. Heathcliff."

There was a start and a troubled gleam of recollection, and a struggle to arrange her ideas. She lifted the letter, and seemed to peruse it; and when she came to the signature she sighed; yet still I found she had not gathered its import, for, upon my desiring to hear her reply, she merely pointed to the name, and gazed at me with mournful and questioning eagerness.

"Well, he wished to see you," said I, guessing her need of an interpreter. "He's in the garden by this time, and impatient to know what answer I shall bring."

As I spoke, I observed a large dog lying on the sunny grass beneath raise its ears as if about to bark, and then smoothing them back, announce, by a way of the tail, that some one approached whom it did not consider a stranger. Mrs. Linton bent forward, and listened breathlessly. The minute after a step traversed the hall; the open house was too tempting for Heathcliff to resist walking in: most likely he supposed that I was inclined to shirk my promise, and so resolved to trust to his own audacity. With straining eagerness Catherine gazed towards the entrance of her chamber. He did not hit the right room directly, she motioned me to admit him, but he found it out ere I could reach the door, and in a stride or two was at her side, and had her grasped in his arms.

He neither spoke nor loosed his h'ld f'r some five minutes, during which period he bestowed more kisses than ever he gave in his life before, I dare say: but then my mistress had kissed him first, and I plainly saw that he could hardly bear, for down-right agony, to look into her face! The same conviction had stricken him as me, from the instant he beheld her, that there was no prospect of ultimate recovery there; she was fated, and sure to die.

QUESTIONS:
1. This passage is taken from a novel entitled _____.
2. Who wrote this novel?
3. The relationship between Mr. Heathcliff and Mrs. Linton is _____.
4. What does this passage mainly talk about?

Exercise 67

"A rise of a shilling or so won't make much difference, and they will go away thinking they've gained their point."

"That's the very thing I object to. They'll think so, and whenever they've a point to gain, no matter how unreasonable, they'll strike work."

"It really injures them more than us."

"I don't see how our interests can be separated."

"The d-d brute had thrown vitriol on the poor fellow's ankles, and you know what a bad part that is to heal. He had to stand still with the pain, and that left him at the mercy of the cruel wretch, who beat him about the head till you'd hardly have known he was a man. They doubt if he'll live."

"If it were only for that, I'll stand out against them, even if it is the cause of my ruin."

"Ay, I for one won't yield one farthing to the cruel brutes; they're more like wild beasts than human beings."

(Well, who might have made them different?)

"I say, Carson, just go and tell Duncombe of this fresh instance of their abominable conduct. He's wavering, but I think this will decide him."

QUESTIONS:
1. This conversation is taken from a novel entitled _____.
2. Who wrote this novel?
3. What is the theme of this novel?
4. Make a brief comment on this novel.

Exercise 68

With fingers weary and worn;
With eyelids heavy and red,
A woman sat, in unwomanly rags,
Plying her needle and thread, —
Stitch! stitch! stitch!
In poverty, hunger and dirt;
And still with a voice of dolorous pitch
She sang the "Song of the Shirt!"

"Work! work! work!"
While the cock is crowing aloof!
And work—work—work—
Till the stars shine through the roof!

It's O! to be a slave

Along with the barbarous Turk,

Where woman has never a soul to save,

If this is Christian work!

QUESTIONS:
1. The poem was written by _____.
2. The title of this poem is _____.
3. What do you think of women workers?

Exercise 69

Break, break, break,

On thy cold grey stones, O Sea!

And I would that my tongue could utter

The thoughts that arise in me.

O, well for the fisherman's boy,

That he shouts with his sister at play!

O, well for the sailor lad,

That he sings in his boat on the bay!

And the stately ships go on

To their haven under the hill;

But O for the touch of a vanish'd hand,

And the sound of a voice that is still!

Break, break, break,

At the foot of thy crags, O Sea!

But the tender grace of a day that is dead

Will never come back to me.

QUESTIONS:
1. This passage is taken from a poem entitled _____.
2. Who wrote this poem?
3. What does the poem describe?

Exercise 70

Sweet and low, sweet and low,
Wind of the western sea,
Low, low, breathe and blow,
Wind of the western sea!
Over the rolling waters go,
Come from the dying moon, and blow,
Blow him again to me;
While my little one, while my pretty one, sleeps.

Sleep and rest, sleep and rest,
Father will come to thee soon;
Rest, rest on mother's breast,
Father will come to thee soon;
Father will come to his babe in the nest,
Silver sails all out of the west
Under the silver moon;
Sleep, my little one, sleep, my pretty one, sleep.

QUESTIONS:
1. What's the title of this poem?
2. Who is the author of this poem?
3. The figures of speech used in this poem are _____, _____ and _____.

Exercise 71

Home Thoughts from Abroad

Oh, to be in England
Now that April's there,
And whoever wakes in England
See, some morning, unaware.
That the lowest boughs and the brushwood sheaf
Round the elm-tree bole are in tiny leaf,
While the chaffinch sings on the orchard bough
In England-now!

And after April when May follows,
And the whitethroat builds, and all the swallows!
Hark, where my blossomed pear-tree in the hedge
Leans to the field and scatters on the clover
Blossoms and dewdrops-at the bent spray's edge—
That's the wise thrush; he sing each song twice over;
Lest you should think he never could recapture
The first fine careless rapture!
And, tho' the fields look rough with hoary dew,
All will be gay when noontide wakes anew
The buttercups, the little children's dower
—Far brighter than this gaudy melon-flower!

QUESTIONS:

1. The poet who wrote this poem is _____, considered to be the most important Victorian poet after Tennyson.
2. The poem contains _____ stanzas of different lengths in combined _____ and interchanging rhymes.
3. Make a brief comment on this poem.

4. The poem ends abruptly with a contrast of two flowers in nature. What is your understanding of this contrast, and how does it help reveal the theme?
5. East or west, home is best. There are some Chinese poems express the same sentiment. Could you give an example?

Exercise 72

How do I love thee? Let me count the ways.
I love thee to the depth and breadth and height
My soul can reach, when feeling out of sight
For the ends of Being and ideal Grace.
I love thee to the level of everyday's
Most quiet need, by sun and candlelight.
I love thee freely, as men strive for Right;
I love thee purely, as they turn from Praise.
I love thee with the passion put to use
In my old griefs, and with my childhood's faith.
I love thee with a love I seemed to lose
With my lost saints—I love thee with the breath,
Smiles, tears, of all my life! —and, if God choose,
I shall but love thee better after death.

QUESTIONS:
1. _____ wrote this poem with the title of _____.
2. This poem is a kind of _____.
3. Please make a comment on this poem.

Exercise 73

Neutral Tones

We stood by a pond that winter day,
And the sun was white, as though chidden of God,
And a few leaves lay on the starving sod;
—They had fallen from an ash, and were gray.

Your eyes on me were as eyes that rove
Over tedious riddles of years ago;
And some words played between us to and fro
On which lost the more by our love.

The smile on your mouth was the deadest thing
Alive enough to have strength to die;
And a grin of bitterness swept thereby
Like an ominous bird a-wing…

Since then, keen lessons that love deceives,
And wings with wrong, have shaped to me
Your face, and the God-curst sun, and a tree,
And a pond edged with grayish leaves.

QUESTIONS:
1. The author of the poem is _____ who is a great _____ as well.
2. The theme of this poem is _____.
3. This poem is a representative one that shows the author's sense of _____.
4. Make a brief comment on this poem.

Exercise 74

The Darkling Thrush

I leant upon a coppice gate
When Frost was spectre-gray,
And Winter's dregs made desolate
The weakening eye of day.
The tangled bine-stems scored the sky
Like strings of broken lyres,
And all mankind that haunted nigh
Had sought their household fires.

The land's sharp features seemed to be
The Century's corpse outleant,
His crypt the cloudy canopy,
The wind his death-lament.
The ancient pulse of germ and birth
Was shrunken hard and dry,
And every spirit upon earth
Seemed fervourless as I.

At once a voice arose among
The bleak twigs overhead
In a full-hearted evensong
Of joy illimited;
An aged thrush, frail, gaunt, and small,
In blast-beruffled plume,
Had chosen thus to fling his soul
Upon the growing gloom.

So little cause for carolings

Of such ecstatic sound

Was written on terrestrial things

Afar or nigh around,

That I could think there trembled through

His happy good-night air

Some blessed Hope, whereof he knew

And I was unaware.

QUESTIONS:

1. This is a poem chosen from a collection _____ written by _____.
2. It is written in four _____ stanzas rhyming _____ with the odd lines in iambic _____, while the even lines in iambic _____.
3. The vocabulary and imagery of the poem are directed mainly toward creating a sense of the bleakness and sadness of the winter landscape, which reflect the poet's _____ at the turn of the century.
4. What's the function of imagery in this poem?

Exercise 75

Her narrative ended; even its re-assertions and secondary explanations were done. Tess's voice throughout had hardly risen higher than its opening tone; there had been no exculpatory phrase of any kind, and she had not wept. ...

Clare performed the irrelevant act of stirring the fire; the intelligence had not even yet got to the bottom of him. After stirring the embers he rose to his feet; all the force of her disclosure had imparted itself now. His face had withered. In the strenuousness of his concentration he treadled fitfully on the floor. He could not, by any contrivance, think closely enough; that was the meaning of his vague movement. When he spoke it was in the most inadequate, commonplace voice of the many varied tones she had heard from him.

"Tess!"

"Yes, dearest."

"Am I to believe this? From your manner I am to take it as true. O you cannot be out of your mind! You ought to be! Yet you are not. ... My wife, My Tess—nothing in your warrants such a supposition as that?"

"I am not out of my mind." she said.

"And yet—"He looked vacantly at her, to resume with dazed senses: "Why didn't you tell me before? Ah, yes, you would have told me, in a way but I hindered you, I remember!"

These and other of his words were nothing but the perfunctory babble of the surface while the depths remained paralyzed. He turned away, and bent over a chair. Tess followed him to the middle of the room where he was, and stood there staring at him with eyes that did not weep. Presently she slid down upon her knees beside his foot, and from this position she crouched in a heap.

"In the name of our love, forgive me!" she whispered with a dry mouth. "I have forgiven you for the same!"

And, as he did not answer, she said again—

"Forgive me as you are forgiven! I forgive you; Angel."

"You—yes, you do."

"But you do not forgive me?"

"O Tess, forgiveness does not apply to the case! You were one person; now you are another. My God—how can forgiveness meet such a grotesque—prestidigitation as that!"

He paused, contemplating this definition; then suddenly broke into horrible laughter—as unnatural and ghastly as a laugh in hell.

"Don't—don't! It kills me quite, that!" she shrieked. "O have mercy upon me—have mercy!"

He did not answer; and, sickly white, she jumped up.

"Angel, Angel! What do you mean by that laugh?" she cried out. "Do you know what this is to me?"

He shook his head.

QUESTIONS:

1. This selection is taken from a well-known novel entitled _____

and the author _____ was also a great _____.
2. "Her narrative" in the first line refers to _____.
3. Make a brief comment on this selection.

Exercise 76

When you are old and gray and full of sleep,
And nodding by the fire, take down this book,
And slowly read, and dream of the soft look
Your eyes had once, and of their shadows deep;

How many loved your moments of glad grace,
And loved your beauty with love false or true,
But one man loved the pilgrim soul in you,
And loved the sorrows of your changing face;

And bending down beside the glowing bars,
Murmur, a little sadly, how love fled
And paced upon the mountains overhead
And hid his face amid a crowd of stars.

QUESTIONS:
1. Mixed into William Butler Yeats's poetry were the _____ of William Blake, the _____ of Percy Bysshe Shelley, and the _____ of the Pre-Raphaelites.
   A. mysticism; Romantic idealism; aesthetic ideas
   B. Romantic idealism; mysticism; aesthetic ideas
   C. Romantic idealism; aesthetic ideas; mysticism
   D. mysticism; aesthetic ideas; Romantic idealism
2. This poem is written in three quatrains of iambic _____ rhyming _____.

3. What's the meaning of images of "this book", "changing face" and "bending"?
4. Make a comment on this poem.

Exercise 77

I will arise and go now, and go to Innisfree,
And a small cabin build there, of clay and wattles made:
Nine bean-rows will I have there, a hive for the honey-bee,
And live alone in the bee-loud glade.

And I shall have some peace there, for peace comes dropping slow,
Dropping from the veils of the morning to where the cricket sings;
There midnight's all a glimmer, and noon a purple glow,
And evening full of the linnet's wings.

I will arise and go now, for always night and day
I hear lake water lapping with low sounds by the shore;
While I stand on the roadway, or on the pavements grey,
I hear it in the deep heart's core.

QUESTIONS:
1. This poem is entitled _____ written by _____.
2. This poem consists of three quatrains of iambic _____ rhyming _____.
3. Innisfree is an inlet in the lake in Irish legends. Here it refers to a place for _____.
4. What's the theme of this poem?

Exercise 78

He looked at his watch. In half an hour the doctor would be back. He must decide! If against the operation and she dies, how face her mother and the doctor afterwards? How face his own conscience? It was his child that she was having. If for the operation—then he condemned them both to childlessness. And for what else had he married her but to have a lawful heir? And his father—at death's door, waiting for the news! "It's cruel!" he thought; "I ought never to have such a thing to settle! It's cruel!" he turned towards the house. Some deep, simple way of deciding! He took out a coin, and put it back. If he spun it, he knew he would not abide by what came up! He went into the dining-room, furthest way from that room whence the sounds issued. The doctor had said there was a chance. In here that chance seemed greater; the river did not flow, nor the leaves fall. A fire was burning. Soames unlocked the tantalus. He hardly ever touched spirits; but now he poured himself out some whisky and drank it neat, craving a faster flow of blood. "That fellow Jolyon," he thought; "he had children already. He has the woman I really loved; and now a son by her! And I—I'm asked to destroy my only child! Annette can't die; it's most possible. She's strong!"

He was still standing sullenly at the sideboard when he heard the doctor's carriage and went out to him. He had to wait for him to come downstairs.

"Well, doctor?"

"The situation's the same. Have you decided?"

"Yes," said Soames; "don't operate!"

"Not? You understand the risk's great?"

In Soames' set face nothing moved but the lips.

"You said there was a chance?"

"A chance, yes; not much of one."

"You say the baby must be born dead if you do?"

"Yes."

"Do you still think that in any case she can't have another?"

"One can't be absolutely sure, but it's most unlikely."

"She's strong," said Soames; "we'll take the risk."

The doctor looked at him very gravely. "It's on your shoulders," he said; with my own wife, I couldn't."

Soames' chin jerked up as if someone had hit him.

"Am I of any use up there?" he asked.

"No; keep away."

"I shall be in my picture-gallery, then; you know where."

The doctor nodded, and went upstairs.

QUESTIONS:
1. This selection is taken from a novel entitled _____ written by _____.
2. The novel is the second of a trilogy entitled _____.
3. Make a comment on this selection.

Exercise 79

It is in the nature of a Forsyte to be ignorant that he is a Forsyte; but young Jolyon was well aware of being one. He had not known it till after the decisive step which had made him an outcast; since then the knowledge had been with him continually. He felt it throughout his alliance, throughout all his dealings, with his second wife, who was emphatically not a Forsyte.

He knew that if he had not possessed in great measure the eye for what he wanted, the tenacity to hold on to it, the sense of the folly of wasting that for which he had given so big a price—in other words, the "sense of property"—he could never have retained her (perhaps never would have desired to retain her) with him through all the financial troubles, slights, and misconstructions of those fifteen years; never have induced her to marry him on the death of his first wife; never have lived it all through, and come up, as it were, thin, but smiling.

He was one of those men who, seated crosslegged like a miniature Chinese idol in the cages of their own hearts, are ever smiling at themselves a doubting smile. Nor that this smile, so intimate and eternal, interfered with his actions, which, like his chin and his temperament, were quite a peculiar blend of softness and determination.

He was conscious, too, of being a Forsyte in his work, that painting of water colours to which he devoted so much energy, always with an eye on himself, as though he could not take so unpractical a pursuit quite seriously, and always with a certain queer uneasiness that he did not make more money at it. It was, then, this consciousness of what it meant to be a Forsyte, that made him receive the following letter from old Jolyon, with a mixture of sympathy and disgust.

QUESTIONS:
1. The novel is the first of a trilogy entitled _____.
2. This novel was written by _____.
3. This passage reveals the author's criticism on the strong sense and all-pervasive sense of property among the _____ or in other words, among the British _____.

Exercise 80

MRS WARREN: (piteously) "Oh, my darling, how can you be so hard on me? Have I no rights over you as your mother?"

VIVIE: "Are you my mother?"

MRS WARREN: (appalled) "Am I your mother! Oh, Vivie!"

VIVIE: "Then where are our relatives? My father? Our family friends? You claim the rights of a mother: the right to call me fool and child; to speak to me as no woman in authority over me at college dare speak to me; to dictate my way of life; and to force on me the acquaintance of a brute whom anyone can see to be the most vicious sort of London man about town. Before I give myself the trouble to resist such claims, I may as well find out whether they have any real existence."

MRS WARREN: (distracted, throwing herself on her knees) "Oh no, no. Stop,

stop. I am your mother: I swear it. Oh, you can't mean to turn on me—my own child! It's not natural. You believe me, don't you? Say you believe me."

VIVIE: "Who was my father?"

MRS WARREN: "You don't know what you're asking. I can't tell you."

VIVIE: (determinedly) "Oh yes you can, if you like. I have a right to know; and you know very well that I have that right. You can refuse to tell me, if you please; but if you do, will see the last of me tomorrow morning."

MRS WARREN: "Oh, it's too horrible to hear you talk like that. You wouldn't—you couldn't leave me."

VIVIE: (ruthlessly) "Yes, without a moment's hesitation, if you trifle with me about this. (Shivering with disgust) How can I feel sure that I may not have the contaminated blood of that brutal waster in my veins?"

MRS WARREN: "No, no. On my oath it's not he, nor any of the rest that you have ever met. I'm certain of that, at least."

Vivie's eyes fasten sternly on her mother as the significance of this flashes on her.

QUESTIONS:
1. This passage is taken from a play entitled _____ written by _____.
2. Mrs. Warren's profession is about _____.
3. Talk about the theme of this play.

Exercise 81

Their two hands lay on the rough stone parapet of the Castle wall. He had inherited from his mother a fineness of mould, so that his hands were small and vigorous. Hers were large, to match her large limbs, but white and powerful looking. As Paul looked at them he knew her. "She is wanting somebody to take her hands—for all she is so contemptuous of us," he said to himself. And she saw nothing but his two hands, so warm and alive, which seemed to live for her. He was brooding now, staring out over the country from under sullen brows. The little, interesting diversity of shapes had vanished from the scene; all that remained was a vast, dark matrix of sorrow and tragedy, the same in all the houses and the river-flats and the people and the birds; they were only shapen differently. And now that the forms seemed to have melted away, there remained the mass from which all the landscape was composed, a dark mass of struggle and pain. The factory, the girls, his mother, the large, uplifted church, the thicket of the town, merged into one atmosphere—dark, brooding, and sorrowful, every bit.

"Is that two o'clock striking?" Mrs. Dawes said in surprise.

Paul started, and everything sprang into form, regained its individuality, its forgetfulness, and its cheerfulness.

They hurried back to work.

When he was in the rush of preparing for the night's post, examining the work up from Fanny's room, which smelt of ironing, the evening postman came in.

"'Mr. Paul Morel,'" he said smiling, handing Paul a package. "A lady's handwriting! Don't let the girls see it."

The postman, himself a favourite, was pleased to make fun of the girls' affection for Paul.

It was a volume of verse with a brief note: "You will allow me to send you this, and so spare me my isolation. I also sympathize and wish you well. —C.D." Paul flushed hot.

"Good Lord! Mrs. Dawes. She can't afford it. Good Lord, who eve'd have thought it!"

He was suddenly intensely moved. He was filled with the warmth of her. In the glow he could almost feel her as if she were present—her arms, her shoulders, her bosom, see them, feel them, almost contain them.

This move on the part of Clara brought them into closer intimacy. The other girls noticed that when Paul met Mrs. Dawes his eyes lifted and gave that peculiar bright greeting which they could interpret. Knowing he was unaware, Clara made no sign, save that occasionally she turned aside her face from him when he came upon her.

QUESTIONS:
1. This passage is taken from a novel entitled _____ written by _____.
2. Mrs. Dawes and Clara are the _____.
3. Talk about your thought on the relationship between Paul and Clara.
4. What's the theme of this novel?

Exercise 82

It rasped her, though, to have stirring about in her this brutal monster! To hear twigs cracking and feel hooves planted down in the depths of that leaf encumbered forest, the soul; never to be content quite, or quite secure, for at any moment the brute would be stirring, this hatred, which, especially since her illness, had power to make her feel scraped, hurt in her spine; gave her physical pain, and made all pleasure in beauty, in friendship, in being well, in being loved and making her home delightful rock, quiver, and bend as if indeed there were a monster grubbing at the roots, as if the whole panoply of content were nothing but self love! This hatred!

Nonsense, nonsense! She cried to herself, pushing through the swing doors of Mulberry's the florists.

She advanced, light, tall, very upright, to be greeted at once by button-faced Miss Pym, whose hands were always bright red, as if they had been stood in cold water with the flowers.

QUESTIONS:
1. This novel is entitled _____ written by _____.
2. The author employs the method of "_____" to draw a vivid sketch of her chief character.
3. Make a brief comment on this novel.

Exercise 83

"It's a stinking mean thing, that's what it is, said Fleming in the corridor as the classes were passing out in file to the refectory, to pandy a fellow for what is not his fault."

"You really broke your glasses by accident, didn't you? Nasty Roche asked.

Stephen felt his heart filled by Fleming's words and did not answer.

"Of course he did!" said Fleming. "I wouldn't stand it. I'd goup and tell the rector on him.

"Yes," sad Cecil Thunder eagerly, "and I saw him lift the pandybat over his shoulder and he's not allowed to do that."

"Did they hurt much?" Nasty Roche asked.

"Very much," Stephen said.

"I wouldn't stand it," Fleming repeated, "from Baldyhead or any other Baldyhead. It's a stinging mean low trick, that's what it is. I'd go straight up to the rector and tell him about it after dinner."

"Yes, do. Yes, do," said Cecil Thunder.

"Yes, do. Yes, go up and tell the rector on him, Dedalus," said Nasty Roche, "because he said that he'd come in tomorrow again to pandy you."

"Yes, yes. Tell the rector, all said."

And there were some fellows out of second of grammar listening and one of them said:

"The senate and the Roman people declared that Dedalus had been wrongly punished."

QUESTIONS:
1. This passage is taken from _____ written by _____.
2. Each chapter in this novel marks the protagonist's _____ growth.
3. This masterpiece is a _____ novel.
   A. Romantic
   B. modern psychological
   C. realistic

4. Make a comment on this novel.

Exercise 84

Do not go gentle into that good night,
Old age should burn and rave at close of day;
Rage, rage against the dying of the light.

Though wise men at their end know dark is right,
Because their words had forked no lightning they
Do not go gentle into that good night.

Good men, the last wave by, crying how bright
Their frail deeds might have danced in a green bay,
Rage, rage against the dying of the light.

Wild men who caught and sang the sun in flight,
And learn, too late, they grieved it on its way,
Do not go gentle into that good night.

Grave men, near death, who see with blinding sight
Blind eyes could blaze like meteors and be gay,
Rage, rage against the dying of the light.

And you, my father, there on the sad height,
Curse, bless, me now with your fierce tears, I pray.
Do not go gentle into that good night.
Rage, rage against the dying of the light.

QUESTIONS:
1. _____ created this poem when his father was dying.

2. It is written in an intricate poetic form of five 3-line stanzas rhyming _____ plus a final quatrain rhyming _____.
3. Explain the "grave men" and "blinding sight" in this poem.
4. Make a brief comment on this poem.

Exercise 85

There we were aimed. And as we raced across
Bright knots of rail
Past standing Pullmans, walls of blackened moss
Came close, and it was nearly done, this frail
Travelling coincidence; and what it held
Stood ready to be loosed with all the power
That being changed can give. We slowed again,
And as the tightened brakes took hold, there swelled
A sense of falling, like an arrow-shower
Sent out of sight, somewhere becoming rain.

QUESTIONS:
1. The poem is entitled _____ written by _____.
2. The poem is written in eight 10-line stanzas of iambic _____ rhyming _____ with the exception of the second line iambic dimeter.
3. Make a general introduction to this poem.

Exercise 86

He frowned, and, tearing the paper in two, went across the room and flung the pieces away. How ugly it all was! And how horribly real ugliness made things! He felt a little annoyed with Lord Henry for having marked it with red pencil.

Victor might have read it. The man knew more than enough English for that.

Perhaps he had read it, and had begun to suspect something. And yet, what did it matter? What had Dorian Gray to do with Sibyl Vane's death? There was nothing to fear. Dorian Gray had not killed her.

His eye fell on the yellow book that Lord Henry had sent him. What was it, he wondered. He went towards the little pearl-coloured octagonal stand that had always looked to him like the work of some strange Egyptian bees that wrought in silver, and taking up the volume, flung himself into an armchair, and began to turn over the leaves. After a few minutes he became absorbed. It was the strangest book that he had ever read. It seemed to him that in exquisite raiment, and to the delicate sound of flutes, the sins of the world were passing in dumb show before him. Things that he had dimly dreamed of were suddenly made real to him. Things of which he had never dreamed were gradually revealed.

QUESTIONS:
1. This excerpt is taken from _____ written by _____.
2. Make a brief outline of this novel.
3. Make a brief comment on the author.

Exercise 87

When the short days of winter came dusk fell before we had well eaten our dinners. When we met in the street the houses had grown sombre. The space of sky above us was the colour of ever-changing violet and towards it the lamps of the street lifted their feeble lanterns. The cold air stung us and we played till our bodies glowed. Our shouts echoed in the silent street. The career of our play brought us through the dark muddy lanes behind the houses where we ran the gantlet of the rough tribes from the cottages, to the back doors of the dark dripping gardens where odours arose from the ashpits, to the dark odorous stables where a coachman smoothed and combed the horse or shook music from the buckled harness. When we returned to the street light from the kitchen window shade filled the areas. If my uncle was seen turning the corner we hid in the shadow until we had seen him safely housed. Or if Mangan's sister came out on the doorstep to call her brother in to his tea we watched her from our shadow peer up and down the street. We waited to see whether she would remain or go in and, if she remained, we left our shadow and walked up to Mangan's steps resignedly. She was waiting for us, her figure defined by the light from the half-opened door. Her brother always teased her before he obeyed and I stood by the railings looking at her. Her dress swung as she moved her body and the soft rope of her hair tossed from side to side.

Every morning I lay on the floor in the front parlour watching her door. The blind was pulled down to within an inch of the sash so that I could not be seen. When she came out on the doorstep my heart leaped. I ran to the hall, seized my books and followed her. I kept her brown figure always in my eye and, when we came near the point at which our ways diverged. I quickened my pace and passed her. This happened morning after morning. I had never spoken to her, except for a few casual words, and yet her name was like a summons to all my foolish blood.

QUESTIONS:
1. This passage is taken from "_____", the third story in _____ written by _____.
2. This collection contains _____ short stories.
3. Make a comment on this story.

Exercise 88

How can I further encourage you to go about the business of life? Young women, I would say, and please attend, for the peroration is beginning, you are, in my opinion, disgracefully ignorant. You have never made a discovery of any sort of importance. You have never shaken an empire or led an army into battle. The plays of Shakespeare are not by you, and you have never introduced a barbarous race to the blessings of civilization. What is your excuse? It is all very well for you to say, pointing to the streets and squares and forests of the globe swarming with black and white and coffee-coloured inhabitants, all busily engaged in traffic and enterprise and love-making, we have had other work on our hands. Without our doing, those seas would be unsailed and those fertile lands a desert. We have borne and bred and washed and taught, perhaps to the age of six or seven years, the one thousand six hundred and twenty-three million human beings who are, according to statistics, at present in existence, and that, allowing that some had help, takes time.

QUESTIONS:
1. This passage is taken from _____ written by _____.
2. In this work, the author created an imaginary figure, Judith, sister of _____, in order to make a _____.
3. This book is author's _____ declaration.
4. Make a brief introduction of this book.

Exercise 89

If I should die, think only this of me:
   That there's some corner of a foreign field
That is forever England. There shall be
   In that rich earth a richer dust concealed;
A dust whom England bore, shaped, made aware,
   Gave, once, her flowers to love, her ways to roam;
A body of England's, breathing English air,
   Washed by the rivers, blest by suns of home.
And think, this heart, all evil shed away,
   A pulse in the Eternal mind, no less
     Gives somewhere back the thoughts by England given;
Her sights and sounds; dreams happy as her day;

And laughter, learnt of friends; and gentleness,
   In hearts at peace, under an English heaven.

QUESTIONS:
1. This poem is entitled _____ written by _____.
2. The author's war sonnets were the last of that period to express idealistic _____ in the face of war.
3. Make a brief comment on this poet.

Exercise 90

And indeed there will be time
For the yellow smoke that slides along the street,
Rubbing its back upon the window-panes;
There will be time, there will be time
To prepare a face to meet the faces that you meet;
There will be time to murder and create,
And time for all the works and days of hands
That lift and drop a question on your plate;
Time for you and time for me,
And time yet for a hundred indecisions
And for a hundred visions and revisions,
Before the taking of a toast and tea.

QUESTIONS:
1. This selection is taken from _____ written by _____.
2. "The taking of a toast and tea" brings the speaker back from his wandering thoughts given above to his trivial _____ of life.
3. The poem is a sort of dramatic _____ in lines of varying lengths and occasional rimes.
4. Make a brief comment on this poem.

Exercise 91

Sir, no man's enemy, forgiving all
But will its negative inversion, be prodigal:
Send to us power and light, a sovereign touch
Curing the intolerable neural itch,
The exhaustion of weaning, the liar's quinsy,
And the distortions of ingrown virginity
Prohibit sharply the rehearsed response
And gradually correct the coward's stance;
Cover in time with beams those in retreat
That, spotted, they turn though the reveres were great;
Publish each healer that in city lives
Or country house at the end of drives;
Harrow the house of the dead; look shining at
New styles of architecture, a change of heart.

QUESTIONS:
1. This poem is entitled _____ written by _____.
2. "Sovereign touch" in Line 3 is regarded as a _____ for disease.
3. Make a brief comment on the author.

Exercise 92

Far from the heart of culture he was used:
Abandoned by his general and his lice,
Under a padded quilt he closed his eyes
And vanished. He will not be introduced

When this campaign is tidied into books:
No vital knowledge perished in his skull;

His jokes were stale; like wartime, he was dull;
His name is lost for ever like his looks.

He neither knew nor chose the Good, but taught us,
And added meaning like a comma, when
He turned to dust in China that our daughter

Be fit to love the earth, and not again
Disgraced before the dogs; that, where are waters,
Mountains and houses, may be also men.

QUESTIONS:
1. This poem is entitled _____ written by _____.
2. This sonnet was written in 1938 after the poet visited the front of the war against _____ invaders in _____.
3. "The Good" in this poem means _____.

Exercise 93

Slatter lived five miles from Turners. The farm boys came to him first, when they discovered the body. And though it was an urgent matter, he ignored the telephone, but sent a personal letter by a native bearer on a bicycle to Denham at the police camp, twelve miles away. The Sergeant sent out half a dozen policemen at once, to the Turners' farm, to see what they could find. He drove first to see Slatter, because the way that letter was worded roused his curiosity. That was why he arrived late on the scene of the murder. The native policemen did not have to search far for the murderer. After walking through the house, looking briefly at the body, and dispersing down the front of the little hill the house stood on, they saw Moses himself rise out of a tangled ant-heap in front of them. He walked up to them and said (or words to this effect): 'Here I am.' they snapped the handcuffs on him, and went back to the house to wait for the police cars to come. There they saw Dick Turner come out of the bush by the house with two Whining dogs at his heels. He was off his head, talking crazily to himself, wandering in and out of the bush with his hands full of leaves and earth. They let him be, while keeping an eye on him, for he was a white man, though mad, and black men, even when policemen, do not lay hands on white flesh.

QUESTIONS:
1. This selection is taken from _____ written by _____.
2. This novel was written before the author left _____.
3. Make a brief introduction of this novel.

Exercise 94

Now is the globe shrunk tight
Round the mouse's dulled wintering heart
Weasel and crow, as if moulded in brass,
Move through an outer darkness
Not in their right minds,
With the other deaths. She, too, pursues her ends,
Brutal as the stars of this month,
Her pale head heavy as metal.

QUESTIONS:
1. The title of this poem is _____.
2. The author of the poem _____ examined in his animal poems the themes of survival and the mystery and destructiveness of the _____.
3. Make a brief comment on the author.

Exercise 95

The coarse boot nestled on the lug, the shaft
Against the inside knee was levered firmly.
He rooted out tall tops, buried the bright edge deep
To scatter new potatoes that we picked
Loving their cool hardness in our hands.
By God, the old man could handle a spade,
Just like his old man.

My grandfather could cut more turf in a day
Than any other man on toner's bog.
Once I carried him milk in a bottle
Corked sloppily with paper. He straightened up
To drink it, then fell to fight away
Nicking and slicing neatly, heaving sods
Over his shoulder, digging down and down
For the good turf. Digging.

QUESTIONS:
1. This selection is taken from _____ written by _____.
2. This poem is the _____ poem in the collection _____.
3. "His old man" in this poem represents _____.
4. Make a brief comment on the author.

上编参考答案

Key to Exercises of Part One

Part I

The Anglo-Saxon Period and the Anglo-Norman Period

I. Fill in the Blanks.

1. the Roman Empire
2. the Jutes; the Angles and Saxons
3. pagan; Christian
4. Caedmon; Cynewulf
5. *The Song of Beowulf*
6. The pagan literature
7. pagan
8. Anglo-Saxon
9. 1066; Hastings; Normans
10. Norman
11. French; Saxon
12. the French thinking
13. Cynewulf
14. Britons; Celts
15. *Sir Gawain and the Green Knight*
16. loyalty
17. Matter of France; Matter of Greece and Rome; Matter of Britain
18. Robin Hood
19. romance
20. French; English; Latin

II. Choose the Best Answer for Each Question.

1-5 C D A C A
6-10 B D D B A
11-15 B B D B C
16 A

III. Match-Making

1-5   e a b c d

IV. Define the Literary Terms.

1. Alliteration

    A rhetorical device. Alliteration refers to the repetition of a particular sound in the first syllables of a series of words or phrases. Alliteration has developed largely through poetry, in which it more narrowly refers to the repetition of a consonant in any syllables that, according to the poems meter, are stressed. Alliteration is commonly used in many languages, especially in poetry, e.g. *steap stone! slopes! paths narrow.*

2. Epic

    A long narrative poem that records the adventures or heroic deeds of a hero enacted in vast landscapes. The style of epic is grand and elevated.

3. Romance

    Romance is the most prevailing kind of literature of the upper class in feudal England in the Medieval Ages. It is a long composition in verse or in prose which describes the life and chivalric adventures of a noble hero. According to national themes or "matter", the great majority of the romances fall into three classes (a) Matter of France (b) Matter of Greece and Rome (c) Matter of Britain.

V. Answer the Following Questions Briefly.

1. Give an account of the history of Britain from the Celtic settlement to the Norman Conquest.

In about 600 B.C., Celts began to migrate to the British Isles. From 55 B.C. to 410 (or 407) A.D., troops led by Julius Caesar of the Roman Empire invaded the British Isles, defeated the Celts and began nearly four centuries of Roman occupation. After the Roman troops withdrew from it in 410 A.D., Britain was successively conquered by the Jutes (449), and later by the Angles and Saxons, who came from Denmark and other places in parts of central Europe, presently Germany. They settled down on the island, and the Angles named the central part Anglia or Angle-land, later shortened as England. In late 8th to 9th century, the Danes from Scandinavia came plundering the Isles and were defeated by the Wessex king, Alfred the Great. The greatest historical event that followed was the Norman Conquest of 1066. The Normans came from Normandy in northern France to attack England and won a decisive victory at the battle of Hastings under the leadership of the Duke of Normandy, usually known as William the Conqueror.

2. What are the main characteristics of Anglo-Saxon literature?

Anglo-Saxon literature is almost exclusively a verse literature in oral form. Most of its creators remain unknown. It was written down long after its composition. Two groups of poetry are found in Anglo-Saxon period. Before Christianity was introduced, there was pagan poetry. The representative is *Beowulf*. After the introduction of Christianity, Christian poetry appeared. The representatives are the poems composed by Caedmon and Cynewulf.

3. What is the difference between pagan literature and Christian literature?

The literature of the Anglo-Saxon period falls into two divisions—pagan and Christian. The pagan literature is represented by the poetry, or sagas, of the Anglo-Saxons originally in oral form. The Christian literature is represented by the writings developed under teaching of the monks who copied the works, in the course of which they made some changes to cater to their religious taste.

4. Please briefly describe the plots of *The Song of Beowulf*.

   There are four plots: The fight against Grendel; The fight against Grendel's mother; The fight against the fire dragon; Beowulf's funeral.

5. What are the features of *The Song of Beowulf*?

   A. It emphasizes stress. Number of stresses, not number of syllables, is important. Normally, there are four stressed syllables in each line and at least three of these syllables alliterate.

   B. Each line is divided into two halves. Each half has two strongly-accented syllables. At least one of the stressed syllables in the first half-line must alliterate with the first accented syllable in the second half-line.

   C. A lot of metaphors and understatements are used in the poem, for example, the sea is referred to as the whale-road or the swan-road; human-body is called the bone-house. The epic presents an all-round picture of the tribal society. One can see the social conditions and customs of that period. So, the epic is also a poem of great social significance.

6. What social significance does *The Song of Beowulf* express?

   The epic poem *The Song of Beowulf* reflects the values of the clan and tribal society. For a warrior, the highest virtues are loyalty and courage. Loyalty to the king means loyalty to the country. The warrior perfects himself by his brave behavior. Although people believe in fate, the brave man will be saved from fate. A brave soldier, before finally being defeated by fate, must make the most heroic deeds. These deeds will make him live forever in the memory of future generations, so that he will be immortal and become an immortal hero.

7. Please briefly describe the plots of *Sir Gawain and the Green Knight*.

   There are four cantos in this story.

   In the first canto, the story starts on New Year's Day, when Arthur and his knights are having a feast, a gigantic knight in green enters the banquet hall on horseback and challenges the bravest knight present to an exchange of blows. Gawain accepts the challenge, takes the battle-ax, and cuts off the giant's head. The Green Knight holds out his head and speaks, warning Gawain to keep his promise and to seek through the world till he finds the Green Chapel. There, on next New Year's Day, the Green Knight will meet him and return the blow.

In the second canto, Gawain keeps his promise. He goes on a long journey full of dangers. Instead of finding the Green Chapel, he enters a great castle and is entertained by the host and his wife. Here he learns that he is near the Green Chapel, and settles down for a little comfort after his long quest.

In the third canto, a compact is made between the host of the castle and Gawain. The compact goes as follows. The host goes hunting every day, and Gawain is to remain in the castle and entertained by the hostess. At night they two shall give each other whatever good thing they got during the day.

The last canto brings Gawain to the Green Chapel. He is repeatedly warned not to break his promise in order to keep his life. The Green Knight appears and Gawain, true to his compact, offers his neck for the blow. Twice the ax swings harmlessly; the third time it falls on his shoulder and wounds him. Then the Green Knight gives an explanation. The first two swings of the ax were harmless because Gawain had been true to his compact. The last blow had wounded him because he concealed the green girdle, which belongs to the Green Knight and was woven by his wife. Full of shame, Gawain throws back the gift and is ready to atone for his deception; but the Green Knight thinks he has already atoned, and presents the green girdle as a free gift. Gawain returns to Arthur's court, tells the whole story frankly, and ever after that all the knights of the Round Table wear a green girdle in his honor.

· 217 ·

8. What are the main features of English literature in the period of Norman Conquest?

The literature the Normans brought to England is characterized by its romantic love stories and adventure stories, unlike stories of strength and somberness in Anglo-Saxon poetry. English literature of this period is also a combination of French and Saxon elements. The Norman Conquest left three chief effects in English literature, namely, the introduction of Roman civilization to England, the sense and growth of nationality, i.e. a strong centralized government instead of the loose union of Saxon tribes, and the new language and literature, represented especially by Geoffrey Chaucer.

In the literature of this period, in terms of matter there are mainly three classes: (a) Matter of France, telling stories about Charlemagne and his peers, mainly singing praise of Roland, *Song of Roland* being the first national epic of France; (b) Matter of Greece and Rome, telling stories about Alexander, and also about the Trojan War; (c) Matter of Britain, telling stories about their own heroes such as Arthur and his knights of the Round Table. From this development, one can detect and recognize the function and significance of borrowing, blending and creating in the making of country's literature.

9. Make a brief comment on *Sir Gawain and the Green Knight*.

This is a wonderful story of adventure. But it is more important as a tale of morality. It is an allegory in which man's virtue is tested. Gawain is the sort of person people admire. He can resist the temptation of beauty and sex, though he also has weakness. But when he knows his weakness, he expresses his wish to be atoned. No matter how long the story is, only one thing is proved. A person should not only keep his promise, but also be honest and sincere.

10. The great majority of the romances fall into three groups, what are they?

(a) Matter of France, telling stories about Charlemagne and his peers, mainly singing praise of Roland, *Song of Roland* being the first national epic of France; (b) Matter of Greece and Rome, telling stories about Alexander, and also about the Trojan War; (c) Matter of Britain, telling stories about their own heroes such as Arthur and his knights of the Round Table. From this development, one can detect and recognize the function and significance of borrowing, blending and creating in the making of country's literature.

Part II

The Age of Geoffrey Chaucer

I. Fill in the Blanks.

1. father of English poetry
2. French; Italian
3. 14th
4. tales and stories
5. humanism
6. 24
7. feudalism
8. earthly happiness
9. court and nobility
10. heroic
11. Poet's Corner
12. the founder of English realism
13. miniature
14. The Prologue
15. London dialect
16. a general prologue
17. realistic
18. iambic pentameter
19. the wife of Bath

II. Choose the Best Answer for Each Question.

1-5 B A C B D   6-10 C D A B A   11-15 D A B A B

III. Answer the Following Questions Briefly.

1. Summarize Geoffrey Chaucer's contribution to the English literature.

Geoffrey Chaucer was the most important poet of England of that age and his contribution can be seen as follows. First, his contribution to English poetry is beyond words. He introduced European air into England, bringing the French and Italian humanistic thoughts to England, which served as a bridge between European Renaissance and England thus preparing the way of Renaissance in England. His work is permeated with lively and swift free-thinking, so characteristic of the age of Renaissance because of which he can be rightly called the immediate forerunner of the English Renaissance. He believed in the right of man to earthly happiness. He was anxious to see man freed from superstitions and a blind belief in fate. He was always keen to praise man's energy, intellect, quick wit and love for life. Second, he greatly enriched the rhyme schemes by introducing from France the rhymed stanzas of various types, especially the rhymed couplet of iambic pentameter, which was later called the "heroic couplet" to English poetry. Alliterative verse of the Old English period was to give way to new poetic forms. Third, with his *The Canterbury Tales*, he declared the greatness of national literature. Fourth, his use of London dialect promoted the position of language used by common people and refined it into an acceptable literary one. Thus he established a language of literature. And the language he used is vivid and smooth, which, together with the rhymed couplet, makes a very easy and good reading. This is a contribution in constructing a nation's vernacular literature. Fifth, with his vivid portrait of people of all walks of life, he began the realistic tradition. He created a strikingly brilliant and picturesque panorama of his time and his country. In this poem, his realism, biting irony and freedom of views reached such a high level of power that it had no equal in all the English literature up to the 16th century. Owing to the true-to-life depiction of characters and the broad reflection of the whole society, Chaucer was properly and rightly praised by Gorky as "founder of English realism".

2. Give a brief introduction of *The Canterbury Tales*.

   The Canterbury Tales consists of about 17,000 lines. It displays Chaucer's acceptance and influence he received from Boccaccio's *Decameron*, which describes the stories told by some ladies and young men who were fleeing the Black Death. These two works, in some sense, become the archetype of such fashion. The whole poem is a collection of tales and stories told by people of different background of that time. On a fine spring morning, the poet who stays in the Tabard Inn in Southwark at the south end of London Bridge joins some pilgrims bound for Canterbury. The host of the inn goes too. The host suggests that their company of 30 people tell stories to kill time during the journey. And he acts as the judge. Each is to tell two stories while going and two while returning. Thus there should be 120 stories, but actually only 24 are written. All but two of these tales are in verse. The tales cover all the major types of medieval literature: romances of knights and ladies, folk tales, animal stories, stories of travel and adventure, and others. Perhaps the "marriage group" is more worth reading. The Prologue is worth special mentioning because it is the first of such kind. It provides a framework of this long poem. Like the host's comments on and steering of the story-telling, the Prologue also serves to connect the individual stories. In this Prologue are included vivid sketches of typical medieval figures. The Prologue is a miniature of the English society of Chaucer's time. In order to have a good understanding of the whole poem, it is advised that one should refer frequently to the Prologue.

3. What is the social significance of *The Canterbury Tales*?

   The Canterbury Tales has its social significance in several ways. First, it represents the spirit of the rising bourgeoisie. People's right to pursue earthly happiness is affirmed by Chaucer. Second, the ideas of humanism are shown in Chaucer's praising of man's energy, intellect, wit and love of life. Third, Chaucer exposed and satirized the evils of the time. Fourth, the corruption of the Church was vigorously attacked. Fifth, Chaucer showed sympathy for the poor to some extent.

4. What is the function of the Prologue to *The Canterbury Tales*?

　　The Prologue is a splendid masterpiece of realistic portrayal, the first of its kind in the history of English literature. From the Prologue, one can see that Chaucer is a talented portrait painter. The broad sweeps of his brush in the Prologue are impressive and unforgettable. Each of the pilgrims or narrators is presented vividly in the Prologue. The pilgrims are people from various parts of England. They are the representatives of various sides of life and social groups, with various interests, tastes and predilections. The pilgrims range from the knight, the squire, the prioress, through the landed proprietor and wealthy tradesman, down to the drunken cook and humble plowman. There are also monks, nuns, priests. And there are also a doctor, a lawyer, a summoner, a sailor, a miller and an Oxford scholar. With a feeling of sympathy Chaucer describes the Clerk, a poor philosopher who spends all his money on books. Among the pilgrims there is a Wife from the town of Bath, a gaily dressed middle-aged widow, who hopes to find a husband in Canterbury. In short, each of the narrators reveals his or her own views and character. Thus Chaucer created a strikingly brilliant and picturesque panorama of his time and his country. And thus Chaucer's realism, trenchant irony and freedom of views reached a high level of power. It is no exaggeration to say that the Prologue supplies a miniature of the English society of Chaucer's time. Looking at his picture gallery, one can know at once how people lived in that era. So Chaucer was praised by Gorky as "the founder of English realism". On the other hand, there is also an intimate connection between the tales and the Prologue, both complementing each other. The Prologue provides a framework for the tales.

Part III

The 15th Century: The Age of Popular Ballads

I. Fill in the Blanks.

1. folk literature
2. England; Scotland
3. stanzas
4. 15th
5. Thomas Percy
6. real; legendary
7. *The English and Scottish Popular Ballads*
8. Robin Hood
9. rebellious
10. The ballads of Robin Hood
11. humorous
12. tetrameter; trimester
13. border ballads
14. *Piers Plowman*
15. English; Scottish
16. simplicity; freshness
17. Popular Ballads
18. oppressors
19. abcb; abab
20. 12th; 13th

II. Choose the Best Answer for Each Question.

1-5 B D C A B   6-10 A C C A D

III. Define the Literary Term.

1. Ballad

   A story told in song, usually in 4-line stanzas, with the 2nd and 4th

· 224 ·

lines rhymed. In many countries, the folk ballad is one of the earliest forms of literature. Folk ballads have no known authors. They were transmitted orally from generation to generation and were not set down in writing until centuries after they were first sung. The subject matter of folk ballads stems from the everyday life of the common people. The most popular subjects, often tragic, are disappointed love, jealousy, revenge, sudden disaster, and deeds of adventure and daring. Devices commonly used in ballads are the refrain, incremental repetition, and code language. A later form of ballad is the literary ballad, which imitates the style of the folk ballad. The most famous English literary ballad is Samuel Taylor Coleridge's *The Rime of the Ancient Mariner.*

IV. Answer the Following Questions Briefly.

1. Summarize the various themes of the ballads.

    The ballads are usually in various English and Scottish dialects. They have a variety of themes: the struggle of young lovers against feudal families, the conflict between love and wealth, the cruel effect of jealousy, the border wars between England and Scotland, and matters of class struggle and so on.

2. Make comments on the character Robin Hood.

    In English history, Robin Hood was a partly real and partly legendary figure. He was a Saxon who lived during the reign of Richard I the Lion-Hearted, and had lost his land and money and fled to the forest as an outlaw. He was the leader of a group of outlaws. They often attacked the rich, waged wars against the bishops and archbishops, but helped the poor people. The rebellious spirit of Robin Hood and his companions often inspired the English people in the struggle against their oppressors. The character of Robin Hood is many-sided. Strong, brave and clever, he is at the same time tender-hearted and affectionate. His hatred for the cruel oppressors is the result of his love for the poor and downtrodden. Although he was a robber, he was as courtly as any knight and was welcomed by the poor and the oppressed.

Part IV

The 16th Century: The Age of Drama and Poetry

I. Fill in the Blanks.

1. feudal relations; capitalism
2. enclosure
3. Church of England
4. War of the Roses
5. the bourgeoisie
6. bourgeois economy
7. ruling classes
8. Renaissance
9. literature; arts; sciences
10. drama; poetry
11. The humanists
12. the people's sufferings; a future happy society
13. *Utopia*
14. Francis Bacon
15. Thomas Wyatt; Henry Howard, Earl of Surrey
16. Petrarch's sonnets; male complaint
17. male complaint
18. lyrical poetry
19. John Lyly
20. Realistic
21. Christopher Marlowe
22. Sir Thomas Wyatt
23. sonnet
24. Geoffrey Chaucer
25. Henry Howard
26. blank verse
27. octave; sestet
28. Edmund Spenser
29. *The Shepherd's Calendar*
30. the prince of poets in his time
31. Westminster Abbey
32. *Amoretti*
33. nationalism; humanism; Puritanism
34. Spenserian stanza
35. Sir Walter Raleigh
36. Sir Philip Sidney

37. Philip Sidney
38. Francis Bacon
39. *Essays*
40. Christopher Marlowe
41. Christopher Marlowe
42. William Shakespeare
43. *Hamlet*; *Othello*; *King Lear*; *Macbeth*
44. philosophical; literary; professional
45. individual behavior
46. Christopher Marlowe
47. two
48. *A Midsummer Night's Dream*; *The Merchant of Venice*; *As You Like It*; *Twelfth Night*
49. *Hamlet*
50. Ben Jonson
51. Three Unities
52. Stratford-on-Avon
53. *Hamlet*
54. Francis Bacon
55. Time; Place; Action
56. Ben Jonson

II. Choose the Best Answer for Each Question.

1-5　C A B A C　　　6-10　B A C B A　　　11-15　D A B B D
16-20　A B B B A　　21-25　B A D A C　　26-30　D B B D A
31-35　C D C A B　　36-38　D A C

III. Match-Making

Group One
1-5　b d c a e
Group Two
1-5　a b d c e
Group Three
1-5　c a e d b
Group Four
1-5　e a b c d

IV. Define the Literary Terms.

1. Renaissance

   The term "Renaissance" refers to the period between the 14th and mid-17th century. "Renaissance" means revival, specifically in this period of history, revival of interest in ancient Greek and Roman culture. Renaissance, in essence, was a historical period in which the European humanist thinkers and scholars made attempts to get rid of conservatism in feudalist Europe and introduce new ideas that expressed the interests of the rising bourgeoisie, to lift the restrictions in all areas placed by the Roman church authorities.

2. Humanism

   Humanism is the essence of the Renaissance. According to humanists, human beings are glorious creatures capable of individual development in the direction of perfection and the world can be questioned, explored and enjoyed. By emphasizing the dignity of human beings and the importance of the present life, in contrast to the medieval emphasis on God and contempt for the things in this world, they voiced their beliefs that man do not only have the right to pursue happiness of this life, but have the ability to perfect himself and to perform wonders.

3. Sonnet

   A sonnet is a 14-line complete poem usually using iambic pentameter. There are basically Italian sonnet and English sonnet. Besides, there are many variations, such as Miltonic sonnet, Spenserian sonnet and other forms. The sonnet, in its original function, is a little love song. Later, the meaning expanded to writings about nature, friendship and many other things. In the 17th century, the sonnet was adapted to other purposes, with John Donne and George Herbert writing religious sonnets, and John Milton using the sonnet as a general meditative poem. The romanticists even used sonnet to write about nature and many more things.

4. Stanza

   The stanza is a group of lines forming a structural unit or division of a poem. Stanzas may be units of form established through similarity in the number of lines, length of lines, meter and rhyme scheme; or stanzas may exist as logical units determined by their thought or content.

5. Spenserian stanza

   The 9-line stanza form, called Spenserian stanza, rhymed abab bcbc c, is one of the inventions made by Edmund Spenser. The first eight are iambic pentameter lines, and the last line is an iambic hexameter line.

6. Blank verse

   Blank verse is a poetic form with regular meter, particularly iambic pentameter, but no fixed rhyme scheme. Loosely, any unrhymed poetry, but more generally, unrhymed iambic pentameter verse (composed of lines of five two-syllable feet with the first syllable accented, the second unaccented). Blank verse has been used by poets since the Renaissance for its flexibility and its graceful, dignified tone. Shakespeare's plays are largely in blank verse. Most of the greatest achievements in English poetry are written in blank verse.

7. Essay

   As a form of literature, essay is a composition of moderate length, usually in prose, which deals in an easy way with the external conditions of a subject, and, in strictness, with that subject, only as it affects the writer.

8. Comedy

   A play written chiefly to amuse its audience by appealing to a sense of superiority over the characters depicted. A comedy will normally be closer to everyday life than a tragedy, and will explore common human failings rather than tragedy's disastrous crimes. Its ending will usually be happy for the leading characters.

9. Tragedy

   A serious play or novel representing the disastrous downfall of a central character, the protagonist. According to Aristotle, the purpose is to achieve a catharsis through incidents arousing pity and terror. The tragic effect usually depends on our awareness of admirable qualities in the protagonist, which are wasted terribly in the fated disaster.

10. Morality plays

    A morality play is essentially an allegory, told through drama, presenting stories containing abstract virtues and vices as characters. They are plays which have a moral message: Good and Evil fight for domination of the human soul.

11. History plays

    History plays aim to present some historical age or character, and may be either a comedy or a tragedy. They almost tell stories about the nobles, the true people in history, but not ordinary people. The principal idea of Shakespeare's history plays is the necessity for national unity under a mighty and just sovereign.

12. Three Unities

    Three rules or absolutes of 16th and 17th century Italian and French drama, broadly adapted from Aristotle's *Poetics*: the Unity of Time, which limits a play to a single day; the Unity of Place, which limits a play's setting to a single location; and the Unity of Action, which limits a play to a single story line.

13. Euphuistic style

    Euphuistic style or euphuism is the peculiar style of *Euphues*. Its principal characteristics are the excessive use of antithesis, which is pursued regardless of sense, and emphasized by alliteration and other devices; and of allusions to historical and mythological personages. This style for a time became the fashion in English literary circles and found many followers and imitators among John Lyly's contemporary writers, including Robert Greene and youthful William Shakespeare.

14. University Wits

The University Wits is a phrase used to name a group of the late 16th century English playwrights who were educated at the universities of Oxford or Cambridge and became popular writers. Prominent members of this group were Christopher Marlowe, Robert Greene from Cambridge, and John Lyly, Thomas Lodge from Oxford. This diverse and talented loose association of London writers and dramatists set the stage for the theatrical Renaissance of Elizabethan England, and prepared the way for William Shakespeare.

15. Epigram

Epigram is a short, pointed and witty statement in the form of a two-line couplet. Ben Jonson's *Epigrams* is a good example of epigram.

16. Farce

Farce is a form of play to provoke laughter through highly exaggerated caricatures of people in improbable or silly situation. Many of William Shakespeare's early works, such as *The Taming of the Shrew*, are considered farces.

17. Allegory

The word allegory loosely describes any writing in verse or prose that has a double meaning. This fictional literary narrative acts as an extended metaphor in which persons, abstract ideas, or events not only represent themselves on the literal level, but also stand for something else on the symbolic level. An allegorical reading usually involves moral or spiritual concepts that may be more significant than the actual, literal events described in a narrative. The most famous allegory in English literature is John Bunyan's *Pilgrim's Progress*, a prose narrative symbolically concerning the human soul's pilgrimage through temptation and doubt to reach salvation. Some other famous allegorical works include Edmund Spenser's *The Faerie Queene* and Jonathan Swift's *Gulliver's Travels*.

18. Soliloquy

A soliloquy is a device often used in drama when a character speaks to himself or herself, relating thoughts and feelings, thereby also sharing them with the audience. Other characters, however, are not aware of what is being said.

V. Answer the Following Questions Briefly.

1. What are the main features of European Renaissance?

Two features of the Renaissance Movement are striking. One is a thirsting curiosity for the classical literature. Old manuscripts were dug out. There arose a current for the study of Greek and Latin authors. While people learned to admire the Greek and Latin works as models of literary form, they caught something in spirit very different from the medieval Catholic dogma. So the love of classics was but an expression of the general dissatisfaction with the Catholic and feudal ideas.

The other feature of the Renaissance is the keen interest in the activities of humanity. People ceased to look upon themselves as living only for God and a future world. Thinkers, artists and poets arose, who gave expression, sometimes in an old guise, though, to the new feeling of admiration for human beauty and human achievement, a feeling in sharp contrast with theology. Hence arose the thought of Humanism. Humanism is the keynote of the Renaissance. Humanism reflected the new outlook of the rising bourgeois class, which saw the world opening before it. According to the humanists, both man and world are hindered only by external checks from infinite improvement. Man could mold the world according to his desires, and attain happiness by removing all external checks by the exercise of reason.

2. What are the features of Renaissance in England?

The Renaissance was a European phenomenon. It had its origin in north Italy in the 14th century, and spread northward to other European countries—to France, to Germany, to the Low Countries, and lastly to England. It revived the study of Roman and Greek classics and marked the beginning of bourgeois revolution. During the period of English Renaissance, England enjoyed stability and prosperity. It became the strong power in the world and "the mistress on the seas". The English Renaissance encouraged the Reformation of the Church. King Henry VIII, who started the Reformation, declared the break with Rome and became head of the Church of England, also called Anglican Church. Thus Catholicism was got rid of in England. Protestantism was established.

The increasing of cloth industry stimulated the greed of the moneyed classes to seize more and more land out of the hands of the peasants. This is known as the enclosure movement. As a result of the movement, thousands upon thousands of peasants lost their land and became hired laborers of the merchants.

In the Renaissance period, scholars and educators who called themselves Humanists began to emphasize the capacities of the human mind and the achievements of human culture, in contrast to the medieval emphasis on God and contempt for the things of secular world. So humanism became the keynote of English Renaissance.

English Renaissance is usually divided into three periods: The first period, called the beginning of the Renaissance, started in 1516 and came to an end in 1578. The second period, known as the flowering time of the Renaissance, was from 1578 to 1625. The third period between 1625 and 1660 is the epilogue of the Renaissance. In the second period, Elizabeth I ruled the country. For this reason it is also called Elizabethan Period. William Shakespeare, the greatest playwright of England, lived in the Elizabethan Period. So, in the history of English literature, this period is often referred to as the Age of William Shakespeare.

3. Summarize the English literature in the Renaissance period.

English literature in the Renaissance period is usually regarded as the highlight in the history of English literature. In the second period of English Renaissance, that is, in Elizabethan Period, English literature developed with a great speed and made magnificent achievements. The greatest and most distinctive achievement of Elizabethan literature is drama, thus appeared a group of excellent dramatists. They are John Lyly, Thomas Kyd, George Peele, Robert Greene, Christopher Marlowe, William Shakespeare and Ben Jonson. Next to drama is the lyrical poetry. Elizabethan poetry is remarkable for its variety, its freshness, its youthfulness and its romantic feeling. A group of great poets appeared, and a large number of noble poems were produced. In that period, writing poetry became a fashion. Elizabeth I herself was a poet. She suggested subjects and rewarded poets. Her ministers and courtiers obeyed her example and tried to rival each other in shaping beautiful verses. The gentry, as a matter of fact, also followed the example; and after the gentry, all educated people. The universities made themselves particularly busy with poetry. England then became "a nest of singing birds". The famous poets of that period were Thomas Wyatt, Henry Howard, Philip Sidney and Edmund Spenser.

Since the English Renaissance was an age of poetry and drama, and was not an age of prose, there were not so many prose writers. In the beginning period, the great humanist, Thomas More wrote his famous prose work *Utopia*, which may be thought of as the first literary masterpiece of the English Renaissance. In Elizabethan Period, Francis Bacon wrote more than fifty excellent essays, which make him one of the best essayists in English literature.

4. What contribution did Thomas Wyatt make to the English literature?

Thomas Wyatt's greatest contribution to English literature is that he introduced into England the sonnet, a 14-line poem with a complicated rhyme scheme, rhyming abba abba cde cde or abba abba cdcd ee. The most common rhyme scheme in Wyatt's sonnets is abba abba cddc ee. The usual Italian structure of an octave (first eight lines) is followed, after a turn in the sense usually appearing in the ninth line, by a sestet (last six lines). He also began to write a kind of sonnet which can be regarded as the early English form of sonnet. Later Henry Howard perfected it and developed it into the rhyme scheme of abab cdcd efef gg.

On the one hand, Wyatt was a forerunner of the Elizabethan poetry. On the other hand, his poems were different from those of his contemporaries like Sidney, Spenser and others. Wyatt's poems are characterized by the directness, simplicity and the emotion toward Nature while the poems of others move people with rich diction and imagery. Wyatt was rather like Chaucer and Chaucer's contemporaries. So, in a sense, Wyatt and Howard built the bridge between the Middle Ages and the Elizabethan Age. Wyatt also wrote a large portion of non-sonnet poems. His temperament and disposition were shown more clearly in these poems.

Wyatt introduced to England not only the Italian sonnet form but also the theme of complaint poetry. The man speaker in the Petrarchan sonnet and many sonnets written by English poets is usually in a mood of doleful despair. The typical poem is essentially a complaint, though the interest lies in following the elaborately worked out "conceits" or comparisons. The man speaker is the lady's slave. The lady's coldness is a perpetual torture to him. That is why we call such poems male complaint poems. But in his non-sonnet poems, a rather gay, manly independence is the characteristic note.

5. What are the characteristics of Edmund Spenser's poetry?

Edmund Spenser's poetry possesses the following main qualities:

A. a perfect melody;

B. a rare sense of beauty;

   C. a splendid imagination;

   D. a lofty moral purity and seriousness;

   E. a delicate realism.

   It is his idealism, his love of beauty and his exquisite melody that make him known as "the poet's poet".

6. Summarize the main story of *The Faerie Queene*.

   The Faerie Queene is a long poem planned in 12 books, of which Edmund Spenser finished only 6. The poem was dedicated to Queen Elizabeth I. The whole poem is suffused with genuine devotion to the queen and the country.

   The plan of the whole poem is like this: the Faerie Queene (who represents Queen Elizabeth) holds a feast of 12 days, and on each day a stranger in distress appears telling a woeful story of dragons and enchantresses and asking the Queen to send a knight to right the wrong and let the oppressed go free. Then a knight is assigned to each guest, and the 12 books are to describe the 12 adventures. Moreover, each knight represents a virtue, as Holiness, Temperance, Chastity, Friendship, Justice and Courtesy. So the long poem is a continued allegory. The knights as a whole symbolize England, and the evil figures stand for her enemies, as King Philip of Spain, Mary Queen of Scots or the Church of Rome. The dominating thoughts of the poem are nationalism (as shown in its celebration of Queen Elizabeth), humanism (as shown in its strong opposition to Roman Catholicism) and Puritanism (as shown in its moral teaching). The stories of the 6 finished books are as follows:

   Book I recounts the adventures of a knight called Redcross, who stand for Holiness. Redcross helps a lady slay a dragon, which is besieging her father's castle.

   Book II tells the adventures of a knight representing Temperance. He captures an enchantress, and destroys her bower of Bliss.

   Book III describes the adventures of a woman knight standing for Chastity, who saves a lady from a magician's hands.

Book IV is the legend of 2 knights, who stand for Friendship. The story symbolizes the eternal friendship and love between the same sex.

Book V recounts the story of a knight standing for Justice.

Book VI tells the adventures of a knight representing Courtesy.

All of the poet's ideas are expressed under the guise of medieval knighthood.

7. What are the writing features of Edmund Spenser's masterpiece *The Faerie Queene*?

The long poem is written in the form of allegory. It has sweet melody and its lines are very musical.

Edmund Spenser invented a new verse form for this poem. The verse form has been called "Spenserian Stanza" since his day. Each stanza has nine lines, each of the first eight lines is in iambic pentameter form, and the ninth line is an iambic hexameter line. Because of its rare beauty, this verse form was much used by nearly all the later poets, especially imitated by the Romantic poets of the 19th century.

8. Comment on Thomas More's *Utopia*.

Utopia is Thomas More's masterpiece, written in the form of a conversation between Thomas More and a returned sailor. The whole work is divided into two books. The first book contains a long discussion on the social conditions of England. In the second book, More describes in detail an ideal society called Utopia. The name "Utopia" comes from two Greek words meaning "no place". It was used by More to name his ideal society.

Book One of *Utopia* is a picture of contemporary England. The author severely criticizes English society and exposes social evils. He points out that the enclosure of land and the ensuing expulsion of peasants are the source of social evils, and that the whole system of society around him seems to him "nothing but a conspiracy of the rich against the poor". He condemns the rich and the ruling class for bringing miseries to the poor peasants. Generally speaking, Book One is a forcible exposure of the evil things of the English society.

Book Two offers us a good picture of an ideal society in some unknown ocean. In this society, property is held in common and there is no poverty.

All citizens in Utopia are politically equal. Everybody takes part in labor. The products of the society are distributed according to the needs of the citizens. More emphasizes the importance of labor for every member of the society, and insists upon working six hours a day. After work, the citizens spend their time in studying literature, science and art. All religions in this ideal society are authorized and tolerance is the law. Life there is pleasant. People enjoy cleanliness, comfort and well-being.

This work became very popular after its publication. It was translated into English in 1551. It is regarded as one of the earliest works of Utopian socialism. Karl Marx highly commended this work and mentioned it in his great work, *The Capital*.

9. Francis Bacon's work can be divided into three classes, what are they?

Bacon's works may be divided into three classes, the philosophical, the literary, and the professional works.

The principal and best known of the philosophical works are: the *Advancement of Learning* published in English in 1605, the *Novum Organum* published in Latin in 1620 and the *De Augmentis Scientiarum* published in Latin in 1623.

Of Bacon's literary works, the most important are the essays. Ten of these were published in 1597, and they were reissued and extended in 1612 and again in 1625. They deal with a great variety of subjects, some quite general like *Of Truth*, and *Of Death*; some on questions of individual behavior like *Of Revenge* and *Of Friend-*

ship; many on problems of statesmanship like *Of the True Greatness of Kingdoms and Estates*.

The largest and most important of his professional works are the treatises entitled *Maxims of the Law* and *Reading on the Statute of Uses*.

10. What is the writing style of Francis Bacon's essays?

    Francis Bacon's essays have a literary style peculiar to their own. They are noted for their clearness, brevity and force of expression. Bacon's chief concern is to express his thought with clearness and in as few words as possible. His sentences are short, pointed, incisive, and often of balanced structure. Many of them have become wise old sayings. Generally speaking, Bacon's literary style has three prominent qualities: directness, terseness, and forcefulness.

11. Summarize the social significance of Christopher Marlowe's plays.

    A. Christopher Marlowe's plays show, in various ways, the spirit of the rising bourgeoisie, its eager curiosity for knowledge, its towering pride, its insatiable appetite for power whether that be won by military might, knowledge, or gold. The heroes of his plays are generally distinguished by a resolute character, a scorn of orthodox creeds, and an overpowering passion: in *Tamburlaine*, it is ambition; in *Doctor Faustus*, desire for knowledge; in the *Jew of Malta*, greed for wealth. They are typical images of the era of the primitive accumulation of capital, about which the *Manifesto of the Communist Party* gives a classical analysis.

    B. The theme of Christopher Marlowe's plays is the praise of individuality freed from the restraints of medieval dogmas and law, and the conviction of the boundless possibility of human efforts in conquering the universe. There is in his plays a combination of the soaring aspiration after power and knowledge and beauty in their ideal forms, and the bold critical, analytic spirit which leads to the questioning of the old traditions and standards of conduct. Here man's reason and power are everything. This is the progressive side of the ideas of the young bourgeoisie. It has played its part in pushing human society a step forward.

C. However, the heroes in Christopher Marlowe's plays are merely individualists. Their individualistic ambition often brings ruin to the world and sometimes to themselves. This reactionary nature of the bourgeois class even in its early stage of development has been pointed out by Marx in the first volume of *The Capital*. In Christopher Marlowe's plays, this is shown through striking, lively and typical images.

12. Summarize the periods of William Shakespeare's literary creation.

William Shakespeare's literary career can be divided into four periods.

A. Period of early experimentation

This period is marked by youthfulness and exuberance of imagination, by extravagance of language, and by the frequent use of rimed couplets with his blank verse. It is the period of apprenticeship in which he made over old plays or wrote new ones largely in imitation of other men. The main plays written in this period are: *Love's Labor's Lost*, *Two Gentlemen of Verona*, *Richard III*. But the typical works of this period are his early poems, such as, *Venus and Adonis* and *The Rape of Lucrece*.

B. Period of rapid growth and development

In this period, which dated from 1595 to 1600, Shakespeare excelled all his contemporaries in historical plays and romantic comedies. Owing to the premature death of his rivals, or their withdrawal from drama, Shakespeare reigned as master at first with no one to challenge his supremacy. The main plays written during this period are *A Midsummer Night's Dream*, *The Merchant of Venice*, *As You Like It*, *Richard II*, *Henry IV*, *Romeo and Juliet* and *Julius Caesar*.

C. Period of gloom and depression

This period, which dated from 1600 to 1607, marks the full maturity of his power; it was devoted largely to tragedies. In this period Shakespeare produced his most powerful works. In depth of thought, in searching analysis of human motive, in the expression of the profoundest feelings, his tragedies make one of the most magnificent creations of the human mind. The main tragedies of this period are *Hamlet, Othello, King Lear* and *Macbeth*. During this period, Shakespeare also wrote his sonnets, in which he expressed his personal disappointment.

D. Period of calm after storm

This period marks the last few years of Shakespeare's literary work. His last few years (1608-1613) had neither the lightness of the beginning nor the somber violence of the middle period of his career. They had a spirit of serenity, and optimism. Shakespeare again turned to comedies. His best plays produced in this period are *The Winter's Tale*, *The Tempest*. But these plays all show a falling off from his previous work.

13. In which period did William Shakespeare write his main comedies? What did he tell us in his comedies?

William Shakespeare wrote his comedies in his second period (1595-1600) in which he wrote his "great comedies". In these plays he portrayed the young people who had just freed from the feudal fetters. He sang of their youth, their love and ideal of happiness. The heroes and heroines are sons and daughters of the Renaissance. They trust not in God or King but in themselves.

Usually there are two groups of characters in Shakespeare's comedies. The first group is composed of characters of young men and young women. They live in the world of youth and dreams and laughter, and fight for their happiness. The second group consists of simple and shrewd clowns and other common people. These characters make the play full of humor and laughter. The success of Shakespeare's comedies owes much to the appearance of clowns. Without them the plays would become dull and humourless.

Shakespeare's comedies lay emphasis on emancipation of women, which played a very important role in anti-feudalism. His comedies are imbued with bourgeoisie ideas and show progressive significance.

14. In which period did William Shakespeare write his main tragedies? What did he write about in his tragedies?

William Shakespeare's main tragedies were written during the period of gloom and depression which dated from 1600 to 1607.

William Shakespeare's great tragedies are associated with a period of gloom and sorrow in his life. During this period, England witnessed a general unrest, social contradictions became very sharp. What caused the writer's personal sadness is unknown to us. It is generally attributed to the political misfortune of his friend and patron, Earl of Essex, who was killed by the Queen.

His main tragedies are: *Hamlet*, *Othello*, *King Lear*, and *Macbeth*. All of these plays express a profound dissatisfaction with life. They show the struggle and conflicts between good and evil of the time, between justice and injustice. Shakespeare depicts the life-and-death struggle between the humanists, who represented the newly emerging forces, and the corrupted King and his feudal followers, who represented the dark power of that time. In these plays, Shakespeare condemns the dark and evil society.

15. What did William Shakespeare express in his historical plays?

William Shakespeare's historical plays are political plays. The principal idea of these plays is the necessity for national unity under one sovereign. At his time, this idea was anti-feudal in nature, and it summed up the general opinion of the rising bourgeoisie in Shakespeare's own day.

William Shakespeare's historical plays reflect the historical events of two centuries from Richard II to Henry VIII. They show the horrors of civil war, the necessity for national unity, the responsibilities of efficient ruler and the importance of legitimate succession to the throne.

Like the majority of humanists of his time, William Shakespeare believed in a wise and humane King who would love to serve his country. But, in the historical plays, William Shakespeare's treatment of real English kings is extremely critical. Richard II is condemned for his vanity, political blindness and inability to subdue the feudal lords. Richard III is represented as a king strong-willed and vicious, who came to power through a series of horrible crimes and turned his country into a dungeon. And Henry IV, though glorified for his suppression of the rebellion of feudal lords, is criticized for his participation in the murder of Richard II and his treacherous arrest of the rebels after the truce.

In William Shakespeare's historical plays there is only one ideal king Henry V, though his real prototype differs little from the other kings. Nevertheless, for English patriots of that time his name was associated with the military victories of England in the Hundred Years' War and became a symbol of English glory in the eyes of the well-to-do citizens of England.

Among William Shakespeare's historical plays, *Henry IV* and *Henry V* are two remarkable plays. *Henry V* is the continuation of *Henry IV*. The two plays deal with the events of the 15th century and give the picture of a troubled reign.

16. What are the features of William Shakespeare's plays?

A. William Shakespeare is a realist. He is one of the founders of realism in English literature. His plays are mirrors of his age, reflecting the major contradictions of that time. He described the decaying of the feudal society and the rising of the young men and women who just freed themselves from the fetters of feudalism and who were striving for individual emancipation. Shakespeare also clearly reflected the contradictions between the rich and the poor. He showed his sympathy to the poor people and disclosed the greed and cruelty of the upper class. Moreover, Shakespeare revealed the emergence of the early colonization and racial problem arising with capitalism. He fully reflected the omnipotent power of money in the age of growing capitalism. He was far-sighted into money, capitalist accumulation and its effect.

B. The stories of William Shakespeare's plays often take place in other countries or in the past instead of in England or in his own age. The characters are clothed in foreign dresses, yet their thought and feelings and their attitude towards life belong to the age of Shakespeare. In fact, his characters are representatives of the people of his time.

C. William Shakespeare's main characters are depicted in typical situations. They are typical characters. Their fundamental traits are revealed in their conflicts with their surroundings, in their relations with their fellowmen (such as Hamlet, whose character is depicted through his relations with his father, mother, uncle, his friend Horatio, his lover Ophelia etc.). Each of his characters is a representative of a group of men (such as Hamlet representing the humanists; Shylock the usurer; Falstaff the relic of chivalry).

D. William Shakespeare's dramatic form fits the content of his plays very well. His plays are not controlled by the rules of the classical unities of time, place and action. The action moves from place. A play covers several days or years. In order to reproduce the manifold image of life, Shakespeare used a peculiar combination in his drama, combination of majestic and funny, of poetic and prosaic, of tragic and comic.

E. William Shakespeare was a great master of English language. The language of each of his characters fits his position in society and reveals the peculiarities of his character. He commanded a vocabulary larger than any other English writer. He used about 16,000 words. He loved to play with words, or to make puns with them. Sometimes we find it very difficult to understand him. Shakespeare also created a lot of new words and expressions, thus enriching English language. (e.g. "Brevity is the soul of wit"; "More matter, with less art"; "cudgel one's brains"; "to be or not to be".)

17. Comment on William Shakespeare's sonnets.

   The sonnet is a poem in 14 lines with one or the other rhyme scheme, a form much in vogue in Renaissance Europe, especially in Italy, France and England.

   In 1609 appeared *Shakespeare's Sonnets, Neuer Before Imprinted*. The collection contains 154 sonnets, commonly thought to be written between 1593 and 1599. They may be roughly divided into three groups. Numbers 1-17 are variations in one theme. A handsome young man is being persuaded to marry and beget offspring who will preserve his beauty in a new generation. Gradually this theme gives place to the idea that the beloved youth will survive through the poet's verse. Numbers 18-126 are on a variety of themes associated with a handsome young man. The poet enjoys his friendship and is full of admiration promising to bestow immortality on the young man by the poems he writes in his honor. The climax of the series comes when the young man seduces the poet's mistress. Then begins a new series, principally about a married woman with dark hair and complexion, the so-called "dark lady of the sonnets", by whom the poet is enthralled, though well aware of her faults. And the "story" in the poems is merely an elusive one: at times it can be sensed, but frequently breaks off, and then reverts to the beginning. For all that, all critics unite in praising these sonnets for a variety of virtues. They express strong feeling. They have a density of thought and imagery that makes them the quintessence of the poetical experience. They delight by a felicity of phrase and verse movement. They also afford the readers hints of Shakespeare's personality and personal life, which, though regrettably scanty and elusive, are tantalizing.

18. Make a brief comment on the character of Hamlet.

   Without knowledge of his character, Hamlet's story would hardly be intelligible. Hamlet is neither a frail and weak-minded youth nor a thought-sick bookworm. The play itself does not bear out such ideas. In the play, nobody thinks of him in that way. Though a scholar, he is at the same time fearless and impetuous in action.

A. Hamlet is a humanist, a man who is free from medieval prejudices and superstitions. He has an unbounded love for the world instead of the heaven. Like other humanists, he cherishes a profound reverence for man, and a firm belief in man's power and destiny: "What a piece of work is a man! How noble in reason…" Such a delight in nature and man is characteristic of the humanist of the Renaissance.

B. Starting from his humanist love for man, he turns to those around him with the same eagerness. He loves good and hates evil. He adores his father, loves Ophelia and greets his school-fellows with hearty welcome, while he is disgusted with his uncle's drunkenness and shocked by his mother's shallowness. In his contact with the people around him, he cares for nothing but human worth and shows contempt for rank and wealth. A king and a beggar are all one to him. His democratic tendency is based on his humanist thought.

C. His intellectual genius is outstanding. He is a close observer of men and manners. He easily sees through people. His quick perception drives him to penetrate below the surface of things and question what others take for granted. So he is forever unmasking his world. His observation of his world is summed up into a bitter sentence: "Denmark is a prison".

From these one may know that Hamlet is not a mere scholar, and his nature is by no means simply meditative. On the contrary, Hamlet is a man of genius, highly accomplished and educated, a man of far-reaching perception and sparking wit. He is a scholar, soldier and statesman. His image reflects the versatility of the men of the Renaissance.

19. What is the theme of *The Merchant of Venice*?

The theme of *The Merchant of Venice* can be summarized as follow:

A. Justice versus mercy: Shakespeare reveals different aspects of justice versus mercy and suggests, through Portia, that all men should be merciful. Human mercy should follow the example of divine mercy. There is a further aspect of justice in this case—injustice revealed in the Christians' treatment of the Jews. In this way Shakespeare gives Shylock a motive in wanting his revenge on Antonio.

B. Appearance versus reality: there are numerous variations on this theme: superficial or external beauty versus moral or spiritual beauty or truth (as in the case of the three caskets); the letters of law versus the spirit of the law.

C. Commercial or material values versus love: Shakespeare puts forward the idea that true love is much more worthwhile than money and material values. Antonio epitomizes true love in his friendship for Bassanio, when he is prepared to lay down his life for his friend. Shylock, on the other hand, does not appear to be able to distinguish his values. When he hears that Jessica has run away, he cannot decide which hurts him more: the loss of his daughter or the loss of his money.

20. Make a brief comment on Ben Jonson's works.

His poetry can be divided into five groups: poems of festive ceremony, poems in imitation of Horace with English tonality, elegies and epitaphs, compliments and tributes, and epigrams.

Ben Jonson was more important as a critic. He advocated classicism, modeling on the old Greek and Roman masters, taking a firm stand for the Three Unities in play-writing.

Ben Jonson, with his *Epitaph on S. P., My Picture Left in Scotland, A Hymn to God the Father* and other poems, was also listed as one of the metaphysical poets.

His literary achievements were not great. But his influence was big in that he gathered many writers around him, encouraged them, helped them and commented on their writing. He was almost worshipped by them. His criticism was insightful.

21. Make a brief comment on Christopher Marlowe's *The Tragical History of Doctor Faustus*.

   According to the conventional view, *Doctor Faustus* is a predominantly Christian play, carrying the essential elements of the medieval morality. Like morality plays, it vindicates humility, faith and obedience to the law of God. By exhibiting the punishment of man for trying through the proud exercise of forbidden knowledge to transcend the bounds of his nature, the Faust-myth is actually a warning against the sin of pride and presumption. The struggle in Dr. Faustus is the same struggle between heaven and hell, between God and Lucifer; Faustus's fall is caused by the same pride and ambition that caused the fall of the angels in heaven; and there is a strong analogue between his state and that of Adam and Eve in the Garden of Aden.

   But in a radical view, the play's dominant moral is human rather than religious. It celebrates the human passion for knowledge, power and happiness; it also reveals man's frustration in realizing the high aspirations in a hostile moral order. And the confinement to time is the cruelest fact of man's condition. Besides, the conflict of choice is made convincing as it would not have been in a medieval play, and the psychology not only of Faustus, but of Mephistophilis is presented with moving insight.

22. What are the limitations in *Utopia*?

   In *Utopia*, we see the ruthless expose of cruelty of the English ruling classes in their oppression and exploitation of peasants and a rather vivid picture of a utopian socialist state. However, it has some limitations at certain levels:

   A. Writing at the dawn of capitalism, Thomas More could not but build his dreams of a communist society on the social foundations of handicrafts manufacture, and this limitation of his age necessarily made him conceive of a society free from oppression and exploitation in a vague and dreamy way, devoid of any solid political and economic foundations.

B. Thomas More's social status as a member of the ruling class manifested itself also in his indifferent attitudes towards slaves and mercenary soldiers and in his actual contempt for physical labor—in spite of his insistence on the need of most Utopians to participate in physical labor.

C. As a great thinker, Thomas More was not so revolutionary as to arouse the people or to start any revolutionary movement among the exploited classes.

D. Living in the Middle Ages, Thomas More could see what was wrong and what was needed, but he could never find at that time the means by which socialism could be realized. Here Thomas More, in common with other Utopians, was at his weakest. He confessed at the end of *Utopia*: "So must I needs confess and grant that many things be in the Utopian weal-public, which in our cities I may rather wish for, than hope after".

E. When we bear in mind that Thomas More's life as a courtier and fervent believer in Catholicism who would rather die than give up his belief in the absolute authority of the Pope in Rome, and compare it with his views on Utopian socialism, the contradictions appear very strange indeed.

Part V

The 17th Century: Revolution, Restoration and New Poetic Expression

I. Fill in the Blanks.

1. metaphysical
2. the individual conscience
3. Oliver Cromwell
4. French
5. family burden
6. frankness; realism; cynicism
7. Cambridge University
8. *Hesperides*; *Noble Numbers*
9. Robert Herrick
10. people's liberties
11. Trinity College
12. *To His Coy Mistress*
13. the First World War; *Metaphysical Lyrics*; T. S. Eliot
14. English Bourgeois Revolution
15. *The Plain Man's Pathway to Heaven*; *The Practice of Piety*
16. *The Pilgrim's Progress*; 1678
17. drawing comparisons; the liturgy
18. Andrew Marvell
19. temptation; fall
20. Puritan
21. Restoration
22. decline
23. John Bunyan
24. *The Pilgrim's Progress*
25. John Dryden
26. conceit
27. *All for Love*
28. Diggers
29. conceit
30. Bourgeois Revolution
31. a military dictatorship
32. Restoration
33. *Samson Agonistes*
34. the Civil War
35. George Herbert
36. Paganism

· 251 ·

37. *Corinna's Going A-Maying*
38. *L'Allegro*
39. God's English Poet; Holy Spirit
40. *Paradise Regained; Samson Agonistes*
41. Spanish
42. *To Althea*
43. Andrew Marvell

II. Choose the Best Answer for Each Question.

1-5   C A B D A   6-10 D A B B C   11-15 C A B D D
16-20 A A D B B   21-25 A D B B D   26-30 B C C A C
31-35 C A C C B   36-37 C A

III. Match-Making

Group One
1-5   c a b e d
Group Two
1-5   b d e a c

IV. Define the Literary Terms.

1. Puritan Age

   In literature the Puritan Age was one of confusion, due to the breaking up of old ideals. Medieval standards of chivalry, the impossible loves and romances perished. The Puritans believed in simplicity of life. They disapproved of the sonnets and the love poetry written in the previous period. The Bible became now the one book of the people. The Puritan influence in general tended to suppress literary art.

2. Metaphysical poetry

The term "metaphysical poetry" refers to the works of the 17th century writers who wrote under the influence of John Donne who made frequent and skilled use of conceit, an extended metaphor in which things quite dissimilar are yoked together by violence of thought. They liked to reason and argue about things rather than to be lyrical in their expression. The metaphysical poets tried to break away from the conventional fashion of Elizabethan love poetry, and favored in poetry for a more colloquial language and tone, a tightness of expression and the single-minded working out of a theme or argument.

3. Cavalier poet

The Cavalier poets were a group of English lyric poets who were active, approximately during the reign of Charles I. This group included Richard Lovelace, Sir John Suckling, Robert Herrick, Thomas Carew and Edmund Waller. These poets virtually abandoned the sonnet form which had been the favored medium for love poems for a century. They were considerably influenced by Ben Jonson. Their lyrics are light, witty, elegant, and for the most part, concerned with love. They showed much technical virtuosity.

4. *Paradise Lost*

Paradise Lost was written by John Milton. It is marked for its intricate and contradictory composition. It is based on the biblical legend of the Adam and Eve, and involves God and his eternal adversary, Satan in its plot.

The poem opens with the description of a meeting among the angels. Led by the freedom-loving Satan, the mutinous angels rise against God himself, but in the battle with the hosts of angels that remain true to God they are finally defeated. Satan and his followers are banished from heavenly domains and sequestered into the nether world. Henceforward infernal torments are to be their lot. But even here, in hell, amidst flames and poisonous fumes, Satan and his adherents are not discouraged. Satan's proud spirit is not subdued. He stoically withstands all agonies and passionately strives for victory.

5. Conceit

An elaborate metaphor comparing two apparently dissimilar objects or emotions, often with an effect of shock or surprise. The metaphysical conceit, as used by John Donne and his followers, applies wit and ingenuity to, in the words of Samuel Johnson, a combination of dissimilar images, or discovery of occult resemblances in things apparently unlike.

6. Restoration literature

Restoration literature is characterized by a cliquish culture centering on the court and deeply influenced by French classical taste. These four things: the tendency to vulgar realism in the drama, a general formalism, the development of a simpler and more direct prose style, and the prevalence of the heroic couplet in poetry are the main characteristics of Restoration literature. They are all exemplified in the works of one man, John Dryden.

V. Answer the Following Questions Briefly.

1. Describe the features of metaphysical poetry in the 17th century.

The marks of the metaphysical poetry in the 17th century are arresting and original images and conceits, wit, ingenuity, dexterous use of colloquial speech, considerable flexibility of rhythm and meter, complex themes, a liking for paradox and dialectical argument, a direct manner, a caustic humor, a keenly felt awareness of mortality, and a distinguished capacity for elliptical thought and tersely compact expression. But for all their intellectual robustness the metaphysical poets were also capable of refined delicacy, gracefulness and deep feeling, passion as well as wit.

2. What does Glorious Revolution symbolize?

It symbolizes the supremacy of Parliament, the beginning of modern England, and the final triumph of the principle of political liberty for which the Puritans had fought and suffered hardship for a hundred years.

3. Make a brief comment on *Paradise Lost*.

The purpose of John Milton in writing *Paradise Lost* is open to interpretation. But some phenomena are worth noticing. This long epic is obviously the product of Milton's Age. Some people say that John Milton sympathizes with Satan because they both love freedom. John Milton praised Satan's challenge and revolt to God. Some readers who had read the whole epic found John Milton's change of attitude toward Satan. From the surface, indeed, the early image of Satan is one of positive figures. The rebellious spirit of Satan is quite like that of Oliver Cromwell. One can also find some similarities in God and the king. God was offended by the rebels, just as the King was offended and beheaded. An interesting thing is that God defeated Satan and his followers and punished them. And the monarchy restored its order while the followers of Oliver Cromwell were persecuted and fled to different places. John Milton the author of such a work could not have opposed God. Anyway, a careful reader cannot fail to understand this: The war between God and Satan echoes the Civil War between the Crown and the parliament headed by Oliver Cromwell.

4. What do you think contributed to John Bunyan's ideas?

A. From the Renaissance he inherited nothing, unlike John Milton who is thought to be the child of the Renaissance. But from the reformation John Bunyan received the spiritual independence which had caused the Puritan struggle for liberty, that is, the English Bourgeois Revolution.

B. The religious ferment of the age made a tremendous impression on Bunyan's sensitive imagination.

C. Two old, threadbare books—*The Plain Man's Pathway to Heaven* and *The Practice of Piety* which were brought by his wife.

D. His attendance at church grew exemplary. He began slowly and painfully to read the Bible for himself, but because of his own ignorance and the contradictory interpretations of the Scripture which he heard on every side, he was tossed about like a feather by all the winds of doctrine.

5. Make a brief comment on John Bunyan's *The Pilgrim's Progress*.

   Though not the earliest novel in England because there were other works that might also be called novels, and also because it is difficult to decide which is the first novel, John Bunyan's *The Pilgrim's Progress* can be said to be the first most influential one. In its simplest definition, a novel is a book-length fictional prose narrative, having many characters and often a complex plot. As a genre, novel was not paid attention to because the age of the Elizabeth and her successors was the age of poetry and drama. Even though many poets also wrote some prose narratives, they were drowned in the sea of poetry and drama. John Bunyan took material from the Bible and wrote to teach people what is good and what is bad, what people should do and what people should not do. In allegorical form, he criticized the evil and praised the kind. In some episodes he gave a realistic description of the evils existing in the society. His puritan ideas were fully displayed.

6. What are the different aspects between the literature of the Elizabethan Period and the literature of the Revolution Period?

   The Revolution Period was of confusion in literature. English literature of the period witnessed a decline and degeneration. One can see that it is different from the literature of Elizabethan Period in three aspects.

   A. Elizabethan literature had the spirit of unity and the feeling of patriotism and devotion to the Queen. However, in the Revolution Period, the king became the open enemies of the people, and the country was divided by the struggle for political and religious liberty. So literature was as divided in spirit as were the struggling parties.

B. Elizabethan literature was generally inspiring. It throbbed with youth and hope and vitality. Literature in the Puritan Age expressed age and sadness. Even its brightest hours were followed by gloom and pessimism.

C. Elizabethan literature was intensely romantic. The romance sprang from the heart of youth. People believed all things, even the impossible. But in literature of the Puritan period, one cannot find romantic ardor.

7. What are the differences between John Milton and John Donne in terms of religious sensibility?

John Milton is a writer at an opposite remove from John Donne in terms of religious sensibility. John Donne questions everything and refuses to untie the knots he creates, yet at the back of John Donne's poetry is the remnant of a Catholic desire to embrace all of experience in a comprehensive and traditional world picture. John Milton, by contrast, a Puritan, and indeed the most eloquent defender of Oliver Cromwell's regime, engages in fundamental religious and political rethinking. John Donne in a sense looks, almost longingly, towards the past, whereas John Milton is interested in the future and in establishing a new order.

8. What are the features of John Milton's poetry?

A. John Milton was a great revolutionary poet of the 17th century. He was also an outstanding political pamphleteer of the Revolution Period. He dedicated himself to the revolutionary cause. He made a strong influence on the later English poetry. Every progressive English poet since John Milton has drawn inspiration from him.

B. John Milton is a great stylist. His poetry has a grand style. That is because he made a life-long study of classical and Biblical literature. His poetry is noted for sublimity of thought and majesty of expression.

C. John Milton is a great master of blank verse. He is the glorious pioneer to introduce blank verse into non-dramatic poetry. He used it as the main tool in his masterpiece *Paradise Lost*. His blank verse is rich in every poetic quality and never monotonous.

9. What's the feature of the literature after Restoration?

In the literature of the Restoration one can note a sudden breaking away from old standards, just as society broke away from the restraints of Puritanism. Many of the literary men had been driven out of England with Charles and his court, or else had followed their patrons into exile in the days of the Commonwealth. On their return they renounced old ideals and demanded that English poetry and drama should follow the style to which they had become accustomed in the gaiety of Paris.

Restoration created a literature of its own, which was often witty and clever, but on the whole immoral and cynical. The most popular genre was that of comedy whose chief aim was to entertain the licentious aristocrats.

10. Make a comparison between *The Pilgrim's Progress* and *Journey to the West*, one of China's classical novels.

The two works are both famous religious works in world literature. Both works are exposure of evil society and cruel reality at that time with romantic ardor through episodes of adventures. Though they share so much in common, they are different in the follow aspects:

A. *Journey to the West* is famous for its complicated and interesting stories while *The Pilgrim's Progress* is dull and boring. The former is full of humorous and satirical descriptions while the latter more of religious preaching and debate.

B. *Journey to the West* is more like a work of the author's self-revelation with religious and mythological cloak, whereas *The Pilgrim's Progress* is a pious Christian allegory.

C. *Journey to the West* is a combination of Buddhism, Confucianism and Daoism; the only concern of *The Pilgrim's Progress* is Christian thinking and principles.

D. The former shows loyalty to the king and rely on the king to solve the social problems while the latter seeks to self-salvation.

Part VI

The 18th Century: The Enlightenment, Neo-classicism and Pre-romanticism

I. Fill in the Blanks.

1. prose
2. the liberal Whigs; the conservative Tories
3. Pamphlets
4. public coffeehouses and private clubs
5. bourgeoisie; feudalism
6. the contradictions of new society
7. *The Spectator*
8. social problems; private life; adventures
9. industry and trade
10. Daniel Defoe; *Robinson Crusoe*
11. Henry Fielding; Tobias George Smollet
12. Jonathan Swift; *Gulliver's Travels*
13. Gothic novel; medieval
14. John Dryden; Oliver Cromwell
15. political; religious; literary
16. Daniel Defoe
17. advertisement or pamphlet
18. Friday
19. *The Battle of the Books*
20. *The Tale of a Tub*; the Tories; *Gulliver's Travels*
21. Horses; Yahoos
22. essay writing
23. *The Tatler; The Spectator*
24. *An Essay on Criticism*; *The Rape of the Lock*
25. *The Iliad; The Odyssey*
26. mock-heroic
27. Neo-classicism
28. burlesques; dramatic satires

29. *Ode to Eden*; *Elegy*
30. poet laureate
31. classicists; sentimentalism and romanticism
32. *The School for Scandal*
33. William Blake; pre-Romantic
34. stanza; blank verse
35. Robert Burns
36. radical
37. realism
38. digression; stream
39. *The Deserted Village*
40. Laurence Sterne
41. press; argument; satire
42. morals and manners; innermost life
43. False virtues; *The School for Scandal*
44. Laurence Sterne
45. Robert Burns; revolutionary romanticism
46. the Restoration
47. *Mac Flecknoe*
48. heroic couplets
49. *The Shortest Way with the Dissenters*
50. *The Life and Strange Surprising Adventures of Robinson Crusoe*
51. clergyman
52. Parliament; Secretary of State
53. *The Tatler*
54. newspaper
55. Catholic; Glorious Revolution
56. Enlightenment
57. *Essay on Criticism*
58. realism
59. *Robinson Crusoe*
60. *Jonathan Wild the Great*
61. manners
62. *The School for Scandal*

II. Choose the Best Answer for Each Question.

1-5   C A D B B   6-10 D A C D A   11-15 B D C B D
16-20 A D D B C   21-25 B A B A C   26-30 B D B D C
31-35 D A B B A   36-40 A A B B B   41-45 D C D C D
46-50 B D A D B   51-55 A C C C A   56-60 D A D A A
61-65 C D B C A   66-70 C A D B D   71-74 C D D B

III. Match-Making

Group One
1-8 c d a e b g h f
Group Two
1-10 e g j h a b c i f d

IV. Define the Literary Terms.

1. The Enlightenment

    The Enlightenment was a progressive intellectual movement throughout Western Europe in the 18th century. It was an expression of struggle of the bourgeoisie against feudalism. The enlighteners fought against class inequality, stagnation, prejudices and other survivals of feudalism. They thought the chief means for bettering society was "enlightenment" or "education" for the people. The English enlighteners were bourgeois democratic thinkers. They were different from those of France, for they appeared not before but after the bourgeois revolution. They set no revolutionary aim before them, and what they strove for was to carry the revolution through to an end.

2. Sentimentalism

    Sentimentalism is a literary tradition followed by some poets and novelists of the 18th century. It indulged in emotion and sentiment, which were used as a sort of relief from the grief and heartaches felt toward the world's wrongs, and as a kind of mild protest against the social injustice. The writers who followed this tradition criticized the cruelty of the capitalist relations and the gross social injustices brought about by the bourgeois revolutions and the Industrial Revolution. They yearned for the return of the patriarchal times. They thought the bourgeois society was founded on the principle of reason, so they began to react against anything rational and to advocate that sentiment should take the place of reason.

In English poetry of the 18th century, sentimentalism first found its full expression in the forties and the fifties, in Edward Young's *Night Thoughts* and in Thomas Gray's *Elegy Written in a Country Churchyard*. In the later decades of the century, it was found in a number of the poems by William Cowper.

3. Neo-classicism

Neo-classicism, as a movement or tendency in art, literature, or music, reflects the principles manifested in the art of ancient Greece and Rome. Classicism emphasizes the traditional and the universal, and places value on reason, clarity, balance and order. The 18th century classicism, with its concern for reason and universal themes, was later opposed by romanticism which is concerned with emotions and personal themes. English neo-classical literature found fine expression in poetry.

4. Elegy

The term "elegy", first used to describe any serious meditative poem, is now used to refer to a poem that laments the death of a particular person. Thomas Gray's poem laments the passing of all people, but ends with an epitaph for a particular person, and is thus an elegy in both senses.

5. Archaism

A word, expression, spelling, or phrase that is out of date in the common speech of an era, but still deliberately used by a writer, poet, or playwright for artistic purposes.

6. Romanticism

Romanticism has six prominent characteristics which distinguish it from the classic literature.

A. The Romantic Movement was marked, and is always marked, by a strong reaction and protest against the bondage of rule and custom, which, in science and theology, as well as in literature, generally tends to fetter the free human spirit.

B. Romanticism returned to nature and to plain humanity for its material, and so is in marked contrast to classicism, which had confined itself largely to the clubs and drawing-rooms, and to the social and political life of London.

C. It brought back the dream of a golden age in which the stern realities of life were forgotten and the ideals of youth were established as the only permanent realities. It is marked by renewed interest in medieval ideals and literature.

D. Romanticism is marked by intense human sympathy, and by a consequent understanding of the human heart. The sympathy for the poor, and the cry against oppression grew stronger and stronger.

E. The Romantic Movement was the expression of individual genius rather than of established rules. In consequence, the literature of romanticism was as varied as the characters and moods of the different writers. In the works of the best romanticists there is endless variety.

F. Edmund Spenser, William Shakespeare and John Milton were inspiration of the Romantic Movement. One can hardly read a poem of the early romanticists without finding a suggestion of the influence of one of these great leaders.

V. Answer the Following Questions Briefly.

1. What are the features of Enlighteners?

    A. The Enlighteners fought against class inequality, stagnation, prejudices and other survivals of feudalism.

    B. They attempted to place all branches of science at the service of mankind by connecting them with the actual deeds and requirements of the people.

C. The Enlighteners criticized the false religious doctrines about the viciousness of human nature, and proved that man is born kind and honest, and if he becomes depraved, it is only due to the influence of corrupted social environment.

D. They were prone to accept bourgeois relationships as rightful and reasonable relationships among people.

2. Why can we call John Dryden a many-sided talent?

A. He wrote *A Song for St. Cecilia's Day*, which is an inventive testimony to the power of music, intended to be sung as well as read.

B. *Mac Flecknoe* is a witty attack on Thomas Shadwell, a minor poet and playwright, showing John Dryden's superb gifts in verse satire.

C. In poetry he set an enduring style with his neat "heroic couplets"—paired lines of rhymed iambic pentameter, which unites a classical conception of order and clarity with traditional English energy and inventiveness.

D. In prose he established the neoclassical standards of order, balance and harmony. Both in his lucid prose and in his balanced, harmonious poetic couplets, he fashioned techniques that would dominate English writing for a century.

E. His greatest work of literary criticism is *An Essay of Dramatic Poesy*, in which appears his famous appreciation of Shakespeare.

3. Make an outline of *Robinson Crusoe*.

This work mainly tells the story of the protagonist Robinson Crusoe who was born in a middle-class family and has a lifelong ambition to travel around the world. He encounters a storm while sailing to Africa, and drifts to an uninhabited desert island alone, and starts a life in isolation. With a strong will and unremitting efforts, he survives tenaciously on the desert island. After living on the island for 28 years, 2 months and 19 days, he is finally able to return to his hometown.

4. What is the significance of *Robinson Crusoe*? What do you think is the value of *Robinson Crusoe*?

Robinson Crusoe is a novel popular with the rising bourgeoisie who believed in the spirit of working hard to gain wealth. The adventurous spirit is also a treasure for those who want to trade with other countries and accumulate their wealth. This novel also touches upon the issue of colony. Daniel Defoe seems to glorify colonization through his relationship with Friday. But one can understand it first of all as a novel publicizing hard work and survival.

Through his characterization of Crusoe, Daniel Defoe depicts a man as a hero struggling against nature and human fate with his indomitable will and hand, and eulogizes creative labor, physical and mental, as an allusion to the glorification of the bourgeois creativity when it was a rising and more energetic class in the initial stage of its historical development. From an individual slave and laborer to a master and colonizer, Crusoe seems to have gone through various phases of human civilization, creating a visual picture that manifests how man's history has developed from the primitive to the feudal, and then to the capitalistic in the eighteenth century. Here dwells the vital significance of the novel.

5. Why is *Gulliver's Travels* called a satirical novel?

A. The Lilliputian scene depicted in the first volume of the novel is a microcosm of Britain. Year-round struggles and foreign wars are essentially just politicians fighting each other on issues that have nothing to do with the national economy and the people's livelihood.

B. The second volume of the novel expresses suspicion and denial of various British systems and political and religious measures through the sharp attacks on the proud policies and various political and religious measures by the king of the adult kingdom.

C. In the third volume of the novel, the author points the irony at contemporary British philosophers, scientists who are divorced from reality and indulged in fantasy, absurd inventors, and critics and historians who turn black and white.

D. In the fourth volume of the novel, the author uses Gulliver to answer a series of questions to expose the essence of war, the hypocrisy of the law, and the shameful behavior of unscrupulous means to obtain officials.

6. What are the features of Henry Fielding's novels?

A. Henry Fielding is both the story-teller and commentator in the novel. First-person narrative and the author's comment coexist. This is commonly called narration mingled with comments.

B. Satire and irony abound everywhere in Henry Fielding's works.

C. Henry Fielding believed in the function of moral teaching. Both drama and novel are weapons of criticizing the social evil.

D. Misunderstanding and sudden discovery set examples for later writings.

E. Henry Fielding is a master of style. His style is easy, unlabored and familiar, but extremely vivid and vigorous. His sentences are always distinguished by logic and musical rhythm. His command of language is remarkable. His language is characterized by clarity and suppleness. The plot construction is usually complicated and masterly made. Each thread is clearly laid out as the story develops, though the story may consist of several major and minor threads.

7. What is Richard Steele's and Joseph Addison's contribution to English literature?

A. Their writings in *The Tatler* and *The Spectator* provided a new code of social morality for the rising bourgeoisie.

B. They gave a true picture of the social life of England in the 18th century.

C. In their hands, the English essay completely established itself as a literary genre. Using it as a form of character sketching and story-telling, they ushered in the dawn of the modern novel.

8. What are the features of Daniel Defoe's novels?

Daniel Defoe is remembered chiefly, for his novels. The central idea of his novels is that man is good and noble by nature but may succumb to an evil social environment. The writer wants to make it clear that society is the source of various crimes and vices.

Daniel Defoe's intention is that the readers should regard his novels as true stories. For that reason, he deliberately avoids all arts, all fine writings, so that the reader should concentrate only on a series of plausible events.

Daniel Defoe's novels all take the form of memoirs or pretended historical narratives, everything in them gives the impression of reality.

9. What are Jonathan Swift's writing features?

Jonathan Swift is one of the realistic writers. His realism is quite different from Daniel Defoe's. Daniel Defoe's stories are based upon the reality of human life, while all of Johnathan Swift's plots come from imagination, which is the chief means he uses in his satires. He drew ruthless pictures of the depraved aristocracy and satirically portrayed the whole of the English state system.

Jonathan Swift is one of the greatest masters of English prose. His language is simple, clear and vigorous. He said, "Proper words in proper place, makes the true definition of a style". There are no ornaments in his writings. In simple, direct and precise prose, Johnathan Swift is almost unsurpassed in English literature.

Jonathan Swift is a master satirist, and his irony is deadly. His satire is masked by an outward gravity, and an apparent calmness conceals his bitter irony. This makes his satire all the more powerful.

Jonathan Swift expresses democratic ideas in his works. This exerts a strong influence on later writers, such as Richard Brinsley Sheridan, Henry Fielding, George Gordon Byron and even George Bernard Shaw.

10. What are the features of Henry Fielding's novels?

A. Henry Fielding's method of relating a story is telling the story directly by the author.

B. Satire abounds everywhere in Henry Fielding's works.

C. Henry Fielding believed in the educational function of the novel. The object of his novels is to present a faithful picture of life, while sound teaching is woven into their very texture.

D. Henry Fielding is a master of style. His style is easy, unlabored and familiar, but extremely vivid and vigorous. His sentences are always distinguished by logic and musical rhythm. His command of language is remarkable.

11. What is William Blake's position in English literature?

The whole temper of William Blake's genius was essentially opposed to the classical tradition of that age. He identifies classicism with formalism. As he put it, the writers of the classical school "knew enough of artifice, but little of art." His lyric poetry displayed the characteristics of the Romantic spirit, according to which natural sentiment and individual originality were essential to literary creation.

William Blake's revolutionary passion came near to that of Percy Bysshe Shelley. There is strong likeness between Percy Bysshe Shelley and William Blake: the imagery and symbolism as well as the underlying spirit. Percy Bysshe Shelley's revolutionary epics, such as *The Revolt of Islam* and *Prometheus Unbound*, find their nearest parallel in William Blake's prophetic book.

For these reasons, William Blake is called a pre-Romantic or a forerunner of the Romantic poetry of the 19th century.

12. What are the three stages of the Enlightenment?

The Enlightenment went through three stages in its development. The first period or the early period of the Enlightenment lasted from the "Glorious Revolution" to the end of the 1730s. This period was characterized by the so-called neo-classicism in poetry, of which the representative poet was Alexander Pope. Meanwhile a new prose literature appeared in the essays of Joseph Addison and Richard Steele and in the first realistic fiction of Daniel Defoe and Johnathan Swift.

The second period—the mature period of the Enlightenment was from 1740s to 1750s. The more important works that appeared during this period were chiefly the novels of Richardson, Henry Fielding and Smollett. The last two writers made rather fierce attacks on the existing social conditions.

The third period or the last period of the Enlightenment, covered the last decades of the 18th century. It was characterized by the appearance of new literary tendencies of sentimentalism and pre-romanticism, both of them served as protests to the social injustices of the day. Sentimentalism found its representative writers in the field of poetry, such as Edward Young and Thomas Gray; in the field of novels, Laurence Sterne and Oliver Goldsmith. Pre-romanticism found its expression chiefly in poetry, represented by William Blake and Robert Burns. The chief realistic dramatist of the century Richard Brinsley Sheridan wrote his plays in this period.

Generally speaking, literature in the 18th century was very complex.

13. What is Alexander Pope's position in English literature?

Alexander Pope was known as a great poet in his day. He exerted much influence upon the other writers of the age.

He popularized the neoclassical literary tradition brought from France.

He was one of the early representatives of the Enlightenment who introduced into English culture the spirit of rationalism and greater interest in the human world. He was a great satirist and a literary critic.

He occupied a prominent place in the literary world of his time. The early period of the 18th century has often been named after him as "The Age of Pope".

His influence on Byron was great and strong, so Byron thought highly of him and defended him while he was criticized by some critics in the 19th century.

14. Are there any differences in William Blake's two collections of lyrics *Songs of Innocence* and *Songs of Experience*? Why?

    There is a sharp contrast between the two collections, though they have many a poem with the same title.

    Songs of Innocence contains poems which were apparently written for children. Using a language which even little babies can learn by heart, William Blake succeeded in depicting the happy condition of a child before it knows anything about the pains of existence. The poet expresses his delight in the sun, the hills, the flowers, in the innocence of the child and of the lamb. Here everything seems to be in harmony.

    In *Songs of Experience*, a much maturer work, entirely different themes are to be found, for in this collection of poems the poet drew pictures of neediness and distress and showed the sufferings of the miserable. The will to freedom must endure, for a time, the limitations of worldly experience, and salvation is still to come through passionate revolt, through revolution. The poet was conscious of "some blind hand" crushing the life of man, as man crushes the fly.

    The contrast between the two collections is of great significance. It marks a progress in the poet's outlook on life. In the earlier collection there seem to be no shadows. In the poet's eyes, the first glimpse of the world is a picture of light, harmony, peace and love. But in the later years, experience brings a fuller sense of the power of evil, and of the great misery and pain of the people's life. Now the poet had to set himself against the current of the capitalist world.

15. Do you know other Chinese sarcastic writers like Johnathan Swift? What's the representative work of him/her?

There is a famous sarcastic Chinese writer called Lau Shaw, who is also a famous modern writer and an outstanding language master. He became one of the most successful writers in the 1930s. With satirical humor, humorous and relaxed style, he has won the love of the people and is known as "people's artist".

One of his representative works is *The Rickshaw Boy*, which tells a story about the life experience of Xiangzi, a young, strong and energetic rickshaw driver in Peking, China.

Part VII

The 19th Century (First Half): The Romantic Period

I. Fill in the Blanks.

1. The Romantic Period
2. late 18th century; 19th century
3. *Lyric Ballads*
4. William Blake
5. William Wordsworth; Samuel Taylor Coleridge; Robert Southey
6. *Don Juan*
7. *Kubla Khan*
8. the Industrial Revolution; the American Revolution; the French Revolution
9. William Blake; Robert Burns
10. revolutionary
11. *Lyrical Ballads*
12. *Childe Harold's Pilgrimage*
13. Percy Bysshe Shelley
14. Walter Scott
15. Jane Austen
16. *Sense and Sensibility*
17. Charles Lamb
18. *Ivanhoe*
19. *Lyrical Ballads*
20. novelists
21. Samuel Taylor Coleridge and Robert Southey
22. Samuel Taylor Coleridge
23. Charles Lamb
24. John Keats
25. William Wordsworth
26. Samuel Taylor Coleridge
27. *Song for the Luddites*
28. the May 4th Movement
29. political lyrics
30. Greek
31. *The Masque of Anarchy*
32. Charles Lamb
33. Burke
34. Walter Scott

35. peasants
36. Coleridge
37. Romantic
38. essays
39. three
40. Romantic
41. Charles Lamb
42. Byron
43. satiric
44. romanticism
45. Shelley
46. Renaissance
47. sensuous
48. Thomas Hood

II. Choose the Best Answer for Each Question.

1-5　B D A A C　　6-10　A D B A B　　11-15 C A B C B
16-20 C A B B D　　21-25 A B A B C　　26-30 D A A A B
31-35 C A D C A　　36-40 A D A A A　　41-45 A B C A D
46-47 C A

III. Match-Making

Group One
1-5　a d c b e
Group Two
1-5　c b e a d
Group Three
1-5　b d a e c
Group Four
1-5　c e d b a
Group Five
1-5　e b d a c

· 274 ·

IV. Define the Literary Terms.

1. Romanticism

    Romanticism is one of the basic creative methods of literature and art. Together with realism, romanticism is the main ideological trend in literature and art. As a creative method, romanticism focuses on the subjective inner world in reflecting the objective reality, expresses the warm pursuit of the ideal world, and often shapes the image with passionate language, magnificent imagination and exaggerated techniques.

2. The Lake Poets

    It refers to an early school in the British Romantic Movement in the 19th century. The representative figures are the three poets living in the lake area of Queensland in northern England, and the poetry school formed by Wordsworth, Coleridge and Southey. The words and sentences in their poems praise the lake and mountain scenery of nature, express lingering love and praise pure friendship. They are mostly characterized by freshness, nature, youth, beauty and philosophy.

3. Byronic Hero

    "Byronic hero" refers to a kind of characters in the works of Byron, an English Romantic poet in the 19th century. They are not only arrogant and stubborn, but also dissatisfied with the reality and demand to rise up and resist. They have a rebellious character; but at the same time, they are melancholy, lonely and pessimistic. For example, Harold, the noble son in the long lyric poem *Childe Harold's Pilgrimage* and so on.

V. Answer the Following Questions Briefly.

1. Briefly describe the characteristics of romanticism.

A. An emphasis on feeling, imagination, intuition and subjectivity;

B. A love for nature—the worshiper of nature; consolation, inspiration and revelation from nature;

C. A belief in individuality and freedom;

D. The glorification of the commonplace—incidents and situations from common life; the language spoken by the ordinary people;

E. An interest in the past and the picturesque scenery.

2. What are the differences between romanticism and realism?

A. The time and historical background of Romantic and realistic movements are different. For the emergence of romanticism from the 18th century to the mid-19th century, the French Revolution is a very important opportunity, which represents individualism. Realism has profound reasons for the development of social history and literature and art itself. Facing the reality, progressive writers reflect some real conditions of society in their own creation.

B. They express different contents. For Romantic writers, the expression of passion and the publicity of personality are their goals. Romantic works must show the writer's love, worship and praise for nature, and express his strong feelings. But the realistic writers pursue the real description of real ordinary life and the description of "typical characters in typical environment". They focus on the objective, specific and historical description of reality and emphasize the realistic relationship between characters and environment.

3. Why is Jane Austen a representative of female writers?

Jane Austen was one of the greatest women writers of the 19th century. She brought something new to the readers of the 19th century when they got tired of the vulgar and boring sentimental novels and Gothic novels: everyday life and pastoral living style of the British countryside gentry who remained unaffected by the capitalist industrial revolution; she was not only concerned about human beings in their personal relationships, but also preoccupied with the relationship between men and women in love. Such as *Pride and Prejudice*, *Sense and Sensibility* and so on.

4. Please briefly describe Samuel Taylor Coleridge.

   English lyrical poet, critic, and philosopher, whose *Lyrical Ballads*, written with Wordsworth, started the English Romantic Movement. Although Coleridge's poetic achievement was small in quantity, his metaphysical anxiety, anticipating modern existentialism, has gained him reputation as an authentic visionary.

   In Cambridge Coleridge met the radical, future poet laureate Robert Southey (1774-1843) in 1794. Coleridge moved with him to Bristol to establish a community, but the plan failed. His famous work is *Kubla Khan*.

   In 1795 he married the sister of Southey's fiancée Sara Fricker, whom he did not really love.

5. Make a brief comment on *Pride and Prejudice*.

   Pride and Prejudice, as the most famous work of Jane Austen's novel, describes a series of events that the squire class of Bennet's family went through for the marriage of their five daughters. In *Pride and Prejudice*, Jane Austen describes four patterns of marriage—marriage based on flesh, money, stabilization and love. The author expresses her view of love by expressing different forms of marriage and using irony.

Part VIII

The 19th Century (Second Half): The Victorian Age and Critical Realism

I. Fill in the Blanks.

1. 1837; 1901
2. The awakened social conscience
3. Whigs; Tories
4. Pauperism
5. *Oliver Twist*; *Bleak House*
6. Chartist Movement
7. Chartism
8. democratic
9. Charles Dickens
10. Chartist
11. proletariat
12. *The Origin of Species*
13. *Sonnets from the Portuguese*
14. Alfred Tennyson
15. love
16. *The Cry of the Children*
17. Robert Browning
18. liberation; child labor
19. Elizabeth Barrett Browning
20. Elizabeth Barrett Browning
21. poet
22. Alfred Tennyson
23. *Idylls of the King*
24. *In Memoriam*
25. dramatic monologue
26. Alfred Tennyson
27. *The Princess*
28. Alfred Tennyson
29. William Makepeace Thackeray
30. 19th
31. *Vanity Fair*
32. William Makepeace Thackeray
33. *Novel Without a Hero*
34. Rebecca Sharp
35. hypocrisy; money-worship
36. Charles Dickens
37. realism
38. *Oliver Twist*
39. *Pickwick Papers*
40. *Oliver Twist*
41. historical
42. middle

43. *A Christmas Carol*
44. *Bleak House*
45. virtue
46. *Great Expectations*
47. Pip
48. characterization
49. reforms
50. *Dorrit*
51. French
52. Robert Browning
53. dramatic monologue
54. Robert Browning
55. sudden discovery
56. humanistic
57. characterization
58. *The Ring and the Book*
59. George Eliot
60. Eliot
61. *Amos Barton*
62. Eliot
63. English
64. provincial
65. realism
66. morality
67. woman
68. *The Mill*
69. *Middlemarch*
70. *Middlemarch*
71. *Marner*
72. Charlotte Brontë; Emily Brontë; Anne Brontë
73. *Jane Eyre*
74. *Wuthering Heights*
75. realism; romanticism; symbolism
76. nature
77. *Wuthering Heights*
78. *The Professor*
79. dignity; love
80. inner life of emotion
81. love
82. *Wuthering Heights*
83. Rochester
84. Matthew Arnold
85. poet
86. *Anarchy*
87. Christina Rossetti
88. Hopkins
89. secret ballot
90. Brontë; Gaskell
91. *Barton*
92. laboring
93. decline
94. *Pauline*
95. passion
96. monologue
97. Byron; Shelley
98. upper
99. Court of Chancery
100. Morris
101. *The Virginians*

II. Choose the Best Answer for Each Question.

1-5　D A A A B　　　6-10　C A A D C　　　11-15 B A D D B
16-20 A C D B A　　21-25 A C D D B　　26-30 B A D C A
31-35 B C A D C　　36-40 B D A D A　　41-45 A C D A B
46-50 B A C D A　　51-55 C B A C B　　56-60 D B B A A
61-65 A C A A C　　66-70 C A B B D　　71-75 A A B A C
76-80 A A B D A　　81-85 A C A A A　　86-90 D A B C B
91　B

III. Match-Making

Group One
1-10　b a d c e i g h f j
Group Two
1-10　a f g d h b j e i c
Group Three
1-10　d j a i e h b f c g
Group Four
1-10　d h a i f g e b j c

IV. Define the Literary Terms.

1. English critical realism

   English critical realism of the 19th century flourished in the forties and in the early fifties. The critical realists described with much vividness and artistic skill the chief traits of the English society and criticized the capitalist system from a democratic viewpoint. The greatest English realist of the time was Charles Dickens. With striking force and truthfulness, he pictures bourgeois civilization, showing the misery and sufferings of the common people. Another critical realist, William Makepeace Thackeray, was a no less severe exposer of contemporary society. Thackeray's novels are mainly a satirical portrayal of the upper strata of society. Other adherents to the method of critical realism were Charlotte and Emily Brontë, and Elizabeth Gaskell. In the fifties and sixties the realistic novel as represented by Dickens and Thackeray entered a stage of decline. It found its reflection in the works of George Eliot, though the life of exposure became weaker in her works. She seemed to be more morally than socially minded. The English critical realists of the 19th century not only gave a satirical portrayal of the bourgeoisie and all the ruling classes, but also showed profound sympathy for the common people.

2. Dramatic monologue

Dramatic monologue is a kind of poem in which a single fictional or historical character other than the poet speaks to a silent "audience" of one or more persons.

Such poems reveal not the poet's own thoughts but the mind of the impersonated character, whose personality is revealed in the presence of a listener, which distinguishes from a soliloquy. Robert Browning is associated with the term. His *My Last Duchess* is a case in point.

3. Characterization

The way of an author or poet using description of dialogue, appearance, and action of a character to create in the reader an emotional or intellectual reaction to the character or to make him more vivid and realistic.

V. Answer the Following Questions Briefly.

1. Please briefly describe the historical background of the Victorian Pe-

riod.

A. The period was from 1836 to 1901 when Queen Victoria ruled over England.

B. After the Reform Bill of 1832, the political power passed from the decaying aristocrats into the hands of the middle-class industrial capitalists.

C. England became the "workshop of the world".

D. Yet beneath the great prosperity and richness, there existed widespread poverty and wretchedness among the working class.

E. The English workers got themselves organized in big cities and brought forth the People's Charter, in which they demanded basic rights and better living and working conditions.

F. At home, the Irish question remained unsolved.

G. The rapid development of science and technology, new inventions and discoveries in geology, astronomy, biology and anthropology drastically shook people's religious convictions.

2. What are the greatness and weakness of English critical realists?

The greatness of the English realists lies not only in their satirical portrayal of bourgeoisie and in the exposure of the greed and hypocrisy of the ruling classes, but also in their profound humanism which is revealed in their sympathy for the laboring people. These writers create positive characters who are quite alien to the vices of the rich and who are chiefly common people.

While the critical realists of the 19th century, due to their world view, could not find a way to eradicate social evils. They did not, and could not, realize the necessity of changing the contemporary social system radically. They only strived to improve it by means of reforms, which brought them to a futile attempt of reconciling the antagonistic class forces—the bourgeoisie and proletariat.

3. Compare the features of William Makepeace Thackeray's works with those of Charles Dickens's.

Though writing about the same time, William Thackeray differs from Charles Dickens in some aspects. First, his criticism of the society is seldom directed at the inhuman institutions and corrupted government which bring great misery and suffering to the poor working class, as is shown in Dickens's works. What Thackeray criticizes is the social moral that makes up the society, not the political structure and organizations that run the society. To him, the society is diseased because it is morally corrupted, because most people are money-oriented. To obtain money and the comfort and luxury it brings, they take every means to fight and cheat each other. Besides, unlike Dickens who has a firm belief in the honesty and respectability of the working class, Thackeray's criticism embraces people of all social strata. Though the world he depicts is predominantly that of the upper class in the early 19th century—with its whirling ballrooms, noisy parties, heavily curtained bedrooms, elegantly dressed ladies and gentlemen at card-tables and billiard rooms, flirting or gambling, where money is made or lost, marriages are contracted, and ambitions are thwarted and stupid favored—his social-climbers and snobs and money-grabbers can be found in any class.

4. Make a comment of the 19th century's critical realists' major contribution.

The major contribution made by the 19th century critical realists is their perfection of the novel. Like the realists of the 18th century, the 19th century critical realists made use of the form of novel for full and detailed representations of social and political events, and of the fate of individuals and of whole social classes. However, the realistic novels of the 19th century went a step further than those of the 18th century in that they not only pictured the conflicts between individuals who stood for definite social strata, but also showed the broad social conflicts over and above the fate of mere individuals. Their artistic representation of vital social movements such as Chartism, and their vivid description of the dramatic conflicts of the time make the 19th century realistic novel "the epic of the bourgeois society."

5. Charlotte Brontë is a writer of realism combined with romanticism. Why is *Jane Eyre* written by her a successful novel?

    A. The story opens with the titular heroine, Jane Eyre, a plain little orphan.

    B. This novel sharply criticizes the existing society, e.g. the religious hypocrisy of charity institutions such as Lowood School where poor girls are trained.

    C. The success of the novel is also due to its introduction to the English novel the first governess heroine Jane Eyre.

6. Based on *Jane Eyre* by Charlotte Brontë, discuss the theme of her works and the image of women protagonists.

    A. Charlotte's works are all about the struggle of an individual consciousness towards self-realization, about some lonely and neglected young women with a fierce longing for love, understanding and a full happy life.

    B. All her heroines' highest joy arises from some sacrifice of self and some human weakness overcome.

    C. The image of women protagonists in her works mostly reflect the life of the middle-class working women, particularly governesses.

    D. Her works present a vivid realistic picture of the English society by exposing the cruelty, hypocrisy and other evils of the upper classes, and by showing the misery and suffering of the poor. Especially in *Jane Eyre*, she sharply criticizes the existing society, e.g. religious hypocrisy of charity institutions.

7. Make a comment on the plot of *Adam Bede*.

    Adam Bede is a novel of moral conflicts, showing the contest of personal desires, passions, temperament, human weaknesses and the claims of moral duty. The theme of social inequality is blended with a moralization typical of the author.

In the novel, the two pairs, Arthur and Hetty on the one hand, and Adam and Dinah on the other, are described in contrast to each other. The former couple are always thinking of their own interests without any consideration of others, while the latter pair endowed with high moral principles which guide their conduct for the good of others and of themselves. The novelist takes her side with the latter party.

8. Summarize the plot of *Vanity Fair*.

Vanity Fair focuses on the lives of two young women, Rebecca Sharp ("Becky") and Amelia Sedley ("Emmy"), and shows the life of the upper class in Britain in the early 19th century. The story of *Vanity Fair* begins with two clues, one of which is about Amelia Sedley, who is a good-natured, simple-minded young girl, of a wealthy London family; the other clue is about Rebecca Sharp, daughter of an art teacher and a French dancer, a strong-willed, cunning, moneyless young woman determined to make her way in society. They left school in 1813. Both married two British officers who were about to participate in the Battle of Waterloo regardless of their families' opposition in 1815. Shortly after the wedding, the historic battle began. Amelia Sedley's husband died on the battlefield, and Becky Sharp's husband survived. In the following ten years, Rebecca Sharp's life was smooth and she was even lucky to meet the king, while Amelia Sedley suffered great misfortune because of her father's bankruptcy. In 1827, their fate was reversed, Rebecca Sharp's life fell into the abyss of destruction owing to her crimes, while Amelia Sedley turned rich and happy.

9. Make a comment on William Makepeace Thackeray's masterpiece *Vanity Fair*.

Vanity Fair is William Thackeray's masterpiece, taking the title from the fair in Bunyan's *The Pilgrim's Progress*, where all sorts of cheats are displayed for sale. The novel presents a panorama of the society of the English upper-middle class of the first half of the 19th century. What is more important, none of his other novels can rival it in width of social life, and in depth of social criticism. The subtitle of the novel—*A Novel Without a Hero*—points to the author's intention to portray not individuals singly but the whole of the notorious "Vanity Fair", a name Thackeray gave English bourgeois and aristocratic society. Thackeray realistically paints a truthful picture of the fortunes and characters of the middle-class people in the middle of the nineteenth century. As the subtitle of the novel suggests, the story is neither with a plot nor a hero. Its whole action revolves two women, Amelia Sedley and Rebecca Sharp. With biting irony Thackeray exposes the vices of this society: hypocrisy, money-worship, and moral degradation. This accounts for the fact that the novel has very few positive characters.

10. Make a brief comment on Rebecca Sharp, the central figure of the novel *Vanity Fair*.

The central figure in the novel is Rebecca Sharp. She is a perfect embodiment of the spirit of Vanity Fair as her only aspiration in life is to gain wealth and position by any means: through lies, mean actions and unscrupulous speculating with every sacred ideal. Thackeray does not, however, regard her as an exception. Everyone wishes to gain something in the Vanity Fair and acts almost in the same manner as Becky. The character of Rebecca Sharp is drawn with admirable skill. She is full-blooded and many-sided. The unprincipled adventurer is a gifted woman, with a keen sense of humor and deep understanding of people. Cringing to the rich and titled snobs, clever Rebecca at the same time perceives how shallow, vain and worthless they are.

11. Summarize the three periods of Charles Dickens's literary career.

The first period of Charles Dickens's literary career is referred to those years from 1836 to 1841. It is marked for youthful optimism. Charles Dickens believed that all the evils of the capitalist world would be remedied if only men treated each other with kindliness, justice and sympathetic understanding. He thought that the whole social question would be solved if only every employer reformed himself according to the model set by the benevolent gentlemen in his novels and if only the rich used their power and wealth sympathetically to assist the poor to escape from poverty. This naive optimism is the characteristic of the petty-bourgeois humanitarians of his time.

His main works written in this period are *The Pickwick Papers, Oliver Twist, Nicholas Nickleby* and *The Old Curiosity Shop.*

The second period of his literary career began from 1842 and ended in 1850. It was a period of excitement and irritation. In this period, Dickens made a trip to America. Before the visit, he thought of the United States as a world in which there were no class division and human relations were humanitarian. But what impressed him most during his visit there was the rule of the dollar and the enormously corruptive influence of wealth and power. Vulgar selfishness, which prevailed everywhere, concealed the fine qualities of the people. Dickens's naive optimism toward the capitalist society was profoundly shaken. His main works produced in this period are *American Notes, Martin Chuzzlewit, Dombey and Son* and *David Copperfield.*

The third period of his literary career refers to the period from 1851 to 1870. Charles Dickens's works in this period show intensifying pessimism. "Dickens, consciously and subconsciously, shows himself more and more at odds with bourgeois society and more and more aware of the absence of any readily available alternative." His main novels produced in this period are *Bleak House, Hard Times, Great Expectations, A Tale of Two Cities*, and *Our Mutual Friend.*

12. Make a brief comment on Charles Dickens's fictional art.

Of Dickens's fictional art, the most distinguished feature is his successful characterization. Charles Dickens had good skills in story-telling. With his well worked-out plots, Dickens displays great skills in the handling of the broad and intricate construction, in giving to his characters exactly the actions and words that fit them in their positions in life and in their given environment, and in his successful use of irony or obvious exaggeration to achieve the penetrating effect of satire. It is all proper to say that Dickens is a great master in the development of English literature.

Dickens liked to use sudden discovery technique in his novels. With this sudden discovery, he usually ended his novels with relative happy scenes. He always tried to soften the problems and wished for reforms rather than revolution.

13. Based on *Oliver Twist*, how does Charles Dickens express his humanitarian thought?

Oliver Twist is a good example to show Dickens's wish for a better society. He uses this novel to publicize the kind and the beautiful nature of mankind. He also believes in benevolence. The benevolent people always hope to create a harmonious life by helping the miserable and the pitiable. He seems to criticize the thieves and robbers on the surface, but he is actually criticizing the environment that made them. One can also find that Dickens advocates that both the kind and the evil get their due fate. Also, he prefers comic ending to tragic ending. In telling the story of Harry Maylie and Rose Maylie, Dickens seems to tell the readers that love can turn a wastrel son or a prodigal not only to a good man but also a divine minister. In this novel, one can also learn something about the heritage system, which can also foster evil ideas and behavior in the case of Monks. He gives a sympathetic description of even a street girl named Nancy, which shows Dickens's humanitarian viewpoint.

14. What contribution does Robert Browning make to the English poetry?

The greatest contribution of Robert Browning to English poetry is his skillful and unmatched use of dramatic monologue. A dramatic monologue is a poem in which a speaker, clearly separate from the poet, speaks to a mock listener, or an implied audience who does not speak but seem to be clearly present in the scene so that he or she triggers the speaker to talk. By using this technique, Browning created different types of character and displayed the psychology of all sorts of people. The dramatic monologue used by Alfred Tennyson and others tends to be talking to oneself. But in Browning's dramatic monologue, the speaker does not speak to himself, but to the mock listener in the poem rather than the reader. The mock listener is always the trigger of the monologue, or a kind of hidden dialogue. One can always feel the presence and existence of the mock listener. In this way, the speaker becomes the independent person rather than the poet himself. So Browning's dramatic monologue is an objective form of drama with a purpose of characterization rather than expressing the poet's feeling or sentiment.

15. What are the characteristics of George Eliot's novels?

    Characteristics of George Eliot's novels are as follows:

    A. Her novels, for the most part, describe rural life, deal with moral problems and contain psychological studies of the characters.

    B. She has rich humor and keen observation, and her characters are real men and women of her time. She writes very faithfully about the rural artisans, farmers, the country clergy, and other native people, and she fully realizes that the working people like Adam Bede and Silas Marner are much better than the landed aristocracy.

    C. Her novels are very philosophical. The philosophy she preached is idealistic. She believes that all contradictions of social life can be solved by converting mankind to the religion of humanity.

    D. With her the transition from critical realism to naturalism began in English literature.

16. Make a brief comment on *Wuthering Heights*.

    Wuthering Heights is Emily Brontë's only novel. This novel alone has attracted one generation of readers after another because it touched upon the utmost intensity of human feeling and sentiment.

Wuthering Heights is a symbolic novel combining the techniques of realism, romanticism and symbolism. Through a series of vivid plots and symbolic descriptions, the novel creates a lot of peculiar characters and writes about the daily life, love and marriage in the English countryside. Besides, the novel uses a lot of symbolic techniques such as use of dream and the supernatural. The description of nature is very important in this novel in that the exterior nature expresses the inner nature of humanity. In some places of the novel, the author uses quite romantic techniques to delineate the love of the hero and the heroine.

This novel has also become an example of the Gothic novel. The description of the natural scenes and the human passions are both scaring and terrifying.

17. Why is Jane Eyre one of the most popular characters for the contemporary readers? Make a brief comment on her.

People like the character of Jane Eyre for the following reasons. She is plain-looking and ordinary, but she has a good personality, a sense of dignity and real love. She would rather go away than remain as a mistress. But when obstacle was removed after Mrs. Rochester died, she resolutely married the disabled Rochester. So she is noble. She is true to her own emotion, faithful to her feeling, constant in her love, resolute in her decision. To her, love, dignity and virtue are of the utmost importance. If she had married Rochester regardless of the fact that Rochester's wife was still alive though mad, her image would have been greatly harmed. If she had followed St. John Rivers to India, she would never have been so praised for her pure love of Rochester. She never based her decisions on economic status. She is not poor in her later life because she inherited a fortune big enough for her, but she is always generous enough to share her inheritance. This is hard enough for a poor girl to choose and pursue. *Jane Eyre* has great appeal to readers. It successfully created the first woman character who takes an independent and freedom-seeking attitude toward love, life and society.

18. Make a brief comment on the characteristics of Alfred Tennyson's poetry.

Characteristics of Alfred Tennyson's poetry can be summarized as follows: Tennyson has a total mastery of the sounds and rhythms of the English Language. Tennyson has a genius for evoking moods and states of mind in his poems. He is able to create a sense of nostalgia, a wistful longing for the past or for remote experiences. No English poet surpasses Tennyson in linking descriptions of nature or setting to state of mind. Some of his poems deal with the main political, religious and scientific issues of his day. His poems reflect his conservative ideas and idealization of the bourgeois social reality.

19. Summarize the four phrases of Matthew Arnold's career as a writer.

Arnold's career as a writer may be divided roughly into four phases.

Most of his poems appeared during the 1850s: a volume entitled *The Strayed Reveller and Other Poems* (1849) was followed by additional volumes in 1852 and 1853.

During the 1860s the focus of his writing shifted from poetry to literary and social criticism. In 1865 the first series of his *Essays in Criticism* was published, and in 1869, *Culture and Anarchy*, a fierce attack on middle-class materialism and narrow-mindedness, considered by many to be his finest work.

In the 1870s Arnold devoted himself mainly to writing about education and religion.

Finally, in the 1880s he returned to literary criticism and wrote the second series of his *Essays in Criticism*, published soon after his death in 1888.

20. What are the characteristics of William Makepeace Thackeray's novels?

   A. Just like Charles Dickens, William Makepeace Thackeray was one of the greatest critical realists of the 19th-century Europe. He paints life as he has seen it. With his precise and thorough observation, rich knowledge of social life and of the human heart, the pictures in his novels are accurate and true to life. He is good at describing the life of the upper class which he is familiar with.

   B. William Makepeace Thackeray is a satirist. His satire is caustic and his humor subtle.

   C. Besides being a realist and satirist, William Makepeace Thackeray is a moralist. His aim is to produce a moral impression in all his novels.

21. Summarize the plot of *Adam Bede*.

   Adam Bede, a local carpenter much admired for his integrity and intelligence, is in love with Hetty. She is attracted to Arthur Donnithorne, the local squire's charming grandson and heir, and falls in love with him. When Adam interrupts a tryst between them, Adam and Arthur fight. Arthur agrees to give up Hetty and leaves Hayslope to return to his militia. After he leaves, Hetty Sorrel agrees to marry Adam but, shortly before their marriage, discovers that she is pregnant. In desperation, she leaves in search of Arthur but cannot find him. Unwilling to return to the village on account of the shame and ostracism she would have to endure, she delivers her baby with the assistance of a friendly woman she encounters. She subsequently abandons the infant in a field but not being able to bear the child's cries, she tries to retrieve the infant. However, she is too late, the infant having already died of exposure.

   Hetty is caught and tried for child murder. She is found guilty and sentenced to hang. Dinah enters the prison and pledges to stay with Hetty until the end. Her compassion brings about Hetty's contrite confession. When Arthur Donnithorne, on leave from the militia for his grandfather's funeral, hears of her impending execution, he races to the court and has the sentence commuted to transportation. Ultimately, Adam and Dinah, who gradually become aware of their mutual love, marry and live peacefully with his family.

22. Summarize the plot of *Wuthering Heights*.

   In 1801, Mr. Lockwood, the new tenant at Thrushcross Grange in Yorkshire, pays a visit to his landlord, Heathcliff, at his remote moorland farmhouse, Wuthering Heights. Mr. Lockwood has a nightmare in which a ghostly Catherine begs to enter through the window. Later Lockwood's housekeeper Ellen "Nelly" Dean tells him the story of the strange family.

   Thirty years earlier, the Earnshaws live at Wuthering Heights with their children, Hindley and Catherine, and a servant—Nelly herself. Returning from a trip to Liverpool, Earnshaw brings home a young orphan whom he names Heathcliff; Earnshaw treats the boy as his favorite. Hindley hates Heathcliff, who gradually becomes close friends with Catherine. Hindley becomes the new master of Wuthering Heights on the death of his father later. Hindley and Edgar make fun of Heathcliff; a fight ensues. Heathcliff is locked in the attic and vows revenge. When Catherine becomes engaged to Edgar, Heathcliff misunderstands Catherine's heart and flees the household.

   Later Heathcliff unexpectedly returns, now a wealthy gentleman. He encourages Isabella's infatuation with him as a means of revenge on Catherine. At Wuthering Heights Heathcliff gambles with Hindley who mortgages the property to him to pay his debts. When Heathcliff discovers that Catherine is dying, he visits her in secret. She dies shortly after giving birth to a daughter, Cathy, and Heathcliff rages, calling on her ghost to haunt him for as long as he lives. Isabella flees south where she gives birth to Heathcliff's son, Linton. Cathy and Linton (respectively at the Grange and Wuthering Heights) gradually develop a relationship. When Linton dies, Cathy has no option but to remain at Wuthering Heights.

Lockwood learns that Cathy and Hareton plan to marry and move to the Grange. Joseph is left to take care of the declining Wuthering Heights. Nelly says that the locals have seen the ghosts of Catherine and Heathcliff wandering abroad together, and hopes they are at peace.

23. Make a brief comment on the Chartist literature.

The working-class literature is represented largely by the Chartist literature.

The Chartist Movement appeared in the thirties of the 19th century. It developed rapidly. It showed that the English workers were able to appear as an independent political force and were already realizing the fact that the industrial bourgeoisie was their principal enemy. During the Chartist Movement, numerous Chartist organizations published newspapers and magazines, which contained poems, short stories and essays. The Chartist writers introduced a new theme into literature—the struggle of the proletariat for its rights. They proclaimed that the struggle between the proletariat and the ruling classes was irreconcilable, and they expressed firm belief in the ultimate victory of the suffering people. The heroic and revolutionary Chartist poetry played an important role in the development of English proletarian literature in connection with the working-class movement. The greatest of Chartist poets was Ernest Jones. Next to him were Thomas Hood, and Thomas Cooper.

In 1864 the First International was formed in London. Under the leadership of Carl Marx and Friedrich Engels, the working-class movement developed quickly.

24. Make a brief comment on Christina Rossetti's works.

Christina Rossetti's works range from poems for children to love lyrics, sonnets and religious poetry. Her poetry is remarkable for its simplicity and singing quality. The recurring theme in her love poems is the unhappy or frustrated love. Her religious poetry often shows a strong sense of duty. Frequently suffering from ill health, Christina wrote poetry that was often melancholy and concerned with thoughts of death. However, she could also be sprightly and fanciful in her writing.

Part IX

The 20th Century: Transition from the 19th to the 20th Century Before 1945

I. Fill in the Blanks.

1. Rudyard Kipling
2. realistic; anti-realistic
3. art for art's sake
4. propertied
5. modernist
6. *Far from the Madding Crowd*
7. *Tess of the D'Urbervilles*; *Jude the Obscure*
8. sexual desire
9. *The Dynasts*
10. *A Pure Woman Faithfully Presented*

11. separate
12. Fabian Society
13. paradox
14. prefaces
15. Napoleon
16. *My Fair Lady*
17. marriage; reconciliation
18. Anglo-Norman
19. Irish National
20. Romantic; rhythms
21. Modernist
22. criticism
23. bourgeois
24. justice; poor; loser
25. immorality; aestheticism; obscurity
26. inner lives
27. impressionistic; poetic
28. comparison
29. stream of consciousness
30. Feminism
31. James Joyce
32. *Dubliners*
33. artist; society
34. actual language
35. narrator
36. mother; distorted
37. sexual relationships
38. patriotism

39. *The Waste Land*
40. logical continuity
41. poetic drama
42. dramatic monologue
43. imagination
44. the ills; religious themes
45. forms; meters
46. symbolism; surrealism
47. death
48. Angel Clare
49. Fabian Society
50. James Joyce
51. David Herbert Lawrence
52. *The Picture of Dorian Gray*
53. *The Picture of Dorian Gray*
54. *Under the Greenwood Tree*
55. *Jude the Obscure*
56. aestheticism
57. October
58. Henry James
59. David Herbert Lawrence
60. John Galsworthy
61. Soames Forsyte
62. *Heartbreak House*
63. *The Quintessence of Ibsenism*
64. *The Apple Cart*
65. *Too True to Be Good*
66. Rupert Brooke
67. Virginia Woolf
68. James Joyce
69. Virginia Woolf
70. *The Waves*
71. *Strife*
72. *The Man of Property*
73. *Ulysses*
74. *Ash Wednesday*
75. *Candida*
76. *Saint Joan*

II. Choose the Best Answer for Each Question.

1-5   B C A C B
6-10   A A B C D
11-15 B B A C C
16-20 D A B A A
21-25 D C A A C
26-30 D B C D B
31-35 B C C B A
36-40 D A B A C
41-45 C A A B C
46-49 C B A D

III. Match-Making

Group One
1-6   b d a c f e

Group Two
1-8　e c a b d h f g
Group Three
1-8　c e a h b g d f
Group Four
1-8　f c a b d g h e

IV. Define the Literary Terms.

1. Stream of consciousness

   It is the style of writing that attempts to imitate the natural flow of a character's thoughts, feelings, reflections, memories, and mental images as the character experiences them.

2. Aestheticism

   Aestheticism (also the Aesthetic Movement) is an intellectual and art movement supporting the emphasis of aesthetic values more than social-political themes for literature, fine art, music and other arts. It was particularly prominent in Europe during the 19th century, but contemporary critics are also associated with the movement. In the 19th century, it was related to other movements such as symbolism or decadence represented in France.

3. Modernism

   Modernism is a philosophical movement that, along with cultural trends and changes, arose from wide-scale and far-reaching transformations in Western society in the late 19th and early 20th centuries. Modernism includes the activities and creations of those who felt the traditional forms like art, architecture and literature, were becoming ill-fitted to their tasks and outdated in the new environment of an emerging fully industrialized world.

   A notable characteristic of modernism is self-consciousness and irony concerning literary and social traditions with the use of techniques that drew attention to the processes and materials used in creation. Modernism explicitly rejects the ideology of realism and makes use of the works of the past by the employment of reprise, incorporation, rewriting, recapitulation, revision and parody.

4. Naturalism

   Naturalism was a literary trend prevailing in Europe, especially in France and Germany, in the second half of the 19th century. According to the theory of naturalism, literature must be "true to life" and exactly reproduce real life, including all its details without any selection. Naturalist writers usually write about the lives of the poor and oppressed, or the "slum life", but by giving all the details of life without discrimination, they can only represent the external appearance instead of the inner essence of real life. However, some of the best naturalistic novels may approach or even become forceful realistic literature because naturalism, in reality, is a development of realism. This may be shown by the works of Emile Zola, the French novelist and the master of modern naturalism. George Gissing is one of the English novelists who wrote under the influence of naturalism.

5. Imagism

   Imagism was an Anglo-American poetic movement flourishing in the 1910s. Its program was formulated about 1912 by the American poet, Ezra Pound, who wrote: "An Image is that which presents an intellectual and emotional complex in an instant of time." In 1915, Richard Aldington, the English poet and novelist, gave another definition of Imagism. So the Imagist poetry is a kind of vers libre (i.e. free verse) shaking off the conventional meters and emphasizing on the use of common speech, new rhythms and clear images. It owed something to Walt Whitman, the American poet who wrote *Leaves of Grass*, and was influenced by the French Symbolist movement. "Whereas Symbolism had an affinity with music, Imagism sought analogy with sculpture", aiming at a "hard and dry" clarity and precision in representing natural objects and ideas. Leading Imagist poets, besides Pound and Aldington, were Hilda Doolittle and Amy Lowell of America, and Thomas Ernest Hulme and Frank Stuart Flint of England. Then the movement soon broke up. But it left a notable impact on the development of both English and American poetry.

V. Answer the Following Questions Briefly.

1. What are William Butler Yeats's four phases of his literature career?

   The four phases of William Butler Yeats's literature career are as follows.

   A. The first phase began from 1889 to 1899. During this period, he lived and wrote in London, as a member of a movement. Their literary purpose was to create beauty in art for its own sake. Yeats became one of the founders of the Rhymers' Club, a group of disciples of Walter Pater.

   B. The second phase began from 1899 to 1909. This is a period of drama to Yeats. Lady Gregory asked him to help establish the Irish National Theater. He did help in writing for the theater, which produced original plays of Irish people and Irish history.

   This was part of the cultural revival accompanying the pressure for national independence. During this period, Yeats mainly wrote poetic drama for the theater.

   C. The third phase was from 1910 to 1918. In his late forties and early fifties, his poetry began to change. He refocused his attention to poetry and its techniques. He was then influenced by the contemporary poets Ezra Pound and T. S. Eliot, beginning to write less romantic and less sensuous poetry. Yeats's style grew more colloquial, reproducing the patterns of ordinary speech. His marriage to Georgie Hyde-Lees in 1917 changed his style again. She wrote whatever came to her mind without any conscious effort to shape the words into a composition. From such natural writings and other sources in occult literature, Yeats began to develop a great historical, mythical, and psychological system that was to provide the set of symbols that dominate his mature poetry.

D. The fourth phase was from 1919 to 1939. This is his mature period. During this phase, he used a set of interlocking symbols—the spiral, the tower, the cycles of motion—that he integrated into a quasi-historical framework for his poetic ideas. Most critics say that he produced his best poems during this period. It is also during this period that he received the Nobel Prize in 1923.

2. Talk about the content and theme of *The Waste Land*.

The Waste Land itself is a desolate and sterile country ruled by an impotent king. The whole poem is divided into five parts: I. "The Burial of the Dead," representing the stirring life in the land after the barren winter; II. "The Game of Chess," contrasting the splendors of the past represented by Cleopatra with uneasiness and despair of modern life; III. "The Fire Sermon," making an imaginative silhouette sketch of the ugliness of cities and the mechanization of modern life and emotion; IV. "Death by Water," presumptively proving in the vision of a drowned Phoenician sailor that water is not only the constructive source of life but also the destructive source of death because of drowning and its absence, which causes drought; and V. "What the Thunder Said," presenting a picture through symbols of the Grail legend, of the drought, the decay and emptiness of modern life.

The theme of the poem is modern spiritual barrenness, the despair and depression that followed World War I, the sterility and turbulence of the modern world, and the decline and break-down of Western culture.

3. Talk about your opinion about heroine Tess in *Tess of the D'Urbervilles*.

Though fateful circumstances and tragic coincidences abound in the novel, though the life of Tess involves a number of accidental events which seem to be decisive to her tragedy, like her father's discovery of their kindred with the noble D'Urberville family, yet the real causes of her tragedy lie in, as seen in the story, the wicked nature and hypocritical morality of the bourgeois society.

Tess, who is well characterized, is a victim of the social changes, and a woman of good nature as suggested by the subtitle of the novel: *A Pure Woman Faithfully Presented*. When she is away from the patriarchal mode of life, her sweet-natured mind, innocence, simplicity, and diligence could not prevent herself from being ruined in the circumstances of bourgeois city-civilization. In characterizing Tess, who is victimized by bourgeois morality and social injustice, Thomas Hardy vividly depicts the process in which she turns from a simple and naive girl to a woman who commits supposedly criminal or immoral actions, with a motive to display that her seeming degeneration is the consequence of not only her poor economic condition but the suppression as well as exploitation from which she suffers morally, physically, and spiritually. Among the English novels of critical realism, the novel stands out for its deep sympathy for the simple rural folk, and for its searing exposition and condemnation of the social injustice and bourgeois morality.

4. Tell the story of *Jude the Obscure*.

Jude and his cousin Sue, who both have unhappy marriage, fall in love with each other, but they soon find it impossible to enjoy real happiness in life, though they live together. Their relationship makes it impossible for Jude, a promising and ambitious youth, to become a priest, nor possible to find a job, for they are prejudiced everywhere because they fail to get legally married. The unexpected difficulties in life and the tragic death of their children lead to their hopelessness over the love and happiness they pursue. In the long run Sue returns to her husband to bear with her earlier suffering, whereas Jude is enticed to go back to his wife though they never love each other. The miserable death of Jude brings an end to the story.

5. Tell the story of *The Man of Property*.

The central figure in *The Man of Property* is Soames Forsyte, who is "the man of property". At the opening scene, Soames has already married Irene, a girl eight years his junior. Irene is young and beautiful. She loves art and cherishes noble ideas of life. But Soames does not pay the slightest attention to her thoughts and feelings, regarding her merely as a piece of his own property. So Irene is very unhappy. Later Soames asks an architect called Bosinney to build a country house for him. In the process of designing and building the house, Irene and Bosinney become more and more attracted to each other because they have a common interest in art. Soon rumors arise. In order to have his revenge on Bosinney, Soames sues him at the court for spending more money than stipulated. The triangular relationship of Soames, Irene and Bosinney ends in the tragic death of Bosinney, who is run over by a car in a London fog. Irene returns to Soames's house, but not to Soames. Soames wins but an empty triumph. In dealing with this story, the author takes the side of Irene and Bosinney, showing much sympathy for them, describing them as people beyond the pale of the practical, money-making world of the Forsytes, as rebels who share a common belief in art and beauty and are engaged in a common struggle against the stifling atmosphere of the bourgeois world. At the same time John Galsworthy seems to blame Soames for extending his sense of property not only to the physical but also to the spiritual possession of his wife, and for using the dirty trick of revenge on his rival by suing him at court. In doing so, John Galsworthy lays bare the oppressive nature of the bourgeois property instinct, and criticizes its sense of property because it stifles the natural and justifiable human desire for art and beauty.

6. Make a comment on John Galsworthy.

John Galsworthy is one of the important English critical realist writers of the 20th century. His works give a comprehensive picture of contemporary England. His satire and criticism are directed especially at the propertied class. Exposing the well-to-do and diagnosing the social disease, he penetrated into the subtlest windings of the human heart and drew human passions with psychological depth yet his criticism of the bourgeoisie was limited to the spheres of ethics and aesthetics only. Being conservative at heart, he suggested no remedies to the social disease. He aimed to improve his class wishing it could retain its ruling position in society. His works show a touch of fatalism and a growing sympathy for the class from which he sprang. His bourgeois conservatism is particularly evident in the works written after World War I and the October Revolution. Facing the crisis of British imperialism and the growing forces of socialism, John Galsworthy began to idealize the decadent bourgeoisie. This is particularly evident in his last trilogy *The End of the Chapter.*

In art he learned much from the French realists and the Russian realists in particular, of the 19th century.

John Galsworthy is a great stylist. His style is remarkable for its strength and elasticity, for its powerful sweep, brilliant illustrations and deep psychological analysis. Everything he touches upon seems to reflect the feelings of the heroes and his power of depicting their fiercest passion is exceptional. His language is concise and exact.

7. Make a comment on George Bernard Shaw.

A. George Bernard Shaw was a critical realist writer. His dramatic works bitterly criticize and attack the English bourgeois society. He tears away the mask of capitalism and deeply exposes the social conflicts.

B. His plays deal with contemporary social problems. He portrays his situations frankly and honestly intending to shock his audiences with a new view of society. He presents many of his characters as fools. He believes in the power of human reason what he called the "Life Force"—to cut through all pretense in the end. In their realism and wit, his plays are largely comedies of ideas in the French dramatist tradition of Moliere and mark a turning to realism and naturalism that is increasingly to dominate British drama.

C. George Bernard Shaw is a humorist. He manages to produce amusing and laughable situations. He delights in ridiculing, upsetting, scandalizing and astonishing his public.

The humor of George Bernard Shaw always has a touch of satire—a sharp social lash that he uses with superb skill for exposing and discrediting vice or folly of the age.

8. Make a brief comment on *Sons and Lovers*.

Sons and Lovers is a semi-autobiographical novel written by David Herbert Lawrence. It is based on Lawrence's early life in the Midland coal-mining village of Eastwood which is called Bestwood in the novel. The novel tells the story of a coal miner's family with the third child Paul as the central character. It is the first novel in the history of English literature that has a truly working-class background. Paul's father, Mr. Morel, is a miner who is driven to drunkenness by the bad working conditions. Paul's mother, Mrs. Morel, is a sensitive and high-minded woman and she is better-educated than her husband. Mrs. Morel's dream is smashed by the surroundings of poverty, heavy labor, illiteracy and her husband's habit of heavy drinking. So she devotes her entire love to her four children, especially for her two eldest sons William and Paul. After William dies of pneumonia, Mrs. Morel turns her whole attention to Paul. Meanwhile Paul also devotes his emotions to his mother. When Paul is on intimate terms with Miriam, Mrs. Morel is filled with resentment and jealousy lest Miriam should possess Paul's entire emotions. And in Paul's heart, there is always a conflict between the two kinds of love—the love for Miriam and the love for his mother. Tired of Miriam's pure spiritual love, Paul turns to Clara, a woman worker who has separated from her husband. Again Paul is dropped into a difficult position of dissensions and contradictions since pure physical warmth cannot bring about long-term happiness for him. He soon gets tired of Clara and later she returns to her husband. Mrs. Morel's death is a sort of release to Paul. But still he refuses to marry Miriam, because he thinks marriage is somewhat a bondage. The novel ends with Paul's drifting away on the sea of life.

The novel certainly reflects the problems of Lawrence's young age. It is taken as a typical example and lively manifestation of Oedipus Complex in fiction, as the result of Lawrence's long-range study of psychoanalytic theories of Sigmund Freud. But the theme of the novel is usually said to concern the effect of maternal love on the development of a son. The didactic elements in the novel and the looseness in structure are often criticized by some critics.

9. What are the characteristics of Thomas Hardy's novels?

Characteristics of Thomas Hardy's novels are as follows:

A. The underlying theme of his writing is the struggle of man against the mysterious force which rules the world and brings misfortune into his life and predetermines his fate.

B. This fatalism is strongly reflected in his writings.

C. In his works the strong elements of naturalism is combined with a tendency towards symbolism. These defects spoil the main realistic effect of his art.

D. Hardy has a strong sense of humor and often describes nature with charm and impressiveness.

10. What do you know about George Bernard Shaw's literary ideas?

George Bernard Shaw held that art should serve social purposes by reflecting human life, revealing social contradictions and educating the common people. Being a drama critic, George Bernard Shaw directed his attacks on the neo-Romantic tradition and the fashionable drawing-room drama. His criticism was witty, biting, and often brilliant. George Bernard Shaw was strongly against the credo of "art for art's sake" held by those decadent aesthetic artists. In his critical essays, he condemned the "well made" but cheap, hollow plays which filled the English theater of the late 19th century to meet the low taste of the middle class.

11. Make a comparison between Tess in *Tess of the D'Urbervilles* and Lu Sifeng in *Thunderstorm* (雷雨).

There are both similarities and differences between the two characters. Their similarities are as follows:

A. They are all innocent girls and work hard to provide for themselves and their families. Born in poor families, they are doomed to be in low social status that is disadvantaged in that environment, which is the starting point of their tragedy. With little education, they have to work for rich families as servants.

B. They are all victims of patriarchal society. In this environment, women are regarded as possession of men. They should obey their fathers' order and arrangement before they get married and then continue to follow their husbands after marriage. This notion causes a wrong sense of virginity and males' double-standard. Sifeng and Tess have a sexual relationship with Zhou Ping and Alec respectively. The former hopes to get married with Zhou who instead reduces Sifeng to a toy and discard her love. The latter believes that she does not deserve the love of her future husband Angel Clare for the loss of virginity and the result is that her husband refuses to accept her although he once lived a dissolute life.

There are also differences between them. Tess is braver to fight against her fate although she at last fails. From the perspective of humanism, however, she succeeds because she becomes a complete human-being that contains contradiction. Compared with Tess, Sifeng seems to be an embodiment of feudalism, which reflects the ruthlessness of feudal society.

12. Make a comment on Oscar Wilde.

   During the height of the prosperity that swept through London in the Victorian Era of the late 19th century, Oscar Wilde wrote rich and dramatic portrayals of the human condition. In his writings, he excelled in a variety of genres: as a critic of literature and of society, and also as a novelist, poet, and dramatist. His most outstanding achievements are his comedies, which were performed in London and New York from 1892 to 1895, including *Lady Windermere's Fan* (1892), *A Woman of No Importance* (1893), *An Ideal Husband* (1895), and *The Importance of Being Earnest* (1895) which is particularly successful.

   As a spokesman for aestheticism, Wilde had many gifts. He was an eloquent conversationalist and a master of paradoxical utterance. In addition, Wilde had the gifts of an actor who delighted in gaining attention.

   Oscar Wilde was making his criticism of the society in his own way, a way different from Charles Dickens and other writers. Oscar voiced his reaction against the high-minded, serious preoccupations of the middle class in Victorian England in the form of search for beauty. Oscar's satiric weapons were aimed against the aristocracy, a class on the verge of ruin, clinging absurdly to his artistic form and standards. He did not try to probe the economic and political problems. He and other aesthetic writers just showed what was wrong. Though his irony did not bring about any change, he, as well as others, was preparing the way for new directions in literature at the turn of the century.

13. Make a comment on Thomas Stearns Eliot.

   Thomas Stearns Eliot (1888-1965) was the leading writer in the English world in the first half of the 20th century. He was not only a great poet, an insightful critic, a fine playwright, but also he sought to become the conscience of his generation.

   As a poet, Eliot was above all an intellectual, one who had put much hard thinking into his verse and who demanded an equal amount of thought from the reader. He could encompass poignant feeling when he chose, but his habitual choice was to establish an exact equation between feeling and thought.

As a critic, he advocated new ideas. He was against the Romantic poetry, insisting that poetry was not turning loose of feeling. He turned to Renaissance poetry and drama for proper technique. It is he who helped to bring metaphysical poetry to intense public attention.

Thomas Stearns Eliot changed the direction of modern writing more sharply than any of his contemporaries did. He changed it in the direction of precision and complexity, and of wide-ranging reference, so that all of history is brought into his poetry. And he moved it toward deep but highly controlled emotion—emotion, as some of his poems imply, that is much too serious to be stated in consciously "poetic" language. In 1948 he was awarded the Nobel Prize in Literature.

14. Make a comment on David Herbert Lawrence.

David Herbert Lawrence, English author of novels, short stories, poems, plays, essays, travel books, and letters. His novels *Sons and Lovers* (1913), *The Rainbow* (1915), and *Women in Love* (1920) made him one of the most influential English writers of the 20th century.

David Herbert Lawrence was a controversial figure because of his frank treatment of sex and his outspoken insistence upon a need for a readjustment in the relationship between the sexes. Lawrence is often criticized for the didactic elements in his novels and the looseness in structure. The short stories he wrote are generally considered to be superior in unity of mood and artistic form.

Lawrence was innovative. He displayed the liberating effect of modernism. He felt free to give up the bondage of realism or critical realism in order to present narratives of the mind and feelings. The narration is freed from traditional ordinary chronological sequence to accommodate the movements of memory and mental pattern of association. The focus of the novel shifted from character's efforts to find their proper roles in society toward an illustration and an examination of states. The freedom of form in the new novel is so extended that they even include a more frank way of presenting sexual relations, which became intolerable to the public.

15. Make a comment on Virginia Woolf.

    Virginia Woolf, originally Virginia Stephen, was an English writer, considered one of the most important modernist 20th-century authors and a pioneer in the use of stream of consciousness as a narrative device.

    Virginia Woolf's greatest contribution to English literature is her use of the "stream of consciousness" technique. This technique is a means of exploring the inner life of the characters. This was rather a new or experimental technique of writing a novel at that time. The pen of the author follows the mind to any place, any person, anything and any time with great freedom. It makes good use of memory and imagination that external events or things or whatever remind the character of.

    Another contribution to the world literature is her concern with the position of women, which ushered the approach of feminism in literary criticism. She had fully noticed that the position of women should be enhanced and women's condition should be improved, especially professional women, and the constrictions they suffered under. She wrote several essays on the subject, notably in *A Room of One's Own* (1929).

16. Make a comment on James Joyce.

    James Joyce was one of the most influential and innovative writers of the 20th century. He is the author of the short story collection *Dubliners* (1914) and the novels *A Portrait of the Artist as a Young Man* (1916), *Ulysses* (1922), and *Finnegans Wake* (1939). He is known for his experimental use of language and exploration of new literary methods, including interior monologue, use of a complex network of symbolic parallels, and invented words, puns, and allusions in his novels.

He felt free to give up the constraints of realism or critical realism in order to present narratives of the mind and feelings. He aimed to give the readers a maze of conflicting and sometimes incoherent thoughts in a character's mind and consciousness. The narration is freed from traditional chronological sequence to accommodate the movements of memory and mental pattern of association. The focus of the novel shifted from character's efforts to find their proper roles in society toward an illustration and an examination of states.

17. Make an introduction of and a comment on *Mrs. Warren's Profession*.

The play *Mrs. Warren's Profession*, written in 1893, was published in 1898. In this play, George Bernard Shaw accuses the bourgeoisie of making profit by fostering prostitution. Mrs. Warren's profession is keeping brothels. Mr. Crofts is her partner in this business. Vivie, Mrs. Warren's daughter, was educated in a very moral atmosphere at a boarding school. On graduating, she returns home and by accident discovers the source of her mother's income. Her conversations with Mrs. Warren and Crofts reveal the cynicism of these members of the ruling class. It must be noted however, that while protesting strongly against bourgeois exploitation and the immorality of the ruling classes of England, Shaw does not point a way out. His heroine Vivie simply leaves her mother and, living independently, tries to earn her bread by honest work. Like Shaw, she is under the delusion that petty and gradual reforms will eventually do away with the evils of capitalism.

This play is a comedy for its witty dialogue and surprising turns of plot, but it does not have the conventional comic ending, for example, the marriage of the lovers and the reconciliation between generations. Its "happy" ending is more modern. Vivie embodies the idea of reforming of Shaw. She finds happiness in not being married and in being free of the duties of a daughter.

18. Make an introduction of and a comment on *A Room of One's Own*.

A Room of One's Own, written by Virginia Woolf, was published in 1929. In Woolf's opinion, to have a private room to think and write is a basic requirement for literary creation, a requirement that, along with economic independence, few women had ever enjoyed in history. After raising the question why women had not written first-class works, Woolf describes poverty, social pressures, family demands, and lack of education that prevented women from writing.

In this work, Woolf creates an imaginary figure, Judith Shakespeare, sister of the playwright Shakespeare, in order to make a comparison. Judith followed the steps of her brother Shakespeare's career. Woolf tries to show how a woman with similar talents would have still been thwarted and opposed. Judith, though mentally as powerful, would not have been sent to school. Instead, she would have been kept at home and betrothed to someone against her own will. If she had run away to avoid the marriage, she would still be in great difficulties and could not find a job in the theater in which there were no actresses then. Unable to survive alone, she would have to degrade herself by doing different things, good and bad, moral and immoral, until death.

This work concerned with the position of women, especially professional women, and the constrictions they suffered under. *A Room of One's Own* is still often popularized by the modern feminists.

19. Make a comment on *Ulysses*.

Ulysses, written by James Joyce, was published in 1922. The main strength of this novel lies in its depth of character portrayal and its breadth of humor. *Ulysses* broke entirely with traditional forms of the realistic novel. Joyce introduced and extended the "stream of consciousness" technique, in which a character presents an unbroken stream of thoughts, feelings, memories and reactions to the current action, with no description or explanation by a separate narrator.

Ulysses has no plot in the usual sense. It moves through a series of episodes, each revealing a pattern of presenting the cycles of life and death. The passage form morning to night suggests the complete and recurring pattern of human existence. This novel is comprehensive and encyclopedic when it focuses on the ordinary events of a single day.

Part X

The 20th Century: Contemporary Literature Since 1945

I. Fill in the Blanks.

1. social conflict; nature
2. Rhodesia; racial politics
3. classicism; politics
4. structured; flexible
5. bird
6. history
7. black; white
8. death
9. racial dilemma
10. frontier
11. *The Children of Violence*
12. single women
13. William Butler Yeats; Thomas Hardy
14. novelist
15. emotions; places; relationships
16. Christian
17. function
18. nature
19. monologue
20. Ireland
21. characters
22. *Digging*

II. Choose the Best Answer for Each Question.

1-5 A B D D A   6-10 D C D C D   11-13 B B A

III. Match-Making

Group One

1-4   b c d a
Group Two
1-4   b c d a
Group Three
1-4   d c a b

IV. Define the Literary Term.

1. Surrealism

    Surrealism was a cultural movement that began in the early 1920s, and is best known for its visual artworks and writings. The aim was to "resolve the previously contradictory conditions of dream and reality".

    Surrealist works feature the element of surprise, unexpected juxtapositions and non sequitur; however, many surrealist artists and writers regard their work as an expression of the philosophical movement first and foremost, with the works being an artifact.

V. Answer the Following Questions Briefly.

1. Make a comment on *The Grass Is Singing*.

    Doris Lessing's first novel *The Grass Is Singing* is a remarkable work. It is mercilessly penetrating and casts a spell all its own. It touches upon the question of black against white which broods over the land like thunder. But above all, it is the story of Mary Turner who is rather a victim of her character and psychology.

    To many readers, this novel is both an attractive chronicle of human disintegration and a beautifully understated social criticism. Mary Turner, a depressed woman and frustrated wife of an ineffectual, unsuccessful farmer, becomes desperate with the dull hard years. Her tragedy is brought about by her complex feeling with Dick and Moses. Her "love" with Moses is not a match. Their psychic tension explodes in an electrifying scene that ends this disturbing tale of racial strife in colonial South Africa. But in another sense, her death brings her freedom from depression and pain. In this sense, Moses is both a murderer and a savior.

2. Make a comment on Seamus Heaney.

In Seamus Heaney's early works, he is a lyrical nature poet, writing with limpid simplicity about the disappearing world of unspoiled rural Ireland. He was evocative yet clear, direct and balanced between the personal and the topical. His poetry is crafted and famous for its powerful images, meaningful content, musical phrasing, and compelling rhythms. His works often deal with "the local" things such as his surroundings and everything inclusive of them, namely, Ireland and particularly Northern Ireland. Hints of sectarian violence can be found in many of his poems. His works always have a sense of historicalness, deeply associated with the lessons of history, sometimes even prehistory. Many of his works concern his own family history and focus on characters in his own family, which can be read as elegies for those family members.

3. The 20th-century English writers fall into three groups. What are they?

Writers of this period fall into three groups.

A. The reactionaries who glorified imperialism and the decadent, whose chief traits were extreme individualism, pessimism and cynicism. The representative writer of this group is Rudyard Kipling.

B. The critical realists who continued and developed the traditions of critical realism. They sought for new ways and means of revealing the truth of life. In the works of these writers, criticism of the bourgeois world reaches considerable depth and poignancy. They condemned the capitalist order of things and uttered cries of suffering and protest. The representative writers of this group are

John Galsworthy, Herbert George Wells and George Bernard Shaw.

C. The progressive writers after the October Socialist Revolution, who were closely connected with the socialist movement of the people. The representatives are Ralph Fox and Robert Tressell.

4. Make a comment on Doris Lessing.

Doris Lessing (1919-2013), whose original name was Doris Taylor, was born in Iran. As a famous and excellent novelist, she produced many masterpieces such as *The Grass Is Singing*, *Children of Violence* and *The Golden Notebook*. She was the 11th female writer who was awarded the Nobel Prize in Literature.

During her long literary career, she wrote extensively and the themes of her works covered a lot of aspects of life. At the beginning of her writing, she attempted to solve the racial dilemma faced in Southern Rhodesia, a place where many of her writings set upon. With the increasingly widened horizon, her works covered various social, political and religious problems, influencing and modeling the life of men on earth. She was engaged in such topics as racialism, generation gap, women's liberation, sexual maladjustment in the early life. Doris Lessing's perception and strong mind was, to a large extent, closely associated with her frontier life in her childhood.

5. Make a comment on Philip Arthur Larkin.

Philip Arthur Larkin was an English poet, novelist, and librarian. He was associated with the writers of "the Movement", a group of young poets and novelists who took a sardonic and anti-romantic view of modern life. Writers of "the Movement" were concerned with creating a less intense and colloquial experience and the changes in everyday English life. Larkin had proved to be one of the best poets of this group.

His poems are marked by a very English, glum accuracy about emotions, places, and relationships, and are described as lowered sights and diminished expectations. He is widely regarded as one of the great English poets during the latter half of the twentieth century.

6. Make a comment on Ted Hughes.

Ted Hughes was an English poet, translator, and children's writer. Critics frequently rank him as one of the best poets of his generation and one of the twentieth century's greatest writers.

Looking at the dark aspects of nature, he stressed the ferocious and demonic rather than the idyllic and beautiful. Within the cruelty and violence of nature, Hughes looked for an understanding of human life and its mysterious bonds with nature.

His works are marked by a mythical framework, using the lyric and dramatic monologue to illustrate intense subject matter. Animals appear frequently throughout his work as deity, metaphor, persona, and icon. Perhaps the most famous of his subjects is "Crow," a mixture of god, bird and man, whose existence seems crucial to the knowledge of good and evil.

下编参考答案

Key to Exercises of Part Two

Exercise 1

1. B
2. Beowulf
3. This excerpt mainly talks about the people of Jutland composed a dirge praising the great deeds of Beowulf after his death.
4. In this story Anglo-Saxons poured out their full-hearted love for a ruler who fought for the good of the people fearing no difficulty and enemy. Even before Beowulf's death, he still thought about telling his successor how to rule and serve the people. He made a will that he would serve to guide people on their journey and voyages even after his death. From this story one can see the wishes of the English people for an able and kind ruler. After the great epics of Homer, namely, *Iliad* and *Odyssey*, *The Song of Beowulf* became the first monumental epic that was written in the vernacular language of a nation. It is the pride of national literature. And this is the most important reason why this work is never neglected in all anthologies of English literature.

Exercise 2

1. the ballad
2. *Robin Hood and Allin-a-Dale*
3. song; 4-line; rhymed; refrain
4. The character of Robin Hood is many-sided. Strong, brave and clever, he is at the same time tender-hearted and affectionate. His hatred for the cruel oppressors is the result of his love for the poor and downtrodden.
5. A. The ballads are in various English and Scottish dialects.
   B. They were created collectively and revised when handed down from mouth to mouth.

C. They are mainly the literature of the peasants, and give an outlook of the English common people in feudal society.
6. English ballads have a variety of themes: the struggle of young lovers against feudal families, the conflict between love and wealth, the cruel effect of jealousy, the border wars between England and Scotland, and matters of class struggle and so on.

Exercise 3

1. *The Canterbury Tales*
2. Geoffrey Chaucer
3. The Prologue
4. As Chaucer's masterpiece and one of the monumental works in English literature, the whole poem of *The Canterbury Tales* is a collection of stories strung together with a simple plan.

   On a spring evening, the poet, moved by the passion for wandering, drops himself at the south end of London Bridge. Here he meets nine and twenty other pilgrims ready for a journey of 60 miles on horseback to Canterbury. Chaucer joins this journey. At the suggestion of the host of the inn, they agree to beguile the journey by story-telling. Each is to tell two stories going and two returning. The best story-teller shall be treated with a fine supper at the general expense at the end. The host is to be the judge of the contest. According to the number of the persons in the company, it should be an immense work of 124 stories. Actually only 24 were written. These tales cover all the main types of medieval literature: courtly romance, folk tale, beast fable, story of travel and adventure, saint's life, allegorical tale, sermon, alchemical account, and others. All these tales but two are written in verse.

   Various in kind as these stories are, the poet succeeded in linking them together through two ways. The personality of the host affords a clear string of connection from the first to the last tale; he gives a unity to the whole work, inviting, criticizing, admiring, denouncing, but always keeping himself in evidence. Then there is an intimate connection between the tales and the Prologue, both of which complement each other. It is of great importance to read the corresponding portion of the Prologue with each tale in order to get a full dramatic, narrative and pictorial effect of the work.

5. *The Canterbury Tales* has its social significance in several ways. First, it represents the spirit of the rising bourgeoisie. People's right to pursue earthly happiness is affirmed by Chaucer. Second, the ideas of humanism are shown in Chaucer's praising of man's energy, intellect, wit and love of life. Third, Chaucer exposed and satirized the evils of the time. Fourth, the corruption of the Church is vigorously attacked. Fifth, Chaucer showed sympathy for the poor to some extent.

Exercise 4

1. *I Find No Peace*
2. Sir Thomas Wyatt; sonnet
3. paradoxes
4. Love that keeps no jail but yet imprisons me.

Exercise 5

1. *The Soote Season*
2. Henry Howard, Earl of Surrey
3. abab abab abab aa
4. A
5. Winter that was the flower's harm is now over.

6. 抬眼一片勃勃生机，一切的愁云都已散却，而悲哀却漫上我心头。

    This is a kind of comparison. The poet compared the beautiful scenery with his own sorrow, creating a strong contrast and emphasizing the frustrated feeling caused by personal emotional experience.

7. Some other Chinese poems on the same topic.

    白居易:《忆江南》
    苏轼:《蝶恋花·春景》
    杜甫:《春夜喜雨》
    朱熹:《春日》
    贺知章:《咏柳》
    张若虚:《春江花月夜》
    王维:《鸟鸣涧》
    高鼎:《村居》
    叶绍翁:《游园不值》

春日
［宋］朱熹
胜日寻芳泗水滨，无边光景一时新。
等闲识得东风面，万紫千红总是春。

This is a seven-character-quatrain mainly based on reasoning. In the poet's description, the spring is full of vigor, all things are revived, all the flowers are blooming, the world is a riot of color in spring. The poet praises the beautiful scene of spring, but also emphasizes that the "east wind" is the source of the colorful spring. East wind implies the profound and penetrating ideas of the Sage such as Confucius, only by pursuing the Sage's way, all things can have vigor and energy, and society can have peace and harmony, just as everything is colorful in the spring.

Both of the "春日" and *The Soote Season* depict the beautiful scenery of spring. "春日" is a seven-character-quatrain mainly based on reasoning. The poem cleverly encapsulates its reasoning in vivid metaphors and descriptions. In *The Soote Season*, the poet compares the beautiful scenery with his own sorrow, creating a strong contrast and emphasizing the frustrated feeling caused by personal emotional experience.

Exercise 6

1. *Amoretti*
2. Edmund Spenser
3. abab bcbc cdcd ee
4. Spenserian sonnet
5. It shows the author's deep love for his beloved and the importance of his beloved to him. In the poem, the poet compares his love journey to the journey of a ship by using three images: ocean, ship and bright star. His lady is important to him as a North Star to a wandering ship. Though a representative of the Renaissance, Spenser frequently uses alliteration in his poems, especially in this poem. Various sound effects, comparisons and vivid images make the poem both readable and enjoyable.

Exercise 7

1. Spenserian; abab bcbc cdcd ee
2. seashore, beach; for the second time, again; to die in dust
3. *The Faerie Queene*; *Amoretti*; *The Shepherd's Calendar*

Exercise 8

1. *The Nymph's Reply to the Shepherd*
2. Sir Walter Raleigh; *The Passionate Shepherd to His Love*

3. 4-line stanzas; aabb
4. No, the woman didn't accept the shepherd's invitation of being his lover, in the fifth stanza, the woman intensified her refutation by saying that "Thy belt of straw and ivy buds, / Thy coral clasps and amber studs, / All these in me no means can move / To come to thee and be thy love."
5. 只有叫青春常驻爱常留，
   叫欢乐无尽，老来没穷愁，
   这些高兴事才使我动心，
   使我与你同住，做你的情人。（黄杲忻 译）

Exercise 9

1. abab cdcd efef gg
2. Philip Sydney
3. What the poet is trying to reject is the earthly momentary love which many people pursue in their life. But the poem describes a love true and eternal in comparison with one "which reachest but to dust", and it is this love for whose sake the poet says farewell to the former kind of love.

Exercise 10

1. *The Faerie Queene*; Edmund Spenser
2. Spenserian stanza; iambic pentameter; iambic hexameter
3. Redcros
4. holiness, or more specifically, the Anglican Church or the patron saint of England
5. She symbolizes the truth of true religion.

Exercise 11

1. Francis Bacon
2. *Of Studies*
3. The language of this essay is peculiar for its clearness, brevity, and force of expression. The sentences are short, pointed, incisive, and often of balanced structure.

Exercise 12

1. Francis Bacon
2. *Of Studies*.
3. 读书使人充实，讨论使人机智，笔记使人准确。因此不常作笔记者须记忆特强，不常讨论者须天生聪颖，不常读书者须欺世有术，始能无知而显有知。读史使人明智，读诗使人灵秀，数学使人周密，科学使人深刻，伦理学使人庄重，逻辑修辞之学使人善辩。（王佐良 译）

Exercise 13

1. *The Passionate Shepherd to His Love*
2. pastoral; Christopher Marlowe
3. *The Nymph's Reply to the Shepherd*; Sir Walter Raleigh
4. The writer used alliteration. In the first sentence, the writer used alliteration connected "live" with "love"; in the second sentence, the writer used alliteration connected "we" and "will", "pleasure" and "prove".
5. It describes a shepherd's invitation to a girl by promising to give her all the pleasures nature can give.
6. With simple language and rich images, the poet displays the innocent happiness of the pastoral life, romantic and moving, though

not quite believable.

Exercise 14

1. *Hamlet*
2. William Shakespeare
3. Hamlet
4. "To be or not to be" means to live or to end one's life by self-destruction. Hamlet has already spoken of suicide as a means of escape, and he dwells on it in a later part of this very speech, giving, however, a different reason for refraining. The notion that in the words "or not to be" he is speculating on the possibility of "something after death"—whether there is a future life—cannot be entertained for a moment. The whole drift of the speech shows his belief in a future life.
5. It is a famous soliloquy by Hamlet. It reflects the inner conflict of Hamlet, a hero of the Renaissance and a representative of humanism. It also reflects the contradictions between thoughts and action, the ideal of a humanist and the sordid reality at that time.

Exercise 15

1. A
2. abab cdcd efef gg
3. The sonnet starts with a question "Shall I compare thee to a summer's day", develops the argument in three quatrains, and concludes with a final couplet that art, in the form of this sonnet, will bring eternity to his friend. It is a typical structure of Shakespeare's sonnets. The first quatrain raises a question or an argument; the second develops it; the third has a change in argument or mood;

while the final couplet gives a solution, thus settles the argument.
4. It follows the traditional theme for poetry in the Elizabethan Period, that is, poetry can bring eternity to the one he loves and eulogizes. Shakespeare's Sonnet 55 and 60, and Spenser's Sonnet 75 all reflect the same theme.

Exercise 16

1. Shakespearean
2. friendship
3. "State" in line 2 means the poet's rejected condition.
   "State" in line 10 means mental mood, state of mind.
   "State" in line 14 means condition and chair of state, throne.
4. joyful spirit, the higher it flies, the louder it sings
5. This poem praises the power of friendship and shows the poet's admiration for the young man in the poem. At the beginning of the poem, the poet feels dejected by his ignored condition and complains of his bad fate and the indifference of people. Then he becomes joyful when thinking of his friend. The poet uses many a poetic device such as rhymes, pun, repetition, contrast, to show the theme of his poem.

   Unlike Petrarchan tradition according to which sonnets are often written to a young lady and they use many rhetorical devices to praise her beauty or persuade her to seize the earthly happiness, this and most Shakespeare's sonnets, written to a male aristocrat, maybe his patron, adopt many conventions of love poetry to express his allegiance to the young man who is vital to his life.

Exercise 17

1. *Song: To Celia*
2. ballad; iambic
3. Ben Jonson; Ben
4. This is a patchwork of five separate prose passages in the *Epistles of Philostratus* by Philostratus, a Greek sophist (3rd century A.D.). Jonson reworded the phrases into this classic lyric. It has been set to music and considered one of the treasured love lyrics in the English language. The poet sings praise of Platonic love in the poem. It is famous for its fresh imagery of "eyes", "kiss" and "wreath". Here changing of eyes represents exchanging of love between lovers; lover's kiss is considered as a divine drink while a wreath of roses as the messenger of love.

Exercise 18

1. *Doctor Faustus*; Christopher Marlowe
2. Doctor Faustus
3. In portraying Doctor Faustus, Christopher Marlowe praises his soaring aspiration for knowledge while warning against the sin of pride.

Exercise 19

1. A
2. *A Valediction: Forbidding Mourning*; John Donne
3. serious and steady; the circumstances of its composition
4. The circle is an emblem of perfection.

Exercise 20

1. *To the Virgins, to Make Much of Time*; Robert Herrick
2. carpe diem; seizing the day; enjoying the pleasure of the moment without concerning about the future
3. Cavalier poetry is verses written by the Cavalier poets who were often courtiers siding with the king. Such poems are usually light, polished, elegant, amorous and gay, but often superficial. Most of them are short songs, madrigals and love fancies characterized by lightness of heart and of morals. Such poems are lighter and neater but less fresh than the Elizabethan's.
4. **劝少女们利用好时光**

   花开堪折直须折，
   时光老人总飞逝。
   今日花笑同一朵，
   明日笑容会消逝。

   太阳华灯天上悬，
   越近高处路越短。
   路程终点越临近，
   越见匆匆向西沉。

   青春年华最美好，
   血气方刚热情高。
   青春年华若虚度，
   剩余时光失美妙。

   故抓时间别羞怯，
   能得悦时及时悦。
   一旦错过好年华，
   千古遗憾悔成河。（李正栓 译）

Exercise 21

1. *Virtue*; George Herbert
2. Sweet day; Sweet rose; comparison; repetition
3. All things in the world, no matter how beautiful and lovely they are, are only short-lived and cannot avoid the fate of death in the end; Only noble virtues can last forever.

Exercise 22

1. *Paradise Lost*; John Milton
2. Satan; God; Raphael; Adam; Eve (任选三个)
3. Crown; parliament; Cromwell
4. Blank verse consists of unrhythmic five-stressed lines, properly, iambic pentameters. Blank verse is the one closest to rhythms of everyday English speech. So dramatists like to use this form for their works. Shakespeare wrote most of his plays in blank verse. By using it, the author can inspire the emotional waves and imagination. The poem is not subject to the constraints of flat tone, which can send out the most beautiful pictures and strongest sounds with the significance of the times.

Exercise 23

1. *The Constant Lover*; John Suckling; Cavalier poet
2. C

Exercise 24

1. *To Lucasta*, *Going to the Wars*; Richard Lovelace; Oxford
2. B

Exercise 25

1. *To His Coy Mistress*; Andrew Marvell
2. carpe diem; four-beat couplet
3. Marvell's poetry is playful, casual, and witty in tone, and always light on metrical feet and exact in diction, displaying depth and intellectual hardness in unexpected places. Its texture is extraordinarily rich.

Exercise 26

1. *The Pilgrim's Progress*; John Bunyan
2. Christian; Destruction; burden; Holy City; ten; Doubting Castle; Hopeful; Delectable Mountains of Youth; All Delight
3. John Bunyan's *The Pilgrim's Progress* can be said to be the first most influential one. Bunyan took material from the Bible and wrote to teach people what is good and what is bad, what people should do and what people should not do. In allegorical form, he criticized the evil and praised the kind. In some episodes he gave a realistic description of the evils existing in the society. His puritan ideas were fully displayed.

Exercise 27

1. *A Song for St. Cecilia's Day*; John Dryden; 3&4
2. England's poet laureate; 1688

Exercise 28

1. *Robinson Crusoe*; Daniel Defoe
2. Crusoe saved Friday from Cannibals
3. Defoe was a great realist and the charm of his novels is their intense sense of reality, which is embodied in succession of thoughts, feelings and incidents that are easily recognized to be credibly true to life. The sense of his realism is also well presented by his first-person narrating. As an accurate observer and story-teller, Defoe was able to give to his story the quality of factual truth from his observation of nature and society. Moreover, his strong imagination makes it possible for him to create his credible adventurous stories through the use of minute and matter-of-fact details. These distinctions of Defoe are best expressed in *Robinson Crusoe*.

Exercise 29

1. *Gulliver's Travels*; Jonathan Swift
2. Lilliput
3. C
4. A. It can create a sense of familiarity, so that the reader may easily believe the narrator's words. B. It can make the novel a story (let it have twists and turns). C. It can make the article more vivid.

Exercise 30

1. Sir Roger at Church; *The Spectator*
2. Sir Roger is a country gentleman, of old-fashioned manners, and of what were even then regarded by some as the old-fashioned virtues of simplicity, honesty and piety. His foibles, which are described with a gentle humor, make a setting for his virtues which point an example to the world of fashion. The reader comes to know him on his estate, in church, wooing his neighbor the widow, or visiting the strange sights of the city. The essays almost make a novel. At all events they create a character.

Exercise 31

1. *An Essay on Criticism*; Alexander Pope
2. C
3. Pope's poems often use "heroic double rhyme". Many of his words are neat, concise and philosophical, and some of his lines almost become maxims. His works were translated into the languages of many European countries.

Exercise 32

1. *The History of Tom Jones, a Foundling*; Henry Fielding
2. The central plot is to describe the life experience of abandoned child Tom Jones. Tom Jones was born out of wedlock and was abandoned soon after his birth. Later, he was adopted by gentleman Allworthy. Allworthy made Tom Jones fall in love with Sophia, the manor owner's daughter. Blifil was very jealous and tried to slander Tom Jones in front of his uncle Allworthy. So Tom Jones

was banished and wandered around. When he arrived in London, he was sent to prison for injuring a hooligan. Sophia's father forced Sophia to marry Blifil. Sophia disobeyed her father's orders and fled to London to find Tom Jones. Finally, the identity of Tom Jones was revealed. It turned out that he was the illegitimate son of Allworthy's respectable sister, and Blifil was his half brother. The book ends with Blifil's plot to persecute Tom Jones, who marries Sophia.

Exercise 33

1. *Elegy Written in a Country Churchyard*; Thomas Gray
2. melancholy; Romantic
3. Although Gray's life was placid, his poetry was venturesome. He inherited the old and started the new. Without discarding what was good in the old or neoclassic tradition, he explored new and unfamiliar areas in poetry. His use of personification, high-flown allusions, and conventional poetic diction are representative of his ties to the earlier style. He was different from Pope who reflected fashionable city taste. He started a fashion that influenced Wordsworth and other Romantic poets who modeled on Gray who turned to country life and humble people for inspiration. This was quite an important signal and transition. He dealt in honest and homely emotion and brought back into poetry the use of the first-person singular, considered a barbarism by 18th-century norms, which dictated suppression of the ego and concealment of emotion. This new tendency helped the later Romantic idea about the spontaneous overflow of human feeling. Not only Gray's treatment of nature, but also his interest in the past, in Celtic and Norse folklore and simple, primitive cultures, has been seen as a foreshadowing of themes that would find their fullest expression in the Romantic Movement of the 19th century.

Exercise 34

1. *The Vicar of Wakefield*; Oliver Goldsmith
2. Primrose; Squire; elder daughter; a lawsuit of Squire Thornhill; avenge his sister; Sir William Thornhill; the Squire's uncle
3. The author shows his sympathy for the family, and condemns Squire Thornhill, who stands for the cruelty, hypocrisy and moral degradation of the wicked feudal landlord and of the city bourgeoisie. But the solution for the righting of the social wrongs is not satisfactory, for the happy ending hints the existence of a good and benevolent landlord in the person of Sir William Thornhill whose righteous intervention alone can check the villainy of Squire Thornhill and restore the vicar's family to happiness. Goldsmith illustrates his view on morality. In his opinion, the good should be developed no matter how late it is. The evil will be found out sooner or later. Each kind deserves its fate.

Exercise 35

1. drama; *The School for Scandal*; Richard Brinsley Sheridan
2. gossips; scandal fair
3. D

Exercise 36

1. *The Tyger*; William Blake
2. B
3. six
4. A
5. The tiger symbolizes the power of the French Revolution. At that

time, the French revolutionary people drove out the feudal forces and foreign armed interveners symbolized by the "forests of the night". The vast revolutionary people were the "craftsmen" who shaped the tiger. The poem is filled with praise for the tiger and the hands and eyes molded into a tiger, that is, the poet's praise for the French revolutionary forces and revolutionary people.

6. 虎，虎，光焰灼灼
   燃烧在黑林之夜；
   怎样的神手和神眼
   构造出你可畏的美健。（卞之琳 译）

Exercise 37

1. *Mary Morrison*; Robert Burns
2. C

Exercise 38

1. *Scots, Wha Hae*; Robert Burns
2. 有谁想当临阵脱逃的叛徒？
   有谁想钻进胆小鬼的棺木？
   有谁愿做下贱无耻的奴仆？
   我放他一条生路！（晚枫 译）

Exercise 39

1. *The Flea*
2. B
3. metaphor

4. reasoning; lyrical; reasoning
5. carpe diem

Exercise 40

1. *Methought I Saw My Late Espoused Saint*
2. John Milton
3. abba abba cdc dcd
4. To Milton, the day without his wife is like the night, while the night with his wife is like the day. The reversed conception of day and night in the last line is a famous paradox, by which, Milton shows his great happiness in seeing his wife in his dream and his deep sorrow when losing her in reality.
5. 江城子·乙卯正月二十日夜记梦
   十年生死两茫茫。不思量，自难忘。千里孤坟，无处话凄凉。纵使相逢应不识，尘满面，鬓如霜。
   夜来幽梦忽还乡。小轩窗，正梳妆。相顾无言，惟有泪千行。料得年年肠断处，明月夜，短松冈。

Exercise 41

1. Robert Burns; ballad stanza
2. It may imply three meanings: the beauty of the flower, the beauty of the girl and deep love of the speaker toward his beloved. Besides, it is an expression of defamiliarization. It makes the image fresh.
3. In this poem, the image of rose embodies the traditional connotations of beauty, passion and love. Incorporating various elements from folk song, the poem is supposed to be a song sung by an Irish sailor to his sweetheart before his ship sailed off the sea. The ex-

aggerated declaration of love—"Till a' the seas gang dry, my dear, And the rocks melt wi' the sun", easily reminds us of the well-known Chinese love oath "海枯石烂". All in all, its pleasant lyrics, frisk rhythm and direct expression of love make this poem a masterpiece of love poetry.

Exercise 42

1. William Wordsworth
2. *I Wandered Lonely as a Cloud.*
3. emotion recollected in tranquility
4. cloud; daffodils
5. In this poem, William Wordsworth sings praise of the beauty of nature and its influence upon people. Key words like "joyful", "gay", "jocund" reflect the bliss that the happy scene in nature gives him. Wordsworth's poetic idea that "poetry should take its origin from emotion recollected in tranquility" is also shown in this poem.

Exercise 43

1. William Wordsworth
2. *The Solitary Reaper*
3. This poem describes vividly and sympathetically a young peasant girl working in the fields and singing as she works.
4. ababccdd

Exercise 44

1. William Wordsworth

2. violet
3. 千唤万唤始出来，犹抱琵琶半遮面

Exercise 45

1. *Kubla Khan*; Samuel Taylor Coleridge
2. *Lyrical Ballads*
3. dream

Exercise 46

1. ballad
2. *The Rime of the Ancient Mariner*
3. A
4. This excerpt is the first part of *The Rime of the Ancient Mariner*, the first poem in *Lyrical Ballads*. The poem is one of the masterpieces of the Romantic poetry. The theme of the poem is about sin and salvation, depravation and redemption. It tells a strange story in the form of ballads. Three guests are on their way to a wedding party, but one of them is detained by an ancient mariner. The mariner tells him of his adventures on the sea. When his ship sails towards the South Pole, an albatross comes through the snow-fog and alights on the rigging. The mariner shoots it. Then misfortune falls on the ship. The whole crew, with the exception of the mariner, die of thirst as a punishment for the act of inhospitality. The spell breaks only when the mariner repents his cruelty. The atmosphere, the beauty of music and imagery make the poem stand alone of its kind.

Exercise 47

1. sonnet; George Gordon Byron
2. *Sonnet on Chillon*
3. This sonnet is composed in memory of a historical figure named Bonnivard, who was an active fighter for the liberation of his native city Geneva from the control of Charles III and who was imprisoned in the Castle of Chillon from 1530 to 1536. This sonnet was written in praise of liberty, in praise of those who remained true to the ideals of freedom even when persecuted by their oppressors. It was a protest against the political reaction of that time. The sonnet was published together with the poem *The Prisoner of Chillon* to which it served as a poetical introduction.

Exercise 48

1. George Gordon Byron
2. *Don Juan*
3. Sappho is an ancient Greek poetess (c. 600 B.C.) of Lesbos, who is renowned for her love lyrics. Phoebus is epithet of Apollo, the Greek sun-god and god of music and poetry.
4. C
5. Lu Xun said this was to show his sympathy for the Greeks ruled by the Turkish invades, to remind the Greeks of their past glory and to arouse the Greeks to rise and fight for the freedom of Greece.

Exercise 49

1. *When We Two Parted*; George Gordon Byron
2. the past; the present; the future

3. This poem uses three tenses to tell the whole story and shows three kinds of emotions the man has after he parted with his love. The sorrow of separation is too cold to tell. Then when hearing the public rumor, the man turns to resent his lover for being frivolous, and the resentment is too deep to tell. Finally, he becomes hopeless and desperate, considering that only silence is left in this relationship. From the beginning to the very end, the poem is filled with emotional burden, such as grief and despair, leaving readers breathless and depressed.

Exercise 50

1. *She Walks in Beauty*; George Gordon Byron
2. 6-lined, iambic tetrameter
3. a cloudless and starry night sky

Exercise 51

1. aabb
2. Percy Bysshe Shelley
3. *A Song: Men of England*
4. contrast (through the whole poem);
   rhetoric question (stanza 4);
   metonymy (stanza 2: from cradle to grave);
   metaphor (bees, drones);
   parallelism (stanza 5 and 6)

Exercise 52

1. Percy Bysshe Shelley
2. In Hebrew, Latin, Greek, and many other languages, the words for winds, breath, soul, and inspiration are all identical or related. Thus Shelley's west wind is a symbol of "spirit", "the breath of Autumn's being," which on earth, in sky and sea declines in the autumn in order to revive in the spring. Around this central symbol, the poem weaves various cycles of death and regeneration—vegetational, human, and divine.
3. This poem is one of Percy Bysshe Shelley's great lyrics, written in Italy in 1819. Shelley expresses his political ideas through the west wind. It is divided into five stanzas. In the five magnificent stanzas of the *Ode*, Shelley addresses the west wind directly as a force that is both destructive and creative. He longs to establish a vital contact between his own poetic powers and the wind, and he begins by focusing on three natural objects of the wind's power: the autumn leaves in stanza 1, the clouds in stanza 2, and the waves in stanza 3. Stanza 4 marks a crisis in the poem, as Shelley longs to identify himself with these objects of the wind's power; but he fails to recover the spontaneous, imaginative confidence of his boyhood, which would link him positively with the wind itself. In stanza 5, Shelley discovers his true relationship to the west wind. Instead of being a passive object of the wind's power, he will be its active, cooperative instrument: he will be its "lyre," receiving its "mighty harmonies" like a wind harp, or like the forest itself, and converting them into words of poetry. These words, like the leaves of stanza 1, will be scattered everywhere to prophesy and to awaken a rebirth of human imagination. The *Ode* itself succeeds in expressing that relationship between imagination and the power of nature which Shelley longs for.

Exercise 53

1. Percy Bysshe Shelley
2. a female bird without companion
3. images;

   天净沙·秋思

   ［元］马致远

   枯藤老树昏鸦，小桥流水人家，古道西风瘦马。
   夕阳西下，断肠人在天涯。

   These two poems are both succinct in wording and dense in images. The images create an artistic conception. The images and artistic conception are quite expressive of mood and atmosphere.

Exercise 54

1. *On First Looking into Chapman's Homer*
2. John Keats
3. sonnet
4. A
5. In this poem, with great enthusiasm, the poet expresses his admiration and wonder at the antique world of epic heroes after he has read Homer's *Iliad* in Chapman's translation. This poem also provides a good instance of the extremely rich and pictorial language employed by Keats.

Exercise 55

1. John Keats
2. *Ode to a Nightingale*
3. three

· 345 ·

4. John Keats's central symbol is the song of the nightingale. In the first stanza the poet is overcome by the song and almost loses himself, so powerful is its effect. In the second stanza he imagines a drink that might take him out of himself completely and carry him off into the nightingale's retreat. The third stanza turns back to the sadness of the world, in which youth dies (as had Keats's brother Tom a few months before the poem was written). The poet's attempted flight from that world takes another form in the fourth stanza—not a liquor, an external thing, but "poesy," is to free him. At this point the poem takes an unexpected turn, almost a somersault, for after proclaiming that the poet is "Already with thee!"—as if he could at a leap join mortal hopes to an eternal being, "a Queen Moon"—he falls back into a world of time and change, a world in which "there is no light" (line 38).

The wood in which the poet finds himself in the fifth stanza is one in which flowers bloom and die and seasons come and go. There he is conscious of his mortality and is drawn by the fantasy of dying to the nightingale's music. In the sixth stanza Keats imagines a death, which is an ecstatic conclusion, but then acknowledges that if he were dead the song would go unheard.

Exercise 56

1. *To Autumn*
2. ababcde cdde/dcce
3. autumn color; autumn people; autumn song; autumn

Exercise 57

1. John Keats; *On the Grasshopper and the Cricket*

2. bright; happy; optimistic
3. The poetry of earth is never dead; the poetry of earth is ceasing never

Exercise 58

1. *Ivanhoe*
2. Walter Scott
3. historical

Exercise 59

1. *Rob Roy*
2. Walter Scott
3. Francis; Rob Roy

Exercise 60

1. *Pride and Prejudice*
2. Jane Austen
3. This selection is taken from the first chapter of the novel *Pride and Prejudice*. Chapter I has been universally acknowledged to be very well-written as an opening chapter. The style is lucid and graceful, with touches of humor and mild satire. The conversations are interesting and amusing, and immediately bring the characters to life. The author only inserts her observations occasionally.
4. Jane Austen holds a view on marriage that an ideal marriage must depend on both love and material guarantee.

Exercise 61

1. *Vanity Fair*
2. *The Pilgrim's Progress*
3. William Makepeace Thackeray
4. *A Novel Without a Hero*;
   The subtitle of the novel points to the author's intention to portray, not individuals singly, but the whole of the notorious "Vanity Fair", an appellative Thackeray bestows on English bourgeois and aristocratic society. With scathing irony the author exposes the vices of this society: hypocrisy, money worship, and moral degradation. This general approach of the author accounts for the fact that the novel has very few positive characters. It gives a panoramic view of English society in the early 19th century.

Exercise 62

1. *David Copperfield*
2. Charles Dickens
3. Master Copperfield, the stranger.
4. *David Copperfield* is, to some extent, an autobiographical novel. It is regarded by many as Charles Dickens's masterpiece. "Of all my books," wrote Dickens himself, "I like this the best." The story is told in the first person, through the mouth of its hero, David Copperfield. Dickens makes good use of his own life experiences to expose the social evils of his day.

Exercise 63

1. *Adam Bede*

2. George Eliot
3. Adam Bede
4. Arthur has flirted and made love with Hetty.

Exercise 64

1. *Jane Eyre*
2. Charlotte Brontë
3. This passage gives a picture of the tyrannical figure of Mr. Brocklehurst and the cruel punishment Jane Eyre received at his hands. It exposes the inhuman treatment of poor girls and orphans in the charity school of the 19th-century England.

Exercise 65

1. *Jane Eyre*
2. The criticism of the bourgeois system of education and the position of women in society.
3. Jane Eyre is a simple, kind-hearted, noble-minded woman who pursues a genuine kind of love. Jane struggles to find a balance between love and freedom and to find others who understood her. Jane voices her radical opinions on religion, social class, and gender.

Exercise 66

1. *Wuthering Heights*
2. Emily Brontë
3. close childhood friends

4. It describes the pathetic scene of the final meeting between Heathcliff and Catherine just before the latter's death.

Exercise 67

1. *Mary Barton*
2. Mrs. Gaskell
3. The theme of the novel is the class struggle between the workers and the capitalists.
4. It is one of the most important social novels of that period. The main characters are John Barton and his daughter Mary. John is an active Chartist, a leader in Chartist Movement. He believes that workers must fight for their own rights. He goes to London as one of the workers' delegates to submit their petition to Parliament. The petition is rejected. Then he is sacked. He and his daughter live in great misery. Later a strike takes place, and John kills a capitalist called Carson. Before that happens, Carson is attracted to Mary Barton. He tries to flatter and make her marry him. The girl is so innocent that she repulses her lover, a young engineer called Wilson, and almost falls into Carson's trap. As no one knows who has killed the capitalist, Mary's lover Wilson is suspected. Mary tries every means to save her lover. Finally, she finds that it is her father who killed the capitalist.

Exercise 68

1. Thomas Hood
2. *The Song of the Shirt*
3. This poem presents a vivid picture of the miserable life of the British seamstresses. The women workers worked hard till their fin-

gers were weary and their eyelids grew heavy, but they still lived in hunger and poverty and dirt. Like prisoners and slaves, they toiled from morning till night without one short hour's rest. Helpless and hopeless and heartbroken, they led a wretched existence, but no one could lend them a hand. The factory-owners gained huge profit from their ruthless exploitation of the poor seamstresses.

Exercise 69

1. *Break, Break, Break*
2. Alfred Tennyson
3. This poem was written in 1842, in memory of Arthur Hallam, the poet's close friend who died at the age of 22 in Vienna in 1833. The poem is full of contrasts—sense vs. sensibility; hardness of nature in contrast to the weakness of the poet's heart; the joyful scene of the fisherman's boy and of a sailor lad vs. the sorrowful state of his mind; the going on of natural things vs. the great change in the poet's life. By the sharp contrast between the outer world and the inner world, it displays the poet's great sorrow over Hallam's death. The whole effect is one of genuine personal grief revealed through simple imagery and very musical language.

Exercise 70

1. *Sweet and Low*
2. Alfred Tennyson
3. alliteration; repetition; catch-word repetition

Exercise 71

1. Robert Browning
2. two; couplets
3. This poem reveals the poet's nostalgic sentiment while he was staying abroad. It begins with the detailed description of beautiful natural scenes of England, and ends suddenly with a central contrast to show the poet's love for his homeland.
4. The poem ends abruptly with a contrast of two flowers in nature, which is the gist of the poem. The buttercups in England are the little children's favorite, which always make them happy in spring. While the melon-flower in Italy is too bright and showy as the poet thinks. The buttercups in England are far more preferable for the poet. This comparison shows the poet's attitude—how he loves his homeland though staying abroad.
5. 月夜忆舍弟

    [唐] 杜甫

    戍鼓断人行，边秋一雁声。

    露从今夜白，月是故乡明。

    有弟皆分散，无家问死生。

    寄书长不达，况乃未休兵。

    This poem is written by the outstanding poet Du Fu in the Tang Dynasty. In this poem, "月是故乡明" means the moon over one's hometown is the brightest, which shows the same nostalgic sentiment like Robert Browning.

Exercise 72

1. Elizabeth Barret Browning; *How Do I Love Thee?*
2. sonnet
3. This is a famous lyric poem by Elizabeth Barrett Browning. The po-

etess shows her passionate love for her husband Robert Browning by listing eight ways how she loves him. The most powerful line appears at the end of the poem: if God chose her, the poet would love her husband better after death.

Exercise 73

1. Thomas Hardy; novelist
2. the disappointment of love and life
3. pessimism
4. This poem mainly talks about the end of a relationship. It expresses the author's disappointment of love and life. In this poem, there is neither apparent anger, nor obvious despair, just like the title shows that the tone may be neutral but the emotions are black and bitter. This poem is a representative one that shows the author's sense of pessimism.

Exercise 74

1. *Poems of the Past and Present*; Thomas Hardy
2. 8-line; ababcdcd; tetrameter; trimeter
3. bewilderment
4. The poet uses a group of gloomy winter images, such as specter, dregs, weakening eyes, broken lyres, to convey his lament over the past and his bewilderment facing the future. The 19th century is compared to corpse. The only bright image in the poem is the old joyfully singing thrush, which may bring some bright color to the gloomy atmosphere of the poem and the poet's mental state.

Exercise 75

1. *Tess of the D'Urbervilles*; Thomas Hardy; poet
2. Tess's affair with Alec
3. In this passage, Tess confesses, after Clare has told her an evening of debauchery in his past and she has forgiven him, of her affair with Alec in the hope of his forgivingness. But to her surprise, Clare is stunned and then feels so hurt that he refuses to speak to her. Clare thinks it is too much for him to forgive, thus he tells Tess that she is not the woman he loves and marries, but a stranger who is beyond his acquaintance. The incident highlights the selfishness and hypocrisy of Clare in striking contrast with the frankness and honesty of Tess.

Exercise 76

1. A
2. pentameter; abba
3. "This book" means the book of poetry William Butler Yeats wrote for Maud Gonne. "Changing face" means the face getting old. "Bending" refers to the bending of her body or the hunchback when she is old.
4. This poem was written in 1891 for Maud Gonne (1866-1953), an actress and Irish revolutionist, for whom William Butler Yeats cherished a lifelong love. By sharp contrast between his love and others', William Butler Yeats shows his deep admiration for her and regret for the passing of love. Though short and simple, it is passionate and moving.

Exercise 77

1. *The Lake Isle of Innisfree*; William Butler Yeats
2. pentameter, abab
3. hermitage
4. The poem is one of William Butler Yeats's best known lyrics. Written in 1893, it is one of the poet's early works under the influence of the Pre-Raphaelites in the late 19th-century England. Tired of the life of his day, William Butler Yeats sought to escape into an ideal "fairy land" where he could live calmly as a hermit and enjoy the beauty of nature. In his opinion, the best remedy for the emptiness of his age seemed to lie in a return to the simplicity of the past. The poem is closely-woven, easy, subtle and musical.

Exercise 78

1. *In Chancery*; John Galsworthy
2. The Forsyte Saga
3. Soames does not pay the slightest attention to his wife's thoughts and feelings, regarding her merely as a piece of his own property. It tells of the birth of Fleur, the only daughter of Soames and Annerre. It vividly describes that Soames has no love for his wife. He marries her only in order to get an heir to carry on the family line and inherit his property.

Exercise 79

1. The Forsyte Saga
2. John Galsworthy
3. Forsyte; bourgeoisie

Exercise 80

1. *Mrs. Warren's Profession*; George Bernard Shaw
2. prostitution
3. It deals with the theme of prostitution as big business in the bourgeois society. The play launches possibly the sharpest and the bitterest attack ever made by George Bernard Shaw upon the very foundations of the "civilized" capitalist world. The play hits the very heart of capitalism as a social system according to which economic exploitation is not only considered the legitimate thing adopted everywhere but is pursued shamelessly by "dignified" members of the society through the lowest and the dirtiest means.

Exercise 81

1. *Sons and Lovers*; David Herbert Lawrence
2. same person
3. Clara is a woman worker, separated from her husband. Paul and Clara begin to attract each other. Though their relationship is full of fervent feelings, it lacks a common belief and mutual understanding.
4. This novel is about lament and protest against the natural environment polluted by the industrial development and the effect of mother-love upon the development of a son or Oedipus complex.

Exercise 82

1. *Mrs. Dalloway*; Virginia Woolf
2. stream of consciousness
3. This novel records only the events of a single day when Mrs. Dallo-

way was giving an evening party at her home in Westminster. The whole book is a reflection of the process of the mind, a moving mirror of consciousness, wherein is shown the author's mastery of her medium.

Exercise 83

1. *A Portrait of the Artist as a Young Man*; James Joyce
2. spiritual
3. B
4. *A Portrait of the Artist as a Young Man* (1916) is James Joyce's first novel, which is largely autobiographical. It describes the childhood, youth and early manhood of Stephen Dedalus, a highly gifted young Irishman. After mental torment and inner conflict, Stephen abandons Catholicism and leaves Ireland making up his mind to devote himself to artistic career in exile. The plot is symbolic of the relation between an artist and society as well as that between art and exile in the modern western world. In the novel, there are changes of vocabulary, idiom, and prose structure to befit the various stages of the hero's development from childhood to early manhood, but the novel presents no difficulty as prose. It is the author's "preliminary canter over the field of infinite stylistic adaptability."

Exercise 84

1. Dylan Thomas
2. aba; abaa
3. Grave men: a pun, referring to both the serious men and the men approaching death. Blinding sight: an oxymoron; a dying person is doomed to have a weakening sight but may have great insight that

can penetrate the nature of life.
4. Written in 1951, this poem is one of Dylan Thomas's most popular poems. By listing four kinds of people's ways of leaving, the poet asks his father not to accept death passively, but to be brave and struggle for life. The subject of death is displayed in different ways as in "night", "close of day", "dying of the light", "dark", etc.

Exercise 85

1. *The Whitsun Weddings*; Philip Larkin
2. pentameter; ababcdecde
3. This is one of the best-known poems by Philip Larkin, published in the 1964 collection of the same name. Larkin describes a stopping-train journey through East Yorkshire from Paragon Station, Kingston upon Hull (where Larkin was a librarian at the university) to Kings Cross, London on a hot Whitsun Saturday afternoon in the late 1950s. At each stop, Larkin becomes aware the train is being joined by parties of newly-weds. The weddings and the journey share one thing in common, that is, change. The theme of the poem is the importance of change.

Exercise 86

1. *The Picture of Dorian Gray*; Oscar Wilde
2. *The Picture of Dorian Gray* (1891) was Oscar Wilde's novel in which the hero Dorian Gray is at first a handsome innocent youth, and the painter Basil Hallward draws a picture of him. Then Dorian becomes a hedonist and indulges in all sorts of depravity under the influence of Lord Henry, an extremely immoral and degenerate hedonist. He even killes Hallward who tries to give him advice. Dorian

continues to look as innocent as before but his picture now looks terrible. Then one night he stabs at the picture with a knife but the result is that he has stabbed himself and now he looks terrible but the picture appears as handsome and as innocent as before.

3. Oscar Wilde made his criticism of the society in his own way, a way different from Dickens and other writers. Oscar voiced his reaction against the high-minded, serious preoccupations of the middle class in Victorian England in the form of search for beauty. Oscar's satiric weapons were aimed against the aristocracy, a class on the verge of ruin, clinging absurdly to his artistic form and standards. He did not try to probe the economic and political problems. He and other aesthetic authors just showed what was wrong. Though his irony did not bring about any change, he, as well as others, was preparing the way for new directions in literature at the turn of the century.

Exercise 87

1. Araby; *Dubliners*; James Joyce
2. 15
3. This is the third of the fifteen stories in *Dubliners*. This tale of the frustrated quest for beauty in the midst of drabness is both meticulously realistic in it handing of details of Dublin life and the Dublin scene and highly symbolic in that almost every image and incident suggests some particular aspect of the theme (e.g., the suggestion of the Holy Grail in the image of the chalice). Joyce was drawing on his own childhood recollections, and the uncle in the story is a reminiscence of Joyce's father.

Exercise 88

1. *A Room of One's Own*; Virginia Woolf
2. Shakespeare; comparison
3. feminist
4. In the autumn of 1928, Woolf, on invitation, made two lectures on the subject of women and fiction. They were expanded and published as *A Room of One's Own*. In Woolf's opinion, to have a private room to think and write is a basic requirement for literary creation, a requirement that, along with economic independence, few women had ever enjoyed in history. After raising the question why women had not written first-class works, Woolf describes poverty, social pressures, family demands, and lack of education that prevented women from writing.

Exercise 89

1. *The Soldier*; Rupert Brooke
2. patriotism
3. Rupert Brooke was a broad-leaved epiphyllum on the stage of English poetry. He could have written better works if he had lived longer. But involvement in affairs with too many women destroyed him because he almost had a collapse in feeling. The free love and sexuality turned out not to be something that lengthened the life of art and poetry. On the contrary, they brought them harm. Brooke was a symbol in England of the tragic loss of talented youth during the war.

Exercise 90

1. *The Love Song of J. Alfred Prufrock*; Thomas Stearns Eliot
2. realities
3. monologue
4. In spite of its title, the poem is not a love song in the normal sense. Or one can say that it is not a love song at all. It contains references to the speaker Prufrock's love affairs, it is true, but the theme of the poem is a much broader one: it deals with the thoughts of the central figure Prufrock intermixed with random descriptions of his environment. *The Love Song of J. Alfred Prufrock* is actually merely the confession of Prufrock, a middle-aged man and a romantic aesthete who is bored with his ineffectual life and is faced with despair because he wishes but is unable to break away from his meaningless existence or to find the right answers to "the overwhelming question" always occurring to him. In this sense, the poem is a mild satire on the decadence and futility of life in the upper classes in bourgeois society.

Exercise 91

1. *Petition*; Wystan Hugh Auden
2. miraculous cure
3. Auden's poetry has been praised for its vitality, variety, and originality. He imposes new and unexpected patterns on a wide range of forms—from archaic ballads to street-corner blues. Perhaps Auden's most important contribution to 20th century poetry is his experimentation in many verse forms and meters, combining an offhand informality with remarkable technical skill.

Exercise 92

1. *Sonnet from China*; Wystan Hugh Auden
2. Japanese; China
3. kindness

Exercise 93

1. *The Grass Is Singing*; Doris Lessing
2. Rhodesia
3. The story in *The Grass Is Singing* takes place in Rhodesia (now Zimbabwe) in southern Africa during the 1940s. It deals with the racial politics between whites and blacks in that country, then a British Colony. The novel created a sensation when it was first published and became an instant success in Europe and the United States. It is often described as a high-tension story of a woman whose life was changed by a few careless words which triggered the hate of the houseboy.

Exercise 94

1. *Snowdrop*
2. Ted Hughes; cosmos
3. Ted Hughes was versatile. He also wrote poems, drama, short stories and criticism. In his poems, he often uses a bird, for example, the crow, to symbolize the wild and predatory nature. He has been named a "survivor-poet" by the critic Alvarez because he parallels human beings with lower animals, creatures that will do anything to ensure survival. Hughes stated that poems, like animals, are each one "an assembly of living parts, moved by a single spirit." Looking

at the dark aspects of nature, he has stressed the ferocious and demonic rather than the idyllic and beautiful. Within the cruelty and violence of nature, Hughes looks for an understanding of human life and its mysterious bonds with nature.

Exercise 95

1. *Digging*; Seamus Heaney
2. first; *Death of a Naturalist*
3. the author's father
4. In his early works, such as *Death of a Naturalist* (1966) and *Door into the Dark* (1969), Heaney is a lyrical nature poet, writing with limpid simplicity about the disappearing world of unspoiled rural Ireland. He is evocative yet clear, direct and balanced between the personal and the topical. His poetry is crafted and famous for its powerful images, meaningful content, musical phrasing, and compelling rhythms. His work has always a sense of historicalness, deeply associated with the lessons of history, sometimes even prehistory. Many of his works concern his own family history and focus on characters in his own family, which can be read as elegies for those family members. He has acknowledged this trend.

附录一

英国文学主要作家作品简录

作家	作品
Part I　The Anglo-Saxon Period and the Anglo-Norman Period	
Unknown（未知）	*The Song of Beowulf* 《贝奥武甫》（约 700—900）
William Langland （威廉·兰格兰，约 1332—约 1400）	*Piers Plowman* 《农夫皮尔斯》（约 1362—1363）
Unknown（未知）	*Sir Gawain and the Green Knight* 《高文爵士与绿衣骑士》（约 14 世纪）
Part II　The Age of Geoffrey Chaucer	
Geoffrey Chaucer （杰弗雷·乔叟，1340—1400）	*The Canterbury Tales* 《坎特伯雷故事集》（1386—1400）
Part III　The 15th Century: The Age of Popular Ballads	
Unknown（未知）	*Get up and Bar the Door* 《起来把门闩上去》（年代未知）
Unknown（未知）	*Robin Hood and Allin-a-Dale* 《罗宾汉和埃林阿代尔》（年代未知）
Part IV　The 16th Century: The Age of Drama and Poetry	
Thomas More （托马斯·莫尔，1478—1535）	*Utopia* 《乌托邦》（1516）
Thomas Wyatt （托马斯·怀亚特，1503—1542）	*Farewell, Love* 《永别了，爱》（年代未知）
	I Find No Peace 《我得不到安宁》（年代未知）
Henry Howard （亨利·霍华德，1517—1547）	*The Soote Season* 《温柔的季节》（年代未知）

续表

作家	作品
Edmund Spenser (埃德蒙·斯宾塞,1552—1599)	*The Shepherd's Calendar* 《牧人月历》(1579)
	The Faerie Queene 《仙后》(1590—1596)
	Amoretti 《小爱神》(1595)
Walter Raleigh (沃尔特·雷利,1552—1618)	*The Nymph's Reply to the Shepherd* 《少女答牧羊人》(1596)
Philip Sidney (菲利普·锡德尼,1554—1586)	*Astrophel and Stella* 《爱星者与星》(16世纪80年代)
Francis Bacon (弗朗西斯·培根,1561—1626)	*Advancement of Learning* 《学术的进步》(1605)
	Novum Organum 《新工具》(1620)
	Of Studies 《论读书》(1625)
Christopher Marlowe (克里斯托弗·马洛,1564—1593)	*Tamburlaine the Great* 《帖木儿大帝》(1587)
	Doctor Faustus 《浮士德博士》(1592)
	The Passionate Shepherd to His Love 《热情的牧羊人致意中人》(1592)
	The Jew of Malta 《马耳他岛的犹太人》(1633)

续表

作家	作品
William Shakespeare （威廉·莎士比亚，1564—1616）	*The Taming of the Shrew* 《驯悍记》(1593) *Romeo and Juliet* 《罗密欧与朱丽叶》(1594) *A Midsummer Night's Dream* 《仲夏夜之梦》(1595) *The Merchant of Venice* 《威尼斯商人》(1596) *King Henry IV* 《亨利四世》(1597) *The Life of King Henry V* 《亨利五世》(1598) *As You Like It* 《皆大欢喜》(1599) *Twelfth Night, or, What You Will* 《第十二夜》(1600) *Hamlet, Prince of Denmark* 《哈姆雷特》(1601) *Othello, the Moore of Venice* 《奥赛罗》(1604) *The Sonnets* 《十四行诗》(1604) *King Lear* 《李尔王》(1605) *The Tragedy of Macbeth* 《麦克白》(1605) *The Life of King Henry VIII* 《亨利八世》(1612)

续表

作家	作品
Ben Jonson (本·琼森，1572—1637)	*Every Man in His Humor* 《个性互异》(1598)
	Sejanus 《塞扬努斯》(1603)
	Volpone 《福尔蓬奈》(1606)
	The Alchemist 《炼金士》(1610)
	Song: to Celia 《西丽亚颂歌》(1616)

Part V　The 17th Century: Revolution, Restoration and New Poetic Expression

作家	作品
John Donne (约翰·多恩，1572—1631)	*Death Be Not Proud* 《死神你莫骄狂》(1610)
	A Valediction: Forbidding Mourning 《别离辞：莫悲伤》(1611)
Robert Herrick (罗伯特·赫里克，1591—1674)	*To the Virgins, to Make Much of Time* 《劝少女珍惜好时光》(1648)
George Herbert (乔治·赫伯特，1593—1633)	*Easter Wings* 《复活节翅膀》(1633)
	The Collar 《衣领》(1633)
	Virtue 《美德》(1633)
John Milton (约翰·弥尔顿，1608—1774)	*Paradise Lost* 《失乐园》(1667)
	Paradise Regained 《复乐园》(1671)
	Samson Agonistes 《力士参孙》(1674)
John Suckling (约翰·萨克林，1609—1642)	*The Constant Lover* 《永恒的爱人》(年代未知)
Richard Lovelace (理查德·洛夫莱斯，1618—1657)	*To Lucasta, Going to the Wars* 《致卢卡斯塔》(1649)

续表

作家	作品
Andrew Marvell （安德鲁·马韦尔，1621—1678）	To His Coy Mistress 《致他娇羞的女友》（1681）
John Bunyan （约翰·班扬，1628—1688）	The Pilgrim's Progress 《天路历程》（1678）
	The Life and Death of Mr. Badman 《恶人传》（1680）
	The Holy War 《圣战》（1682）

Part VI The 18th Century: The Enlightenment, Neo-classicism and Pre-romanticism

作家	作品
John Dryden （约翰·德莱顿，1631—1700）	A Song for St. Cecilia's Day 《圣塞西莉亚节的赞歌》（1687）
Daniel Defoe （丹尼尔·笛福，1660—1731）	The Life and Strange Surprising Adventures of Robinson Crusoe 《鲁滨逊漂流记》（1719）
Jonathan Swift （乔纳森·斯威夫特，1667—1745）	The Battle of the Books 《书的战争》（1704）
	The Tale of a Tub 《一只桶的故事》（1704）
	Gulliver's Travels 《格列佛游记》（1726）
	A Modest Proposal 《一个温和的建议》（1729）
Joseph Addison （约瑟夫·阿狄生，1672—1719）	Campaign 《远征》（1704）
Richard Steele （理查德·斯蒂尔，1672—1729）	The Christian Hero 《基督教徒的英雄》（1701）
Alexander Pope （亚历山大·蒲柏，1688—1744）	An Essay on Criticism 《批评论》（1711）
	The Rape of the Lock 《夺发记》（1712）
	The Dunciad 《愚人志》（1742）

续表

作家	作品
Henry Fielding （亨利·菲尔丁，1707—1754）	*The Life of Mr. Jonathan Wild the Great* 《大伟人江奈生·魏尔德传》（1743）
	The History of Tom Jones, a Foundling 《弃婴汤姆·琼斯的故事》（1749）
Thomas Gray （托马斯·格雷，1716—1771）	*Elegy Written in a Country Churchyard* 《墓园挽歌》（1751）
Oliver Goldsmith （奥利弗·戈尔德史密斯，1730—1774）	*The Vicar of Wakefield* 《威克菲尔德牧师传》（1766）
	The Good-Natured Man 《善性之人》（1768）
	She Stoops to Conquer 《屈身求爱》（1773）
Richard Brinsley Sheridan （理查德·布林斯利·谢里丹，1751—1816）	*A Trip to Scarborough* 《斯卡勃勒之行》（1777）
	The School for Scandal 《造谣学校》（1777）
	The Critic 《批评家》（1779）
William Blake （威廉·布莱克，1757—1827）	*The Chimney Sweeper* 《擦烟囱的少年》（1789）
	London 《伦敦》（1794）
	The Sick Rose 《病玫瑰》（1794）
	The Tyger 《老虎》（1794）

续表

作家	作品
Robert Burns （罗伯特·彭斯，1759—1796）	*Mary Morrison* 《玛丽·莫里森》（1780） *Auld Lang Syne* 《友谊地久天长》（1788） *My Heart's in the Highlands* 《我的心儿在高原》（1789） *John Anderson, My Jo* 《约翰·安德森，我的爱人》（1789） *Scots, Wha Hae* 《苏格兰勇士》（1793） *A Red, Red Rose* 《一朵红红的玫瑰》（1794）
Part VII　The 19th Century (First Half): The Romantic Period	
William Wordsworth （威廉·华兹华斯，1770—1850）	*She Dwelt Among the Untrodden Ways* 《她住在人迹罕至的地方》（1798） *I Wandered Lonely as a Cloud* 《我独自漫游，像一朵浮云》（1807） *The Solitary Reaper* 《孤独的刈麦女》（1807） *The Prelude* 《序曲》（1850）
Walter Scott （沃尔特·司各特，1771—1832）	*Rob Roy* 《罗布·罗伊》（1817） *Ivanhoe* 《艾凡赫》（1819）
Samuel Taylor Coleridge （塞缪尔·泰勒·柯尔律治，1772—1834）	*Kubla Khan* 《忽必烈汗》（1797） *The Rime of the Ancient Mariner* 《古舟子咏》（1798）

续表

作家	作品
Jane Austen （简·奥斯汀，1775—1817）	*Lady Susan* 《苏珊夫人》（1794） *Sense and Sensibility* 《理智与情感》（1811） *Pride and Prejudice* 《傲慢与偏见》（1813） *Mansfield Park* 《曼斯菲尔德庄园》（1814） *Emma* 《爱玛》（1815） *Northanger Abbey* 《诺桑觉寺》（1818） *Persuasion* 《劝导》（1818）
Charles Lamb （查尔斯·兰姆，1775—1834）	*Essays of Elia* 《伊利亚随笔》（1823） *Last Essays of Elia* 《伊利亚续笔》（1833）
George Gordon Byron （乔治·戈登·拜伦，1788—1824）	*Childe Harold's Pilgrimage* 《恰尔德·哈罗德游记》（1812—1818） *She Walks in Beauty* 《她走在美的光彩中》（1814） *When We Two Parted* 《我们俩分别时》（1817） *Don Juan* 《唐璜》（1818—1823）

续表

作家	作品
Percy Bysshe Shelley （珀西·比希·雪莱，1792—1822）	*Queen Mab* 《麦布女王》（1813）
	The Revolt of Islam 《伊斯兰的反叛》（1818）
	Ode to the West Wind 《西风颂》（1819）
	Prometheus Unbound 《解放了的普罗米修斯》（1819）
	Song to the Men of England 《给英格兰人的歌》（1819）
	To a Skylark 《致云雀》（1820）
John Keats （约翰·济慈，1795—1821）	*On First Looking into Chapman's Homer* 《初读恰普曼译荷马史诗》（1816）
	On the Grasshopper and the Cricket 《蝈蝈和蟋蟀》（1816）
	Ode on a Grecian Urn 《希腊古瓮颂》（1819）
	Ode on Melancholy 《忧郁颂》（1819）
	Ode to a Nightingale 《夜莺颂》（1819）
	To Autumn 《秋颂》（1819）
	Bright Star 《灿烂的星》（1821）
Thomas Hood （托马斯·胡德，1799—1845）	*Odes and Addresses to Great People* 《大人物之歌》（1825）
	The Song of the Shirt 《衬衫之歌》（1843）

续表

作家	作品
Part VIII　The 19th Century (Second Half): The Victorian Age and Critical Realism	
Elizabeth Barrett Browning （伊丽莎白·巴雷特·布朗宁，1806—1861）	*Sonnets from the Portuguese* 《葡萄牙人十四行诗集》（1850） *Aurora Leigh* 《奥萝拉·莉》（1857）
Alfred Tennyson （阿尔弗雷德·丁尼生，1809—1892）	*Break, Break, Break* 《冲激，冲激，冲激》（1842） *Morte d'Arthur* 《亚瑟王之死》（1842） *Locksley Hall* 《洛克斯利大厅》（1842） *The Princess* 《公主》（1847） *The Eagle* 《鹰》（1850） *Queen Mary* 《玛丽女王》（1875） *Crossing the Bar* 《过沙洲》（1880）
William Makepeace Thackeray （威廉·梅克皮斯·萨克雷，1811—1863）	*The Book of Snobs* 《庸人之书》（1846） *Vanity Fair* 《名利场》（1848） *The History of Henry Esmond* 《亨利·艾斯蒙》（1852） *The Rose and the Ring* 《玫瑰与戒指》（1855） *The Adventures of Philip* 《菲利浦的冒险》（1862）

· 373 ·

续表

作家	作品
Charles Dickens （查尔斯·狄更斯，1812—1870）	*Oliver Twist* 《雾都孤儿》(1837—1838) *Nicholas Nickleby* 《尼古拉斯·尼克贝》(1838—1839) *The Old Curiosity Shop* 《老古玩店》(1840—1841) *Barnaby Rudge* 《巴纳比·拉奇》(1841) *American Notes* 《美国纪行》(1842) *A Christmas Carol* 《圣诞颂歌》(1843) *Dombey and Son* 《董贝父子》(1847—1848) *David Copperfield* 《大卫·科波菲尔》(1849—1850) *Bleak House* 《荒凉山庄》(1852—1853) *Hard Times* 《艰难时世》(1854) *Little Dorrit* 《小杜丽》(1855—1857) *A Tale of Two Cities* 《双城记》(1859) *Great Expectations* 《远大前程》(1860—1861) *Our Mutual Friend* 《我们共同的朋友》(1864—1865) *The Mystery of Edwin Drood* 《艾德温·德鲁德之谜》(1870)

续表

作家	作品
Robert Browning （罗伯特·布朗宁，1812—1889）	*Porphyria's Lover* 《波菲利雅的情人》（1836） *My Last Duchess* 《我的前公爵夫人》（1842） *The Ring and the Book* 《指环与书》（1868—1869）
Charlotte Brontë （夏洛蒂·勃朗特，1816—1855）	*Jane Eyre* 《简·爱》（1847） *Shirley* 《谢利》（1849） *Villette* 《维莱特》（1853） *The Professor* 《教师》（1857）
Emily Brontë （艾米莉·勃朗特，1818—1848）	*Wuthering Heights* 《呼啸山庄》（1847）
George Eliot （乔治·艾略特，1819—1881）	*Adam Bede* 《亚当·比德》（1859） *The Mill on the Floss* 《弗洛斯河上的磨坊》（1859—1860） *Silas Marner* 《织工马南传》（1861） *Romola* 《罗慕拉》（1862—1863） *The Spanish Gypsy* 《西班牙吉卜赛人》（1868） *Middlemarch* 《米德尔马契》（1871—1872）
Matthew Arnold （马修·阿诺德，1822—1888）	*Dover Beach* 《多佛滩》（1851） *Culture and Anarchy* 《文化与无政府》（1869）

续表

作家	作品
Christina Georgina Rossetti (克里斯蒂娜·杰奥尔吉娜·罗塞蒂, 1830—1894)	*A Birthday* 《生日》(1861)
	Goblin Market 《精灵市集》(1862)
	Remember 《记住我》(1862)
Gerard Manley Hopkins (杰勒德·曼利·霍普金斯, 1844—1889)	*Pied Beauty* 《斑驳之美》(1918)
	The Windhover 《风鹰》(1918)
Part IX The 20th Century: Transition from the 19th to the 20th Century Before 1945		
Thomas Hardy (托马斯·哈代, 1840—1928)	*Under the Greenwood Tree* 《绿荫下》(1872)
	Far from the Madding Crowd 《远离尘嚣》(1874)
	The Return of the Native 《还乡》(1878)
	Two on a Tower 《塔上恋人》(1882)
	Tess of the D'Urbervilles 《德伯家的苔丝》(1891)
	Jude the Obscure 《无名的裘德》(1896)
Oscar Wilde (奥斯卡·王尔德, 1854—1900)	*The Portrait of Dorian Gray* 《道林·格雷的画像》(1891)
	Lady Windermere's Fan 《温夫人的扇子》(1892)
	A Woman of No Importance 《无足轻重的女人》(1893)
	The Importance of Being Earnest 《不可儿戏》(1895)

续表

作家	作品
George Bernard Shaw （乔治·萧伯纳，1856—1950）	*Arms and the Man* 《武器和人》（1894） *Candida* 《念珠菌》（1897） *The Man of Destiny* 《风云人物》（1897） *Mrs. Warren's Profession* 《华伦夫人的职业》（1898） *Man and Superman* 《人与超人》（1904） *Major Barbara* 《巴巴拉少校》（1907） *Pygmalion* 《卖花女》（1912） *Saint Joan* 《圣女贞德》（1923）
William Butler Yeats （威廉·巴特勒·叶芝，1865—1939）	*The Lake Isle of Innisfree* 《茵梦湖岛》（1890） *When You Are Old* 《当你老了》（1893） *In the Seven Woods* 《在七片树林里》（1903） *The Wild Swan at Coole* 《库尔的野天鹅》（1917） *Sailing to Byzantium* 《驶向拜占庭》（1928）

续表

作家	作品
John Galsworthy (约翰·高尔斯华绥, 1867—1933)	*From the Four Winds* 《天涯海角》(1897)
	The Island Pharisees 《岛国的法利赛人》(1904)
	The Man of Property 《有产业的人》(1906)
	In Chancery 《骑虎》(1920)
	To Let 《出租》(1921)
James Joyce (詹姆斯·乔伊斯, 1882—1941)	*Dubliners* 《都柏林人》(1914)
	A Portrait of the Artist as a Young Man 《一个青年艺术家的画像》(1916)
	Ulysses 《尤利西斯》(1922)
	Finnegans Wake 《芬尼根守灵夜》(1939)
Virginia Woolf (弗吉尼娅·伍尔夫, 1882—1941)	*The Voyage Out* 《远航》(1915)
	Jacob's Room 《雅各的房间》(1922)
	Mrs. Dalloway 《达洛维夫人》(1925)
	To the Lighthouse 《到灯塔去》(1927)
	Orlando: A Biography 《奥兰多》(1928)
	A Room of One's Own 《一间自己的房间》(1929)

续表

作家	作品
David Herbert Lawrence （戴维·赫伯特·劳伦斯，1885—1930）	*The White Peacock* 《白孔雀》（1910）
	Sons and Lovers 《儿子与情人》（1913）
	The Rainbow 《虹》（1915）
	The Lost Girl 《误入歧途的女人》（1920）
	Sea and Sardinia 《大海与撒丁岛》（1921）
	Women in Love 《恋爱中的女人》（1921）
	Aaron's Rod 《亚伦的手杖》（1922）
	The Plumed Serpent 《羽蛇》（1926）
	Lady Chatterley's Lover 《查泰莱夫人的情人》（1959）
Rupert Brooke （鲁伯特·布鲁克，1887—1915）	*The Soldier* 《士兵》（1915）
Thomas Stearns Eliot （托马斯·斯特恩斯·艾略特，1888—1965）	*The Love Song of J. Alfred Prufrock* 《艾尔弗雷德·普鲁弗洛克的情歌》（1915）
	The Waste Land 《荒原》（1922）
	Dante 《但丁》（1929）
	Ash Wednesday 《圣灰星期三》（1930）
	Murder in the Cathedral 《大教堂谋杀案》（1935）
	Four Quartets 《四个四重奏》（1943）

续表

作家	作品
Robert Graves （罗伯特·格雷夫斯，1895—1985）	Claudius the God 《克劳迪斯神》（1934） I, Claudius 《我，克劳迪斯》（1934） Count Belisarius 《贝利萨里乌斯伯爵》（1938）
Wystan Hugh Auden （威斯坦·休·奥登，1907—1973）	The Ascent of F6 《F6 的高升》（1936） Spain 《西班牙》（1937） For the Time Being 《暂时》（1944） The Age of Anxiety 《焦虑的时代》（1947）
Dylan Thomas （狄兰·托马斯，1914—1953）	The Map of Love 《爱的地图》（1939） Deaths and Entrances 《死亡与出场》（1946） Do Not Go Gentle into That Good Night 《不要温顺地走进那个良宵》（1951） In Country Sleep 《在乡间安息》（1951）
Part X The 20th Century: Contemporary Literature Since 1945	
Doris Lessing （多丽丝·莱辛，1919—2013）	The Grass Is Singing 《野草在歌唱》（1950） Children of Violence 《暴力的孩子们》（1952—1969） The Golden Notebook 《金色笔记》（1962） The Summer Before the Dark 《天黑前的夏天》（1973） The Memoirs of a Survivor 《幸存者回忆录》（1975）

附录一　英国文学主要作家作品简录

续表

作家	作品
Philip Arthur Larkin （菲利普·阿瑟·拉金，1922—1985）	*The Less Deceived* 《较小之欺诈》（1955）
	The Whitsun Weddings 《伟森的婚礼》（1964）
	High Window 《高窗》（1974）
Ted Hughes （特德·休斯，1930—1998）	*Snowdrop* 《雪花莲》（1960）
	Hawk Roosting 《鹰之栖息》（1960）
Seamus Heaney （谢默斯·希尼，1939—2013）	*Eleven Poems* 《十一首诗》（1965）
	Door into the Dark 《进入黑暗之门》（1969）

附录二

常用文学术语

AESTHETICISM（唯美主义）

A literary and artistic tendency of the late 19th century which regards beauty as an end in itself and attempts to separate art from real life and moral, didactic or political purposes. Art for art's sake is their slogan. Walter Pater and Oscar Wilde are representatives of aestheticism in England.

ALEXANDRINE（亚历山大诗行）

An iambic hexameter line—that is, a poetic line consisting of six iambic feet. The last line of a Spenserian stanza is an alexandrine. The following alexandrine is from a stanza of John Keats's *The Eve of St. Agnes*:

She sighed for Agnes dreams, the sweetest of the year.

ALLEGORY（寓言）

A story or visual image with a symbolic meaning, distinct from and more important than, the literal meaning. An allegory often uses personifications to convey its meanings, in which abstract ideas or moral qualities are given human shape. John Bunyan's *The Pilgrim's Progress* is one of the most famous allegories in English literature.

ALLUSION（用典）

The reference to some event, person, place or artistic work. It is commonly used in poetry. The classical myths and works provide the major sources for allusions. In *To Helen*, Edgar Allan Poe alludes to the divine figures in Greek mythology to show his admiration for the lady he truly cares about:

Helen, thy beauty is to me
Like those Nicean barks of yore,
That gently, o'er a perfumed sea,
The weary, way-worn wanderer bore
To his own native shore.

Helen is a beautiful woman in Greek mythology, whose love for Paris a prince of Troy is the cause of the Trojan War. The Trojan War lasted ten years with Troy destroyed. Odysseus is one of prominent Greek leaders, who spent ten more years getting back home. The meaning of the allusion is not explained by the poet but relies on the reader's familiarity with what is thus mentioned.

ANALOGY（类比）

A comparison made between two things to show the similarities between them. Analogies are often used for illustration (to explain something unfamiliar by comparing it to something familiar) or for argument (to persuade that what holds true for one thing holds true for the thing to which it is compared). Samuel Johnson draws an analogy for the sake of argument in his *Preface to Shakespeare* when he compares a work of art to a work of nature:

> As among the works of nature no man can properly call a river deep or a mountain high, without the knowledge of many mountains and many rivers; so in the productions of genius, nothing can be styled excellent till it has been compared with other works of the same kind.

ANTAGONIST（反面人物）

A person or force opposing the protagonist in a narrative; a rival of the hero or heroine. Famous antagonists in literature include Professor Moriarty, Sherlock Holmes's antagonist in Arthur Conan Doyle's detective stories, and the monster Grendel, Beowulf's antagonist in the Anglo-Saxon epic poem *Beowulf*.

ANTITHESIS（对照）

The balancing of two contrasting ideas, words, phrases, or sentences. An antithesis is often expressed in a balanced sentence, that is, a sentence in which identical or similar grammatical structure is used to express contrasting ideas. A famous example of antithesis is this line from Alexander Pope's *An Essay on Criticism*: "To err is human, to forgive divine."

APOSTROPHE（顿呼）

A figure of speech in which an absent or a dead person, an abstract quality, or something nonhuman is addressed directly. George Gordon Byron uses apostrophe in *Childe Harold's Pilgrimage* when he addresses the ocean: "Roll on, thou deep and dark blue Ocean—roll!"

BALLAD（民谣）

A story told in song, usually in 4-line stanzas, with the 2nd and 4th lines rhymed. In many countries, the folk ballad was one of the earliest forms of literature. Folk ballads have no known authors. They were transmitted orally from generation to generation and were not set down in writing until centuries after they were first sung. The subject matter of folk ballads stems from the everyday life of the common people. The most popular subjects, often tragic, are disappointed love, jealousy, revenge, sudden disaster, and deeds of adventure and daring. Devices commonly used in ballads are the refrain, incremental repetition, and code language. A later form of ballad is the literary ballad, which imitates the style of the folk ballad. The most famous English literary ballad is Samuel Taylor Coleridge's *The Rime of the Ancient Mariner*.

BALLAD STANZA（民谣体诗节）

The usual form of the folk ballad and its literary imitations, consisting of a quatrain in which the first and third lines have four stresses while the second and fourth have three stresses. Usually only the second and fourth lines rhyme. The rhythm is basically iambic. For example, in Robert Burns's *A Red Red Rose*:

O my Luve's like a red, red rose,

    That's newly sprung in June;

O my Luve's like the melodie

    That's sweetly played in tune.

BLANK VERSE（无韵诗）

Verse written in unrhymed iambic pentameter. Blank verse is used in some of the greatest English poetry, including that of William Shakespeare and John Milton. Henry Howard wrote the first English blank verse, Marlowe first made it the principal instrument of English drama, while Milton first used it in non-dramatic works, for example *Paradise Lost*.

BYRONIC HERO（拜伦式英雄）

Characters in George Gordon Byron's works, usually men of noble birth, with fiery passions and unbending will. They rise against tyranny and injustice, express the poet's own ideal of freedom, but they are merely lone fighters striving for personal freedom and some individualistic ends. Don Juan is a typical Byronic hero.

CARPE DIEM TRADITION（只争朝夕诗歌传统，亦译及时行乐诗歌传统）

A tradition dating back to classical Greek and Latin poetry and particularly popular among English Cavalier poets. Carpe diem means, literally, "seize the day"—that is, "live for today". The carpe diem theme is epitomized in a line from Robert Herrick's *To the Virgins, to Make Much of Time*: "Gather ye rosebuds while ye may". But carpe diem is not necessarily totally passive. It is an attitude toward life.

CLASSICISM（古典主义）

A movement or tendency in art, literature, or music that reflects the principles manifested in the art of ancient Greece and Rome. Classicism emphasizes the traditional and the universal, and places value on reason, clarity, balance and order. Classicism, with its concern for reason and universal themes, is traditionally opposed to romanticism, which is concerned with emotions and personal themes. Alexander Pope is a famous representative in English classicism.

CLIMAX（层进法）

The point of greatest intensity, interest, or suspense in a narrative. The climax usually marks a story's turning point. The action leading to the climax and the simultaneous increase of tension in the plot are known as the rising action. In William Shakespeare's *Macbeth*, the climax occurs during the banquet scene in Act Three. Macbeth, overcome by guilt and nervousness over the murders of Duncan the King and Banquo, sees the ghost of Banquo in the banquet hall. This tense moment is the play's turning point. After this moment, events turn against Macbeth and lead to his final downfall. Events that occur after the climax are referred to as the falling action, or resolution. The term crisis is sometimes used interchangeably with climax.

COMEDY（喜剧）

A play typically dealing with common people and dominated by a light tone that encourages laughter (or at least amusement or entertainment), which ends happily, often with the uniting of a pair of young lovers. The comic protagonist is usually a person of ordinary character and ability. Comedies are often concerned, at least in part, with exposing human folly, and frequently depict the overthrow of rigid social fashions and customs. Wit, humor, and a sense of festivity are found in many comedies. Shakespeare wrote many comedies, such as *Twelfth Night*, *The Merchant of Venice* and *As You Like It*, etc.

CONCEIT（奇喻）

A kind of metaphor that makes a comparison between two startlingly different things. A conceit may be a brief metaphor, but it usually provides the framework for an entire poem. An especially unusual and intellectual kind of conceit is the metaphysical conceit, used by certain 17th-century poets, such as John Donne. In *A Valediction: Forbidding Mourning*, Donne compares the souls of lovers to compasses in an extended simile that begins with these lines:

If they be two, they are two so
As stiff twin compasses are two,
Thy soul the fixed foot, makes no show
To move, but doth, if th' other do.

COUPLET（双偶句）

The rhymed pair of poetic lines. The most commonly used form is Heroic Couplet, a rhymed pair of iambic pentameter lines. It was established by Chaucer as a major English verse form for narrative and other kinds of non-dramatic poetry which dominated English poetry of the 18th century notably in the poetry of Pope, before declining in importance in the early 19th century. Here is an example from *The Rape of the Lock*:

But when to mischief mortals bend their will,
How soon they find fit instruments of ill!

CRITICAL REALISM（批判现实主义）

English critical realism flourished in the 1840s and the early 1850s, which found the best expression in novel. The critical realists vividly described the English society with artistic skill. They showed hatred for the ruling classes and sympathy for the poor. Humor and satire abound in their works where they also expressed democratic and humanistic ideas. However, they were unable to find a good solution to the social problems. Charles Dickens, William Makepeace Thackeray, Brontë sisters, Elizabeth Cleghorn Gaskell, and George Eliot are all its representatives. Among them Dickens is the greatest.

DÉNOUEMENT（结局）

The outcome of a plot. The dénouement is that part of a play, short story, novel, or narrative poem in which conflicts are resolved or unraveled, and mysteries and secrets connected with the plot are explained.

DICTION（措辞）

A writer's choice of words, particularly for clarity, effectiveness, and precision. A writer's diction can be formal or informal, abstract or concrete, simple or ornate. In choosing "the right word", writers must think of their subject and their audience. Words that are appropriate in informal dialogue would not always be appropriate in a piece of formal writing.

DRAMATIC MONOLOGUE（戏剧独白）

A kind of narrative poem in which one character speaks to one or more listeners whose replies are not given in the poem. The occasion is usually a crucial one in the speaker's life, and the dramatic monologue reveals the speaker's personality as well as the incident that is the subject of the poem. Dramatic monologues occurred frequently in Renaissance poetry, especially in metaphysical poetry. But people often consider the best example of dramatic monologue is *My Last Duchess* written by Robert Browning.

ELEGY（挽诗）

A poem of mourning, usually over the death of an individual. It may also be a lament over the passing of life and beauty or a meditation on the nature of death. An elegy is a type of lyric poem, usually formal in language and structure, and solemn or even melancholy in tone. Among the best are Thomas Gray's *Elegy Written in the Country Churchyard* and John Milton's *Lycidas*. But John Donne wrote some elegies which were actually love poems.

EPIC（史诗）

A long narrative poem of great scale and grand style telling about the deeds of a great hero and reflecting the values of the society from which it originated. Many epics were drawn from an oral tradition and were transmitted by song and recitation before they were written down. Two of the most famous epics of Western civilization are Homer's *Iliad* and *Odyssey*. The great epic of the Middle Ages is the *Divine Comedy* by the Italian poet Dante. The Anglo-Saxon poem *Beowulf* is the oldest surviving national epic poem.

EPIGRAM（隽语）

A short, witty, pointed statement often in the form of a poem. Here is an example from Alexander Pope's *Essay on Criticism*:

Be not the first by whom the new are tried,
Nor yet the last to lay the old aside.

EPIGRAPH（题词）

A quotation or motto at the beginning of a chapter, book, short story, or poem that makes the point about the work. One of the epigraphs preceding Thomas Sterns Eliot's *The Hollow Men* is a reference to Guy Fawkes Day, when English children carry stuffed effigies, or likenesses, of the traitor Fawkes. The epigraph serves as a motif throughout the poem for the ineffectuality Eliot identifies with his generation of "stuffed men."

EPILOGUE（后记）

A short addition or conclusion at the end of a literary work. In the epilogue to *Pygmalion*, George Bernard Shaw tells his readers what happened to his characters after the conclusion of the play.

EPIPHANY（顿悟）

A moment of illumination, usually occurring at or near the end of a work. In James Joyce's story *Araby*, the epiphany occurs when the narrator realizes, with sudden clarity, that his dream of visiting the splendid bazaar has resulted only in frustration and disillusion.

EPITAPH（碑文）

An inscription on a gravestone or a short poem written in memory of someone who has died. Many epitaphs are actually epigrams, or short witty sayings, and are not intended for serious use as monument inscriptions.

Here is an example:

Life is a jest, and all things show it.
I thought so once; but now I know it.
　　　　—John Gay, *My Own Epitaph*

ESSAY（随笔）

A piece of prose writing, usually short, that deals with a subject in a limited way and expresses a particular point of view. An essay is never a comprehensive treatment of a subject (the word comes from a French word, essai, meaning "attempt" or "try"). An essay may be serious or humorous, tightly organized or rambling, restrained or emotional.

The two general classifications of essay are the informal essay (also called the familiar or personal essay) and the formal essay. An informal essay is usually brief and is written as if the writer is talking informally to the reader about some topic, using a conversational style and a personal or humorous tone. In an informal essay, the writer might digress from the topic at hand, or express some amusing, startling, or absurd opinions. In general, an informal essay reveals as much about the personality of its author as it does about its subject. By contrast, a formal essay is tightly organized, dignified in style, and serious in tone. Francis Bacon's *Of Studies* is an example of a formal essay and must be learned by heart.

FABLE（寓言）

A brief story that is told to present a moral, or practical lesson. The characters of fables are often animals that speak and act like human beings.

FARCE（滑稽剧）

A type of comedy based on a ridiculous situation, often with stereotyped characters. The humor in a farce is largely slapstick—that is, it often involves crude physical action. The characters in a farce are often the butts of practical jokes: flying cream-pies hit them in the face and beds cave in on them.

FLASHBACK（倒叙）

A scene in a short story, novel, play, or narrative poem that interrupts the action to show an event that happened earlier. Most narratives present events in chronological order—that is, as they occur in time. Sometimes, however, a writer interrupts this natural sequence of events and "flashes back" to tell the reader what happened earlier in the story or in a character's life. Often a flashback takes the form of a character's recollection. Katherine Mansfield, in *A Dill Pickle*, and Elizabeth Bowen, in *Tears, Idle Tears*, both use this technique.

FORESHADOWING（伏笔）

The use of hints or clues in a narrative to suggest what will happen later. Writers use foreshadowing to create interest and to build suspense. Sometimes foreshadowing also prepares the reader for the ending of the story. In Graham Greene's *Across the Bridge*, the ending of the story is foreshadowed in the fifth paragraph when the narrator refers to Mr. Calloway's story as a tragedy.

FREE VERSE（自由诗）

Verse that has either no metrical pattern or an irregular pattern. Although most free verses belong to the nineteenth and twentieth centuries, it can be found in earlier literature, particularly in the Psalms of the Bible. But do not totally believe that free verses have no rhythm and rhyme—they are merely different from traditional poems.

HYPERBOLE（夸张）

A figure of speech using exaggeration, or overstatement, for special effect. In Robert Burns's *A Red, Red Rose*, the speaker expresses his constant love for his beloved girl:

> Till a' the seas gang dry, my Dear,
> And the rocks melt wi' the sun;
> O I will love thee still, my Dear,
> While the sands o' life shall run.

Surely the exaggerated statement is not meant to be taken literally, but we are deeply moved by the passion between the lines.

IMAGERY（意象）

Words or phrases that create pictures, or images, in the reader's mind. Images are primarily visual, as in these lines from William Wordsworth's *Lines Composed a Few Miles Above Tintern Abbey*:

> Once again I see
> These hedgerows, hardly hedgerows, little lines
> Of sportive wood run wild: these pastoral farms,
> Green to the very door; and wreaths of smoke
> Sent up, in silence, from among the trees!

Images can appeal to other senses as well: touch, taste, smell, and hearing.

IMAGISM（意象主义）

An Anglo-American poetic movement flourishing in the 1910s. Led at first by Ezra Pound, the Imagists shake off the conventional meters and emphasize the use of common speech, new rhythms and clear images. Hilda Doolittle is one of the representative writers.

IRONY（反讽）

A contrast or an incongruity between what is stated and what is really meant, or between what is expected to happen and what actually happens. Three kinds of irony are (1) verbal irony, in which a writer or speaker says one thing and means something entirely different; (2) dramatic irony, in which a reader or an audience perceives something that a character in the story or play does not know; (3) irony of situation, in which the writer shows a discrepancy between the expected results of some action or situation and its actual results.

An example of verbal irony occurs in this speech from *Macbeth*. Lennox, a Scottish nobleman, tells another Lord how Macbeth responded to Duncan's murder by killing the two grooms:

How it did grieve Macbeth! Did he not straight
In pious rage the two delinquents tear,
That were the slaves of drink and thralls of sleep?
Was not that nobly done?
　　(III, 6,11-14)

The real meaning of this speech, of course, is that Macbeth acted to cover his own crimes.

An example of dramatic irony can be found in Scene 6 of Act 1. We know that Macbeth and Lady Macbeth are plotting to murder Duncan, but Duncan does not know that he is walking into a trap. The irony is intensified by the opening lines of the scene in which Duncan and Banquo remark on the serenity and loveliness of the setting.

In Thomas Hardy's *The Three Strangers*, an irony of situation occurs when the two strangers at the chimney corner turn out to be the hangman and his intended victim.

KENNING（复合比喻）

In Old English poetry, an elaborate phrase that describes persons, things, or events in a metaphorical and indirect way. The Anglo-Saxon poem *The Seafarer* contains kennings, such as "whales' home" for the sea.

LYRIC（抒情诗）

A poem, usually a short one that expresses a speaker's personal thoughts or feelings. Elegy, ode and sonnet are all forms of lyric poetry. As its Greek name indicates, a lyric was originally a poem sung to the accompaniment of a lyre, and lyrics to this day have retained a melodic quality. Lyrics may express a range of emotions and reflections: Robert Herrick's *To the Virgins, to Make Much of Time* reflects on the brevity of life and the need to live for the moment, while Thomas Stearns Eliot's *Preludes* observes the sordidness and depression of modern life.

MASQUE（假面剧）

An elaborate and spectacular dramatic entertainment that was popular among the English aristocracy in the late sixteenth and early seventeenth centuries. Masques were written as dramatic poems and made use of songs, dances, colorful costumes, and startling stage effects.

MELODRAMA（情节剧）

A drama that has stereotyped characters, exaggerated emotions, and a conflict that pits an all-good hero or heroine against an all-evil villain. The good characters always win and the evil ones are always punished. Originally, melodramas were so called because melodies accompanied certain actions (*melos* means "song" in Greek). Also, each character in a melodrama had a theme melody, which was played each time he or she made an appearance on stage.

METAPHOR（隐喻）

A figure of speech that makes a comparison between two things that are basically dissimilar. "Life is a dream", "Life is a vale of tears", and "Life is a hard road" are all examples of metaphor. Unlike a simile, a metaphor does not use a connective word such as "like", "as", or "resemble" in making the comparison. Many metaphors are implied, or suggested. An implied metaphor does not directly state that one thing is another, different thing. Alfred Tennyson uses an implied metaphor in these lines from *Crossing the Bar*:

> I hope to see my Pilot face to face
> When I have crossed the bar.

By capitalizing the word Pilot, the poet implies a comparison between the maker and the pilot of his ship.

An extended metaphor is a metaphor that is extended throughout a poem. In *Crossing the Bar*, Tennyson compares death to a voyage at sea, at the end of which he will meet the "Pilot".

A dead metaphor is a metaphor that has become so commonplace that it seems literal rather than figurative. Some examples are the foot of a hill, the head of the class, a point in time, and the leg of a chair.

A mixed metaphor is the use of two or more inconsistent metaphors in one expression. When they are examined, mixed metaphors make no sense. Mixed metaphors are often unintentionally humorous: "The storm of protest was nipped in the bud" or "To hold the fort, he'd have to shake a leg."

METAPHYSICAL POETRY（玄学派诗歌）

The poetry of a group of 17th-century English poets including John Donne, Andrew Marvell, George Herbert, Henry Vaughan and Richard Crashaw with John Donne the leader. Metaphysical poetry is notable for surprising conceits, strange paradoxes and far-fetched imagery. But none of the above-mentioned poets knew they were metaphysical poets.

METER（格律）

A generally regular pattern of stressed and unstressed syllables in poetry. Meter is the rhythm and essential feature of poetry. There are various types of meter. The four popular types in English are illustrated as follows.

(1) Iamb（iambic, *adj*., 抑扬格ˇˊ）

For example,

She walks in beauty, like the night

(2) Trochee（trochaic, *adj*., 扬抑格ˊˇ）

For example,

Tell me not, in mournful numbers,

(3) Anapest（anapestic, *adj*., 抑抑扬格ˇˇˊ）

For example,

And a sound of a voice that is still!

(4) Dactyl(dactylic, *adj.*, 扬抑抑格 ´ ˇ ˇ)

For example,

´　ˇ　ˇ　´　ˇ　ˇ
Gently and Humanly

Except the four major types of meter, there are also other variations:

(5) Spondee(扬扬格 ´ ´)

For example,

　　　　´　　　´
Rough winds do shake the darling buds of May,

(6) Pyrrhic(抑抑格 ˇ ˇ)

For example,

　　ˇ　ˇ
Thou art more lovely and more temperate.

METONYMY(转喻)

A figure of speech in which something very closely associated with a thing is used to stand for or suggest the thing itself. "Three sails came into the harbor" is an example of metonymy; the word "sails" stands for the ships themselves. Other common examples of metonymy are crown to mean a king, hardhat to mean a construction worker, and White House to mean the President. William Shakespeare uses metonymy in the following lines from his play *Cymbeline*:

The scepter, learning, and physic, must
All follow this, and come to dust.

The words "scepter", "learning", and "physic" stand for the king, the scholar, and the doctor.

MIRACLE PLAY(奇迹剧)

A popular religious drama of medieval England. Miracle plays are based on stories of the saints or on sacred history.

MODERNISM（现代主义）

A movement of experiments in new technique in writing, which in English literature prevailed during the 1920s and 1930s. The major landmarks are James Joyce's *Ulysses* and Thomas Stearns Eliot's *The Waste Land*.

MORALITY PLAY（道德剧）

An outgrowth of miracle plays. Morality plays were popular in the fifteenth and sixteenth centuries. In them, virtues and vices are personified.

MOTIF（主旨）

A recurring feature (such as a name, an image, or a phrase) in a work of literature. A motif generally contributes in some way to the theme of a short story, novel, poem, or play. For example, a motif used by David Herbert Lawrence in his story *The Rocking-Horse Winner* is the word luck. The main character of the story, a boy named Paul, discovers that he has the power to predict the winner in a horse race. However, this becomes an ironic kind of luck, for Paul grows obsessed with his power and is finally destroyed by it.

At times, motif is used to refer to some commonly used plot or character type in literature. The "ugly duckling motif" refers to a plot that involves the transformation of a plain-looking person into a beauty. Two other commonly used motifs are the "Romeo and Juliet motif" (about doomed lovers) and the "Horatio Alger motif" (about the office clerk who becomes the corporation president).

MYTH（神话）

A story, often about immortals and sometimes connected with religious rituals, that is intended to give meaning to the mysteries of the world. In myths, gods and goddesses are usually identified with the immense powers of the universe: in the Greek myths, Zeus is associated with the sky, Hades with the underworld, Poseidon with the sea, Apollo with the sun, Athena with wisdom, Ares with war. But the gods are also given the forms and feelings of human beings. Thus, myths make it possible for people to understand and deal with things that they cannot control and often cannot see.

A body of related myths that is accepted by a people is known as its mythology. A mythology tells a people what it is most concerned about: where it came from, who its gods are, what its most sacred rituals are, and what its destiny is.

NARRATIVE POEM（叙事诗）

A poem that tells a story. It is always told by a narrator. Narrative poetry is written with the poet standing outside his or her material, representing human experiences by what is often called the "objective" method. It aims primarily at telling a story in a sequence of events. Epic, ballad and metrical romance are three main categories of narrative poetry.

NARRATOR（叙事者）

One who narrates, or tells, a story. A story may be told by a first-person narrator, someone who is either a major or minor character in the story. Or a story may be told by a third-person narrator, someone who is not in the story at all.

The word narrator can also refer to a character in a drama who guides the audience through the play, often commenting on the action and sometimes participating in it. In Thornton Wilder's play *Our Town*, the Stage Manager serves as the narrator.

NATURALISM（自然主义）

A literary trend prevailing in Europe in the second half of the 19th century which focuses on the "true to life" description and exact reproduction of real life, including all its details without any selection. Naturalist writers usually write the lives of the poor and oppressed, but they can only represent the external appearance instead of the inner essence of real life. It can be taken as an extreme form of realism. George Gissing's *New Grub Street* is an example in English.

NEO-CLASSICISM（新古典主义）

A revival in the seventeenth and eighteenth centuries of classical standards of order, balance, and harmony in literature. John Dryden and Alexander Pope were major exponents of the neoclassical school.

NEO-ROMANTICISM（新浪漫主义）

A literary trend prevailing at the end of the 19th century which lays emphasis upon the invention of exciting adventures and fascinating stories to entertain the reading public instead of dealing with the social reality. Robert Louis Stevenson's *Treasure Island* is an example.

NOVEL（小说）

A book-length fictional prose narrative, having many characters and often a complex plot. Some important English novels are *Tom Jones* by Henry Fielding, *Pride and Prejudice* by Jane Austen, *Great Expectations* by Charles Dickens, and *Ulysses* by James Joyce.

ODE（颂诗）

A complex lyric poem of some length, dealing with a noble theme in a dignified manner and originally intended to be sung. Odes are often written for a special occasion, to honor a person or a season or to commemorate an event. John Keats is famous for his odes such as *Ode to a Nightingale*, *Ode on a Grecian Urn* and *To Autumn*.

ONOMATOPOEIA（拟声）

The use of a word whose sound in some degree imitates or suggests its meaning. The names of some birds are onomatopoetic, imitating the cry of the bird named: cuckoo, whippoorwill, owl, crow, towhee, bobwhite. Some onomatopoetic words are hiss, clang, rustle, and snap. In these lines from *The Rime of the Ancient Mariner*, Coleridge reproduces the fearful sounds of the land of ice:

It cracked and growled, and roared and howled
Like noises in a swound!
(lines 61-62)

OTTAVA RIME（八行体诗节）

A form of eight-line stanza. The rhyme scheme is abababcc. *Don Juan* by George Gordon Byron is written in this form.

OXYMORON（矛盾修饰）

A figure of speech that combines opposite or contradictory ideas or terms. An oxymoron suggests a paradox, but it does so very briefly, usually in two or three words, such as "living death," "dear enemy," "sweet sorrow," and "wise fool."

PARADOX（似非而是）

A statement that reveals a kind of truth, although it seems at first to be self-contradictory and untrue. One of the best examples appears in John Milton's *On His Deceased Wife*.

But O, as to embrace me she inclined,
I waked, she fled, and day brought back my night.

By the famous paradox in the last line, Milton shows his great happiness in seeing his wife in his dream and his deep sorrow when he has lost her in reality.

PARALLELISM（排比）

The use of phrases, clauses, or sentences that are similar or complementary in structure or in meaning. Parallelism is a form of repetition. In Alfred Tennyson's poem *Sweet and Low*, the first and third lines of the first stanza are parallel in structure:

Sweet and low, sweet and low
Wind of the western sea,

Low, low, breathe and blow,
Wind of the western sea.

PARODY（戏仿）

The humorous imitation of a work of literature, art, or music. A parody often achieves its humorous effect through the use of exaggeration or mockery. In literature, parody can be made of a plot, a character, a writing style, a sentiment or theme. The poet Algernon Charles Swinburne parodies his own verse in a humorous poem called *Nephelidia*. In these lines, Swinburne is mocking a kind of lush verse that makes excessive use of alliteration:

Pallid and pink as the palm of the flag flower that
flickers with fear of the flies as they float,

PASTORAL（牧歌）

A type of poem that deals in an idealized way with shepherds and rustic life. It describes the loves and sorrows of shepherds, and the rustic innocence and idleness. A popular pastoral is Christopher Marlowe's *The Passionate Shepherd to His Love*.

PATHOS（悲情）

The quality in a work of literature or art that arouses the reader's feelings of pity, sorrow, or compassion for a character. The term is usually used to refer to situations in which innocent characters suffer through no fault of their own. An example of a scene with pathos is Scene 2 in Act 4 of *Macbeth* in which Lady Macduff and her son are ruthlessly murdered by Macbeth's assassins.

PERSONIFICATION（拟人）

A figure of speech in which something nonhuman is given human qualities. Percy Bysshe Shelley, in his *Ode to the West Wind*, says that "O wild West Wind, thou breath of Autumn's being", as if Autumn were a human that had breath. In this famous ode, he further compares the west wind to both destroyer and preserver, as if the west wind were a powerful man that could destroy all the old and decayed, and preserve the new and fresh. The west wind represents the great power of the revolutionary people. The comparison makes this concept vivid and alive.

PLOT（情节）

The sequence of events or actions in a short story, novel, play, or narrative poem. Plots may be simple or complicated, loosely constructed or close-knit. But every plot is made up of a series of incidents that are related to one another.

Conflict, a struggle of some kind, is the most important element of plot. Conflict may be external or internal, and there may be more than one form of conflict in a work. As the plot advances, we learn how the conflict is resolved, either through the action or through major changes in the attitudes or personalities of the characters.

Action is generally introduced by the exposition, information essential to understand the situation. The action rises to a crisis, or climax. This movement is called the rising action. The falling action, which follows the crisis, shows a reversal of fortune for the protagonist. In a tragedy this reversal leads to disaster; in a comedy, it leads to a happy ending.

The denouement or resolution is the moment when the conflict ends and the outcome of the action is clear.

POINT OF VIEW（视角）

The vantage point from which a narrative is told. There are two basic points of view: first-person and third-person. In the first-person point of view, the story is told by one of the characters in his or her own words. The first-person point of view is limited, since the reader is told only what this character knows and observes. Here is an example of first-person point of view from Jonathan Swift's *Gulliver's Travels*: "The King was struck with horror at the description I had given of those terrible engines, and the proposal I had made. He was amazed how so impotent and groveling an insect as I (these were his expressions) could entertain such inhuman ideas..."

In the third-person point of view, the narrator is not a character in the story. The narrator may be an omniscient, or "all-knowing", observer who can describe and comment on all the characters and actions in the story. Thomas Hardy's *The Three Strangers* is written from a third-person omniscient point of view: "Shepherdess Fennel fell back upon the intermediate plan of mingling short dances with short periods of talk and singing, so as to hinder any ungovernable rage in either."

On the other hand, the third-person narrator might tell a story from the point of view of only one character in the story, as Virginia Woolf does in *The New Dress*. All the action in that story is told by the third-person narrator, from the limited point of view of Mable Waring.

PROTAGONIST（主要人物）

The central character of a drama, novel, short story, or narrative poem. The protagonist is the character on whom the action centers and with whom the reader sympathizes most. Usually the protagonist strives against an opposing force, or antagonist, to accomplish something. The protagonist can be either heroic or ordinary, good or bad. For example, Beowulf is brave and good. Macbeth is noble and honorable at first, but becomes increasingly hateful.

PSALM（赞美诗）

A song or lyric poem in praise of God. The term usually refers to the one hundred and fifty sacred lyrics in the Book of Psalms in the Bible. Now any praise of anything may be named "psalm", for example, *A Psalm of Life* written by Henry Wadsworth Longfellow.

PUN（双关）

The use of a word or phrase to suggest two or more meanings at the same time. Puns are generally humorous. In Act 2, Scene 3 of *Macbeth*, the Porter plays on the two meanings of the word "goose" in this line: "Come in tailor, here you may roast your goose." The goose was a tailor's pressing iron.

REALISM（现实主义）

The attempt in literature and art to represent life as it really is, without sentimentalizing or idealizing it. Realistic writing often depicts the everyday life and speech of ordinary people. The rise and growth of the realistic novel is the most prominent achievement in the 18th-century English literature. Daniel Defoe, Jonathan Swift and Henry Fielding are its representatives.

REFRAIN（叠句）

A word, phrase, line, or group of lines repeated regularly in a poem, usually at the end of each stanza. Refrains are often used in ballads and narrative poems to create a songlike rhythm and to help build suspense. Refrains can also serve to emphasize a particular idea. A familiar example is *Auld Lang Syne* written by Robert Burns. Here the second stanza is the refrain that is repeated in the poem and song.

>   Should auld acquaintance be forgot,
>   And never brought to mind?
>   Should auld acquaintance be forgot,
>   And days o'lang syne?

>   For auld lang syne, my dear,
>   For auld lang syne,
>   We'll tak'a cup o' kindness yet,
>   For auld lang syne.

A modern example of the use of refrain appears in Dylan Thomas's *Do Not Go Gentle into That Good Night*.

RENAISSANCE（文艺复兴）

The "rebirth" of literature, art and learning that progressively transformed European culture from the mid-14th century in Italy to the mid-17th century in England and other countries, strongly influenced by the rediscovery of classical

Greek and Latin literature, and promoted by the development of printing. In the Renaissance period, man began to live for his own sake more than for God and for the future world. The Renaissance is commonly held to mark the close of the Middle Ages and the beginning of the modern Western world.

RHYME（韵）

The repetition of certain sounds in words that appear close to each other in a poem, usually at the end of poetic lines. For example: river/shiver, song/long, leap/deep. Approximate rhyme is rhyme in which only the final consonant sounds of the words are identical (as opposed to exact rhyme). Cook/look is an exact rhyme; cook/lack is an approximate rhyme. To poetry composition, rhyme, wherever it may exist, is quite important, though we cannot say rhyme is the soul of poetry.

A. Types of rhyme according to its position
(1) End rhyme（尾韵）

The repetition of the last stressed vowel in a line and all the following syllables. End rhyme is the commonest type of rhyme in English poetry after the medieval period. Here is an example from William Blake's *The Tyger*:

> In what distant deeps or skies
> Burnt the fire of thine eyes?
> On what wings dare he aspire?
>   What the hand, dare seize the fire?

(2) Internal rhyme（行内韵）

If the rhyme occurs within a line, it is called internal rhyme. Here is an example from *The Rime of the Ancient Mariner*: "The guests are *met*, the feast is *set*".

B. Types of rhyme according to its structure
(1) Masculine rhyme（阳韵）

The repetition of one syllable at the end of respective lines. For example,

Under the green wood tr*ee*
Who loves to lie with m*e*.

(2) Feminine rhyme（阴韵）

A rhyme that matches two or more syllables, usually at the end of respective lines, in which the final syllable or syllables are unstressed. Feminine rhyme is relatively rare in English poetry and usually appears as a special effect.

C. Other types of rhyme

Besides the above rhymes, there are other types of rhyme frequently used in English poetry as follows.

(1) Alliteration（also called head rhyme or initial rhyme, 头韵）

The repetition of the same sounds—usually initial consonants of words or of stressed syllables—in any sequence of neighboring words. Although alliteration sometimes appears in prose, it is mainly a poetic device. For example, in Shelley's *Ode to the West Wind*: "O *w*ild *W*est *W*ind, thou *b*reath of Autumn's *b*eing."

(2) Assonance（腹韵，亦称元音韵）

The repetition of vowel sounds within a noticeable range. Assonance occurs in words as fight/bike; fat/map; morning/falling. In poetry, it goes as follows in George Gordon Byron's *She Walks in Beauty*:

She walks in beauty, l*i*ke the n*i*ght
Of cloudless cl*i*mes and starry sk*i*es.

(3) Consonance（辅音韵）

The repetition of consonant sounds before and after different vowels. Consonance occurs in words as *bl*ock/*bl*ack; *cr*eak/*cr*oak.

(4) Eye rhyme or sight rhyme（眼韵）

Eye rhyme occurs when the spelling of the rhyming element match, but the sound does not. For example,

Come live with me and be my L*ove*,

And we will all the pleasures pr*ove*.

D. Rhyme scheme（押韵格式，亦称韵式或韵制）

The pattern of rhymes in a poem. English poetry has various rhyme schemes. Here we take the 4-line stanza as an example to illustrate its diverse patterns.

(1) abab（crossed rhyme / alternating rhyme, 隔行押韵 / 交叉韵）

For example,

Gather ye rosebuds while ye may,

Old time is still a-flying;

And this same flower that smiles today,

Tomorrow will be dying.

(2) aabb（双偶四行）

For example,

Come live with me and be my Love,

And we will all the pleasures prove

That valleys, groves, hills and fields,

Woods, or steepy mountain yields.

(3) aaaa（通韵，一韵到底）

For example,

The woods are lovely, dark, and deep,

But I have promises to keep,

And miles to go before I sleep.

And miles to go before I sleep.

(4) abba（enclosed rhyme, 抱韵）

For example,

I envy not in any moods

The captive void of noble rage,

The linnet born within the cage,

That never knew the summer woods;

(5) aaba（Tang poetry rhyme, 唐诗韵）

For example, the first three stanzas of *Stopping by Woods on a Snowy Evening* written by Robert Frost:

Whose woods these are I think I know.

His house is in the village, though;

He will not see me stopping here

To watch his woods fill up with snow.

My little horse must think it queer

To stop without a farmhouse near

Between the woods and frozen lake

The darkest evening of the year.

He gives his harness bells a shake

To ask if there is some mistake.

The only other sound's the sweep

Of easy wind and downy flake.

ROMANCE（骑士文学；传奇文学）

Any imaginative literature in verse or prose that deals with idealized characters' heroic adventures in some remote setting. Originally, the term referred to a medieval tale dealing with the loves and adventures of kings, queens, knights, and ladies, and including unlikely or supernatural happenings. *Sir Gawain and the Green Knight* is the best of the medieval romances. John Keats's *The Eve of St. Agnes* is one of the greatest metrical romances ever written.

ROMANTICISM（浪漫主义）

A movement that flourished in literature, philosophy, music, and art in Western culture during most of the 19th century, beginning as a revolt against classicism. There have been many varieties of romanticism in many different times and places. It prevailed in England during the period 1798-1832. Many of the ideas of English romanticism were first expressed by the poets William Wordsworth and Samuel Taylor Coleridge. But before William Wordsworth stated his manifesto of Romantic poetry, William Blake and Robert Burns had already broken with classicism and begun to write Romantic poems. Walter Scott is also a great Romantic poet.

SATIRE（讽刺）

A kind of writing that holds up to ridicule or contempt the weaknesses and wrongdoings of individuals, groups, institutions, or humanity in general. The aim of satirists is to set a moral standard for society, and they attempt to persuade the reader to see their point of view through the force of laughter. The most famous satirical work in English literature is Jonathan Swift's *Gulliver's Travels*. In the distant land of Brobdingnag, where people are twelve times as tall as a normal human being, Gulliver is brought before the King to describe the English people. Swift satirizes the English people through the King's response:

> He was perfectly astonished with the historical account I gave him of our affairs during the last century, protesting it was only a heap of conspiracies, rebellions, murders, massacres, revolutions, banishments; the very worst effects that avarice, faction, hypocrisy, perfidiousness, cruelty, rage, madness, hatred, envy, lust, malice, and ambition could produce.

SENTIMENTALISM（感伤主义）

A movement popular in the poetry and novels in the latter part of the 18th century. The writers regarded sentiment as a sort of relief for the social evils and a mild protest against the social injustice. They advocated that sentiment should take the place of reason. Sentimental poetry is represented by Edward Young's *Night Thoughts* and Thomas Gray's *Elegy Written in a Country Churchyard*. Samuel Richardson's *Pamela* and *Clarissa*, Oliver Goldsmith's *The Vicar of Wakefield*; and Laurence Sterne's *Tristram Shandy* are all sentimental novels.

SETTING（背景）

The time and place in which the events in a short story, novel, play or narrative poem occur. A setting may serve simply as the physical background of a story, or a skillful writer may use setting to establish a particular atmosphere, which in turn contributes to the plot and theme of the story.

SIMILE（明喻）

A comparison made between two things through the use of a specific word of comparison, such as "like", "as", "than", or "resembles". The comparison must be between two essentially unlike things. To say "Susan is like her grandmother" is not to use a simile, but to say "Susan is like a golden flower" is to use a simile. In *To a Skylark*, Percy Bysshe Shelley uses a simile to describe the flight of the bird:

> Higher still and higher
> From the earth thou springest
> Like a cloud of fire...

SOLILOQUY（独白）

In drama, an extended speech delivered by a character alone on the stage. The character reveals his or her innermost thoughts and feelings directly to the audience, as if thinking aloud. One of the most famous soliloquies in literature occurs at the end of Shakespeare's *Macbeth*, when Macbeth, near defeat, expresses a bleak and bitter vision of life:

> Tomorrow, and tomorrow, and tomorrow,
> Creeps in this petty pace from day to day

To the last syllable of recorded time

And all our yesterdays have lighted fools

The way to dusty death. Out, out, brief candle!

Life's but a walking shadow, a poor player

That struts and frets his hour upon the stage

And then is heard no more. It is a tale

Told by an idiot, full of sound and fury,

Signifying nothing.

SONG（歌）

A short lyric poem with distinct musical qualities, normally written to be set to music. It expresses a simple but intense emotion. *She Walks in Beauty* by George Gordon Byron is a song. Robert Burns wrote over 300 songs. Percy Bysshe Shelley's *A Song* is a very good example:

A widow bird sat mourning for her love

Upon a wintry bough;

The frozen wind crept on above;

The freezing stream below.

There was no leaf upon the forest bare,

No flower upon the ground,

And little motion in the air

Except the mill-wheel's sound.

SONNET（十四行诗）

A lyric poem consisting of a single stanza of fourteen iambic pentameter lines linked by an intricate rhyme scheme. There are mainly two major patterns of rhyme scheme in sonnets written in English. The Italian or Petrarchan sonnet comprises an octave (eight lines) rhyming abbaabba and a sestet (six lines) rhyming cdecde or cdccdc. The transition from octave to sestet usually coincides with a "turn" in the argument or mood of the poem, usually in line 9. The

English or Shakespearean sonnet comprises three quatrains and a final couplet, rhyming abab cdcd efef gg. The "turn" comes with the final couplet, which may sometimes achieve an epigram. Yet, one can still find the influence of the Italian form, that is, in some sonnets the turn comes in line 9. There was one notable variant, the Spenserian sonnet, in which Spenser linked each quatrain to the next by a continuing rhyme: abab bcbc cdcd ee. There are three famous sonnet sequences in the Elizabethan Age in England: Spenser's *Amoretti*, Shakespeare's sonnets and Sidney's *Astrophel and Stella*. Sonnet later was used to describe other feelings rather than love alone.

SPENSERIAN STANZA（斯宾塞诗节）

The 9-line stanza form rhymed ababbcbcc, in which the first eight lines are in iambic pentameter while the ninth in iambic hexameter. It was invented by Edmund Spenser who first used it in his masterpiece *The Faerie Queene*.

SPRUNG RHYTHM（跳韵）

A term created by the poet Gerard Manley Hopkins to designate a variable kind of poetic meter in which a stressed syllable may be combined with any number of unstressed syllables. Poems with sprung rhythm have an irregular meter and are meant to sound like natural speech.

STEREOTYPE（类型人物）

A commonplace type or character that appears so often in literature that his or her nature is immediately familiar to the reader. Stereotypes, also called stock characters, always look and act the same way and reveal the same traits of character. Examples of stereotypes are the temperamental movie star, the talkative cab driver, the mad scientist, the villain with a waxed mustache, and the wise-cracking, hard-boiled private detective.

STREAM OF CONSCIOUSNESS（意识流）

The style of writing that attempts to imitate the natural flow of the characters' mental and emotional reactions to external events rather than the events themselves. The school of "stream of consciousness" refers to a group of novelists in the 20th century who followed this style. James Joyce and Virginia Woolf are the two best-known novelists of this school.

SUSPENSE（悬念）

The quality of a story, novel, or drama that makes the reader or audience uncertain or tense about the outcome of events. Suspense makes readers ask, "What will happen next?" or "How will this work out?" and impels them to read on. Suspense is greatest when it focuses attention on a sympathetic character. Thus, the most familiar kind of suspense involves a character in mortal danger: hanging from the ledge of a tall building; tied to railroad tracks as a train approaches; or alone in an old house, ascending a staircase to open the attic door. But suspense may simply arise from curiosity, as when a character must make a decision, or seek an explanation for something.

SYMBOL（象征）

Any object, person, place, or action that means not only what it is, but something else as well, especially something larger than itself, such as a quality, an attitude, a belief, or a value. A symbol can be universal or unique. For example, as is known to all, a dove suggests peace and a rose signifies love. But in Donne's poetry, a flea, which is a common, ugly insect to others, can be the symbol of love.

SYMBOLISM（象征主义）

A literary movement that arose in France in the last half of the 19th century and that greatly influenced many English writers, particularly poets, of the 20th century. To Symbolist poets, an emotion is indefinite and therefore difficult to communicate. Symbolist poets tend to avoid any direct statement of meaning. Instead, they work through emotionally powerful symbols that suggest meaning and mood.

SYNECDOCHE（提喻）

A figure of speech that substitutes a part for a whole. An example is Thomas Stearns Eliot's use of "feet" and "hands" to stand for "people" in the poem *Preludes*.

TERZA RIMA（三行体诗节）

An Italian verse form consisting of a series of three-line stanzas in which the middle line of each stanza rhymes with the first and third lines of the following stanza, as follows: aba bcb cdc, etc. Percy Bysshe Shelley's *Ode to the West Wind* is written in *terza rima*. Here are the first two stanzas:

O wild West Wind, thou breath of Autumn's being,	a
Thou, from whose unseen presence the leaves dead,	b
Are driven, like ghosts from an enchanter fleeing,	a
Yellow, and black, and pale, and hectic red,	b
Pestilence-stricken multitudes: O thou,	c
Who chariotest to their dark wintry bed...	b

THEME（主题）

The general idea or insight about life that a writer wishes to express in a literary work. All the elements of a literary work—plot, setting, characterization, and figurative language—contribute to the development of its theme. A simple theme can often be stated in a single sentence. But sometimes a literary work is rich and complex, and a paragraph or even an essay is needed to state the theme. Not all literary works have a controlling theme. For example, the purpose of some simple ghost stories is to frighten the reader, and some detective stories seek only to thrill.

TONE（基调）

The attitude a writer takes toward his or her subject, characters, or audience. It could be happy or sad, gloomy or light, serious or satiric, calm or excited, etc. Tone is found in every kind of writing. It is created through the choice of words and details. In writing about his childhood in his poem *Fern Hill*, Dylan Thomas's tone is nostalgic. In *Preface to Shakespeare*, Samuel Johnson's tone is serious and admiring.

TRAGEDY（悲剧）

Traditionally, a play dominated by a serious tone, concerns characters of noble birth, perhaps a king like Oedipus or a prince like Hamlet, deals with profound issues, and usually concludes with the death of the leading character. Shakespeare is famous for his four great tragedies *Hamlet*, *Othello*, *King Lear* and *Macbeth*.

UNDERSTATEMENT（低调陈述）

An expression with less strength than what would be expected. This is not to be confused with euphemism, where a polite phrase is used in place of a harsher or more offensive expression. No strong feeling is shown in words when William Wordsworth says in his *She Dwelt Among the Untrodden Ways*: "But she is in her grave, and, oh, / The difference to me!" But everyone knows how mournful the speaker is and what great changes has happened after the death of Lucy.

VILLANELLE（维拉内拉诗）

An intricate verse form of French origin, consisting of several three-line stanzas and a concluding four-line stanza. The first and third lines of the first stanza are used as refrains in the succeeding stanzas and as the last two lines of the concluding stanza. Only two rhymes are allowed in a villanelle. A famous modern villanelle is Dylan Thomas's *Do Not Go Gentle into That Good Night*.

WIT（巧智）

A brilliance and quickness of perception combined with a cleverness of expression. In the 18th century, wit and nature were related-nature provided the rules of the universe; wit allowed these rules to be interpreted and expressed.

· 415 ·

参考文献

Abrams, M. H. A Glossary of Literature Terms [M]. Beijing: Foreign Language Teaching and Research Press, 2004.

Chace, William & Collier, Peter. An Introduction to Literature [M]. New York: Harcourt Brace Jovanovich, Inc., 1985.

Greenblatt, Stephen. The Norton Anthology of English Literature [M]. 8th ed. New York: W. W. Norton & Company, 2006.

Peck, John & Coyle, Martin. A Brief History of English Literature [M]. Beijing: Higher Education Press, 2010.

陈嘉. 英国文学史 [M]. 北京：商务印书馆，1986.

陈嘉. 英国文学作品选读 [M]. 北京：商务印书馆，1981.

刁克利. 英国文学经典选读 [M]. 北京：外语教学与研究出版社，2008.

桂扬清，吴翔林. 英美文学选读 [M]. 北京：中国对外翻译出版公司，1991.

胡家峦. 英美诗歌名篇详注 [M]. 北京：中国人民大学出版社，2008.

李正栓. 英国文学简史与选读 [M]. 清华大学出版社，2016.

李正栓. 英美诗歌欣赏 [M]. 北京：清华大学出版社，2021.

李正栓，白凤欣. 英语诗歌教程 [M]. 北京：高等教育出版社，2009.

李正栓，申玉革. 英国诗歌欣赏教程 [M]. 上海：复旦大学出版社，2022.

李正栓，申玉革. 英美诗歌欣赏教程 [M]. 北京：北京师范大学出版社，2014.

李正栓，吴伟仁，吴晓梅. 英国文学史及选读：第一册 [M]. 第二版. 北京：外语教学与研究出版社，2021.

李正栓，吴伟仁，吴晓梅. 英国文学史及选读：第二册 [M]. 第二版. 北京：外语教学与研究出版社，2021.

刘炳善. 英国文学简史 [M]. 新增订版. 郑州：河南人民出版社，2007.
刘炳善，罗益民. 英国文学选读 [M]. 郑州：河南人民出版社，2006.
罗经国. 新编英国文学选读 [M]. 第三版. 北京：北京大学出版社，2011.
王佐良等. 英国文学名篇选注 [M]. 北京：商务印书馆，1999.